T0133781

# DATA PRIVACY
## Principles and Practice

# DATA PRIVACY
## Principles and Practice

Nataraj Venkataramanan
Ashwin Shriram

CRC Press
Taylor & Francis Group
Boca Raton   London   New York

CRC Press is an imprint of the
Taylor & Francis Group, an **informa** business

A CHAPMAN & HALL BOOK

CRC Press
Taylor & Francis Group
6000 Broken Sound Parkway NW, Suite 300
Boca Raton, FL 33487-2742

### Library of Congress Cataloging-in-Publication Data

Names: Venkataramanan, Nataraj, author.
Title: Data privacy : principles and practice / Nataraj Venkataramanan and Ashwin Shriram.
Description: Boca Raton, FL : CRC Press, 2017. | Includes bibliographical references and index.
Identifiers: LCCN 2016009691 | ISBN 9781498721042 (alk. paper)
Subjects: LCSH: Data protection. | Management information systems--Security measures. | Computer networks--Security measures. | Privacy, Right of. | Customer relations.
Classification: LCC HF5548.37 .V46 2017 | DDC 005.8--dc23
LC record available at https://lccn.loc.gov/2016009691

In memory of my parents

*V. Sulochana and E. Venkataramanan*

and my Guru

*Sri Chandrasekharendra Saraswathi*

**Nataraj Venkataramanan**

Seeking God's blessings, I dedicate this book to my

wonderful parents, my lovely wife, and daughter,

who have sacrificed so much to make this happen.

**Ashwin Shriram**

# Contents

# Preface

The ubiquity of computers and smart devices on the Internet has led to vast amounts of data being collected from users, shared, and analyzed. Most of these data are collected from customers by enterprises dealing with banking, insurance, healthcare, financial services, retail, e-commerce, manufacturing, and social networks. These data consist of transactional data, search data, and health and financial data, almost always including a lot of personal data. On the one hand, these data are considered valuable for the enterprise as they can be used for a variety of purposes, such as knowledge discovery, software application development, and application testing. At the same time, these data are considered to be sensitive as they contain their customers' personal information. Therefore, sharing, offshoring, or outsourcing of such data for purposes like data mining or application testing should ensure that customers' personal information is not compromised in any way. Many countries have stringent data protection acts, such as the Health Insurance Portability and Accountability Act of 1996 (HIPAA) in the United States, the EU Data Protection Act, and the Swiss Data Protection Act, which mandate high standards of data privacy. In this context, data privacy, which pertains to protecting the identity of the customers, is high priority for all enterprises as any data privacy loss would result in legal issues with hefty fines, erosion of customer confidence, and customer attrition. To this effect, data privacy as a subject of study is being introduced in some universities at the postgraduate level. Various certifications like PrivacyTrust and CIPP also exist, which endorse an individual's knowledge of privacy laws.

Data privacy as a subject of study and practice is relatively young; in particular, many of the techniques used for data protection are still evolving. Currently, many companies are adopting these data privacy techniques as they try to leverage the opportunities provided by offshoring and outsourcing while at the same time complying with regulatory requirements. This book provides a comprehensive guidance on the implementation of many of the data privacy techniques in a variety of applications. An enterprise's data architecture consists of a wide variety of data structures like multidimensional data, also known as relational data, which are the most widely used data structure, and complex data structures like transaction data, longitudinal data, time series data, graph data, and spatiotemporal data. Multidimensional data are simple in structure, and a rich set of anonymization algorithms are in use currently for such data, but anonymization techniques for other complex data structures are still evolving. Chapters 2 through 4 attempt to provide a detailed coverage on the various anonymization approaches for both multidimensional and complex data structures. Chapters 5 and 6 focus on applications such as privacy preserving data mining and privacy preserving test data management. Chapter 7 focuses on synthetic data that are used as an alternative to anonymization. There is a requirement for protection of data during run-time—dynamic data protection—which is covered in Chapter 8. Here, the techniques of one-way and two-way tokenization are covered. Appendix A provides a detailed set of anonymization design principles, which serve as guidelines to the practitioner. The salient features of this book are

- Static data anonymization techniques for multidimensional data
- Clear-cut guidelines on anonymization design
- Analysis of anonymization algorithms
- Static data anonymization techniques for complex data structures like transaction, longitudinal, time series, and graph data
- Emphasis on privacy versus utility in the techniques
- Applications of anonymization techniques on a variety of domains like privacy preserving data mining and privacy preserving test data management
- Use of synthetic data in place of anonymized data
- Use of tokenization algorithms for dynamic data protection

# *Acknowledgments*

Writing a book is never easy. It requires hard work, research, collaboration, and support from various quarters. Both of us thank our management at HCL Technologies Ltd. for providing a wonderful environment conducive to learning and innovation. We thank our colleague, Harikrishnan Janardhanan, for his selfless support during this endeavor.

We thank N. Krishna and Dr. K. R. Gunasekar of the Indian Institute of Science, Bangalore, India, for helping us with our research in this field. We sincerely thank Aastha Sharma and the members of the editorial group at CRC Press/Taylor & Francis Group for their support in completing this work.

Writing a book is hard and one needs to spend a lot of time on it. This reduces the amount of time one gets to spend with one's family. Nataraj owes special thanks to his wife, Kalyani, and his two sons, Balaji and Srihari, for providing constant encouragement throughout this period. Ashwin thanks his parents for their blessings and support. He appreciates his wife, Deepa, for taking over the entire responsibility of raising their little daughter, Srishti, during this time.

Finally, we collectively thank God for giving us the courage, perseverance, and diligence to contribute to an area that we firmly believe is extremely important in today's world.

# Authors

**Nataraj Venkataramanan** is currently an associate vice president at HCL Technologies Ltd., India. He has previously worked in some of India's major information technology (IT) companies and has over two decades of experience in computing. He has worked across different domains such as banking, financial services, insurance, government, oil and gas, retail, and manufacturing. His main research interests are in large-scale software architecture, quality attributes of software architecture, data privacy, privacy preserving data mining, data analytics, pattern recognition, and learning systems. He has published refereed technical papers in journals and conferences. He is a member of IEEE and ACM. Nataraj can be reached at nataraj.venkataramanan@gmail.com.

**Ashwin Shriram** works for HCL Technologies as a solution architect. As an engineer in computer science, he has a strong technical background in data management. At HCL, Ashwin is a senior member of the Test Data Management Center of Excellence. His current research interests include data privacy, data analytics, pattern recognition, and big data privacy. Prior to joining HCL, he was working in the United States for customers in public as well as in private sectors. Ashwin can be reached at ashwin.shriram@gmail.com.

# List of Abbreviations

| | |
|---|---|
| AG-TS | Attribute generalization–tuple suppression |
| API | Application programming interface |
| BPO | Business process outsourcing |
| CCN | Credit card number |
| CIPP | Certified information privacy professional |
| CM | Classification metric |
| DGH | Domain generalization hierarchy |
| DMV | Department of motor vehicles |
| DOB | Date of birth |
| DPA | Data Protection Act (UK) |
| EC | Equivalence class |
| ECG | Electrocardiogram |
| EI | Explicit identifier |
| FADP | Federal Act on Data Protection |
| FERPA | Family Educational Rights and Privacy Act |
| FIPPA | Freedom of Information and Protection of Privacy Act |
| HIPAA | Health Insurance Portability and Accountability Act |
| IDAS | Information discovery and analysis systems |
| IDSG | Information discovery scenario generator |
| IOT | Internet of things |
| ISI | International Statistical Institute |
| LDAP | Lightweight Directory Access Protocol |
| LM | Information loss metric |
| LOC | Lines of code |
| MBA | Market basket analysis |
| MTBF | Mean time between failures |
| MTTR | Mean time to recovery |
| NFR | Nonfunctional requirements |
| NSD | Nonsensitive data |
| ODS | Operational data store |
| OECD | Organization for Economic Cooperation and Development |
| PAN | Permanent account number |
| PCI | Payment card industry |
| PCI DSS | Payment Card Interface Data Security Standard |
| PHI | Protected health information |
| PII | Personally identifiable information |
| PPDM | Privacy preserving data mining |
| PPTDM | Privacy preserving test data manufacturing |
| QI | Quasi-identifier |
| SD | Sensitive data |

| | |
|---|---|
| SDC | Statistical disclosure control |
| SDDL | Synthetic data description language |
| SDG | Synthetic data generation |
| SDLC | Systems development life cycle |
| SMC/MPC | Secure multiparty computation/multiparty computation |
| SSN | Social security number |
| TDM | Test data manufacturing/test data management |
| TSG | Threat stream generator |
| VIN | Vehicle identification number |
| ZKP | Zero-knowledge proof |

# 1

## Introduction to Data Privacy

## 1.1 Introduction

Organizations dealing with banking, insurance, retail, healthcare, and manufacturing across the globe collect large amounts of data about their customers. This is a valuable asset to the organizations as these data can be mined to extract a lot of insights about their customers. For example, mining these data can throw light on customers' spending/buying, credit card usage, and investment patterns and health issues, to name a few. This information is used by companies to provide value-added services to their customers, which in turn results in higher revenue and profit. But these data might contain customers' personal identification information, and when in the hands of a data snooper, they can be exploited.

Large companies across the globe outsource their IT and business process work to service providers in countries like India, China, Brazil, etc. The outsourced work may involve application maintenance and development, testing, data mining/analysis, statistical analysis, etc. Business applications contain sensitive information, such as personal or financial and health-related data. Sharing such data can potentially violate individual privacy and lead to financial loss to the company. Serious concerns have been expressed by general public about exposing person-specific information. The issue of data leakage, either intentional or accidental exposure of sensitive information, is becoming a major security issue.

An IDC survey [19] claims that data leakage is the number one threat, ranked higher than viruses, Trojan horses, and worms. To address the privacy of an individual's data, governments across the globe have mandated regulations that companies have to adhere to: HIPAA (Health Insurance Portability and Accountability Act) in the United States, FIPPA (Freedom of Information and Protection of Privacy Act) in Canada, Sarbanes–Oxley Act, Video Privacy Protection, U.S. Declaration of Human Rights, and the EU's Data Protection Directive are just a few examples. Companies need to look into methods and tools to anonymize sensitive data. Data anonymization techniques have been the subject of intense investigation in recent years for many kinds of structured data, including tabular, transactional data, and graph data.

In Chapter 2, Static Data Anonymization, we discuss relational data, also known as multidimensional data, which are the most widely found data structure in enterprises currently. This chapter focuses on privacy preservation methods for multidimensional data. Multidimensional data are simple in structure, and a rich set of data protection algorithms, such as randomization, generalization, k-anonymization, *l*-diversity, and t-closeness, is described.

Anonymization techniques for multidimensional data are simple in structure and very commonly found across enterprises. Apart from multidimensional data, other types of data structures, such as graph, longitudinal data, sparse high-dimensional transaction data, time series data, spatiotemporal data, semistructured XML data, and big data, are also present across enterprises. These data structures are complex, contain sensitive customer information, and should therefore be protected. There are unique challenges in designing anonymization techniques for these complex data structures, though. Anonymization techniques used for the protection of multidimensional data are not directly applicable to these complex data structures. Chapter 3 discusses some of the anonymization techniques for complex data structures.

Any anonymization design is a function of many inputs. One of the important inputs is, "who are we protecting these data from?" The answer builds a profile of adversaries who are expected to attack the data. Chapter 4 explains various profiles of adversaries, their techniques, and what safeguards can be implemented against such threats.

Data mining is the first application of data privacy that we discuss. We explore two areas of mining: association rule mining and clustering. Each of these areas works with the goal of knowledge discovery. However, ensuring privacy is important for users/customers/patients to willingly share their data for analysis. In Chapter 5, we explore a few prominent privacy preservation algorithms and conclude with a discussion on their impact on the utility of data.

The second application of privacy, test data, is increasingly becoming an area for privacy preservation. High-quality testing requires high-quality test data. Outsourcing of testing has brought data privacy concerns to the fore. Hence, in Chapter 6, we discuss the need for privacy and current trends and list appropriate algorithms for each class of data. Measuring the utility of test data and also ascertaining the overall quality of test data are important to understand if a balance between privacy and utility has been achieved. Finally, the chapter also highlights some problems with the current anonymization options available.

In data mining and testing, there are times when a need arises to create external supplementary data. Classifiers require training data, which are not available initially. While testing too, special processes like error data handling, performance benchmarking, etc., require data not available in the original source data. Synthetic data generation solves both these issues.

In Chapter 7, we visit each class of personally identifiable information (PII) and explore the techniques available to generate synthetic data. The safety aspects of synthetic data are also covered in this chapter.

Run-time preservation of privacy is needed in cases where changes to the data itself cannot be made. Another challenge is that different roles of users require different levels of protection. In such cases, tokenization is a good solution. Tokens preserve the formats of sensitive data, which make them look just like the original data. Chapter 8 covers use cases, implementation and examples.

Chapter 9, the final chapter, explores the compliance side of data privacy. Most privacy implementations are direct results of compliance mandates at the regional or organizational level. In this chapter, we explain the rules and definitions in some of the relevant privacy regulations. Most of this chapter is dedicated to HIPAA, which is the definitive privacy law in the United States for healthcare data.

Appendix A lists the principles of anonymization that are referred throughout this book. These principles are applicable across domains, thus providing a concrete guideline for data privacy implementations.

Appendix B (PPTDM Manifesto) summarizes the best practices to be applied while preserving privacy in a test data setting.

## 1.2 What Is Data Privacy and Why Is It Important?

Thousands of ambulance service staff and housing benefits claimants have had their personal information accidently leaked in the latest UK data breach blunder (January 4, 2014; news in www.infosecurity-magazine.com/news/thousands-of-personal/-details.)

Natural healthcare chain Community Health Systems (CHS) says that about 4.5 million pieces of "non-medical patient identification data related to our physician practice" have been stolen .... August 18, 2014/News www.infosecurity-magazine.com/news/45-million-records-stolen-from/

NASDAQ-listed outsourcing firm EXL Service has lost a key client due to the breach of confidential client data by some of its employees.

- *Economic Times* (India) on November 6, 2013

There are numerous such incidents where customers' confidential personal information has been attacked by or lost to a data snooper. When such untoward incidents occur, organizations face legal suits, financial loss, loss of image, and, importantly, the loss of their customers.

There are many stakeholders of data privacy in an organization; these are shown in Figure 1.1. Let us define these stakeholders.

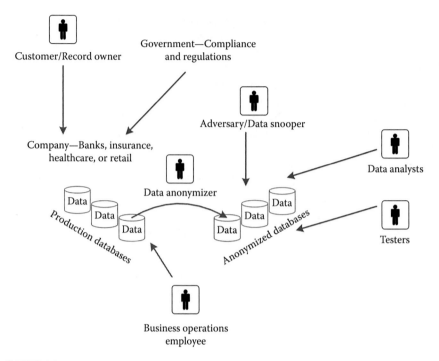

**FIGURE 1.1**
Data privacy—stakeholders in the organization.

*Company*: Any organization like a bank, an insurance company, or an e-commerce, retail, healthcare, or social networking company that holds large amounts of customer-specific data. They are the custodians of customer data, which are considered very sensitive, and have the responsibility of protecting the data at all costs. Any loss of these sensitive data will result in the company facing legal suits, financial penalties, and loss of reputation.

*Customer/record owner*: An organization's customer could be an individual or another organization who share their data with the company. For example, an individual shares his personal information, also known as PII, such as his name, address, gender, date of birth, phone numbers, e-mail address, and income with a bank. PII is considered sensitive as any disclosure or loss could lead to undesired identification of the customer or record owner. It has been shown that gender, age and zip code are sufficient to identify a large population of people in the United States.

*Government*: Government defines what data protection regulations that the company should comply with. Examples of such regulations are the HIPPA Act, the EU Data Protection Act, and the Swiss Data Protection Act. It is mandatory for companies to follow government regulations on data protection.

*Data anonymizer*: A person who anonymizes and provides data for analysis or as test data.

*Data analyst*: This person uses the anonymized data to carry out data mining activities like prediction, knowledge discovery, and so on. Following government regulations, such as the Data Moratorium Act, only anonymized data can be used for data mining. Therefore, it is important that the provisioned data support data mining functionalities.

*Tester*: Outsourcing of software testing is common among many companies. High-quality testing requires high-quality test data, which is present in production systems and contains customer-sensitive information. In order to test the software system, the tester needs data to be extracted from production systems, anonymized, and provisioned for testing. Since test data contain customer-sensitive data, it is mandatory to adhere to regulatory compliance in that region/country.

*Business operations employee*: Data analysts and software testers use anonymized data that are at rest or static, whereas business operations employees access production data because they need to support customer's business requirements. Business operations are generally outsourced to BPO (business process outsourcing) companies. In this case too, there is a requirement to protect customer-sensitive data but as this operation is carried out during run-time, a different set of data protection techniques are required to protect data from business operations employees.

*Adversary/data snooper*: Data are precious and their theft is very common. An adversary can be internal or external to the organization. The anonymization design should be such that it can thwart an adversary's effort to identify a record owner in the database.

Companies spend millions of dollars to protect the privacy of customer data. Why is it so important? What constitutes personal information? Personal information consists of name, identifiers like social security number, geographic and demographic information, and general sensitive information, for example, financial status, health issues, shopping patterns, and location data. Loss of this information means loss of privacy—one's right to freedom from intrusion by others. As we will see, protecting one's privacy is nontrivial.

## 1.2.1 Protecting Sensitive Data

"I know where you were yesterday!" Google knows your location when you use Google Maps. Google maps can track you wherever you go when you use it on a smart phone. Mobile companies know your exact location when you use a mobile phone. You have no place to hide. You have lost your privacy. This is the flip side of using devices like smart phones, Global positioning systems (GPS), and radio frequency identification (RFID). Why should others know where you were yesterday? Similarly, why should others know your health issues or financial status? All these are sensitive data and should be well protected as they could fall into the wrong hands and be exploited. Let us look at a sample bank customer and an account table. The customer table taken as such has nothing confidential as most of the information contained in it is also available in the public voters database and on social networking sites like Facebook. Sensitiveness comes in when the customer table is combined with an accounts table. A logical representation of Tables 1.1 and 1.2 is shown in Table 1.3.

Data D in the tables contains four disjointed data sets:

1. *Explicit identifiers (EI)*: Attributes that identify a customer (also called record owner) directly. These include attributes like social security number (SSN), insurance ID, and name.

2. *Quasi-identifiers (QI)*: Attributes that include geographic and demographic information, phone numbers, and e-mail IDs. Quasi-identifiers are also defined as those attributes that are publicly available, for example, a voters database.

3. *Sensitive data (SD)*: Attributes that contain confidential information about the record owner, such as health issues, financial status, and salary, which cannot be compromised at any cost.

4. *Nonsensitive data (NSD)*: Data that are not sensitive for the given context.

**TABLE 1.1**

Customer Table

| Explicit Identifiers | | Quasi-Identifiers | | | | |
|---|---|---|---|---|---|---|
| ID | First Name | DOB | Gender | Address | Zip Code | Phone |
| 1 | Ravi | 1970 | Male | Fourth Street | 66001 | 92345-67567 |
| 2 | Hari | 1975 | Male | Queen Street | 66011 | 98769-66610 |
| 3 | John | 1978 | Male | Penn Street | 66003 | 97867-00055 |
| 4 | Amy | 1980 | Female | Ben Street | 66066 | 98123-98765 |

**TABLE 1.2**

Account Table

| | Sensitive Data | | | | |
|---|---|---|---|---|---|
| ID | Account Number | Account Type | Account Balance | Credit Limit | Nonsensitive Data |
| 1 | 12345 | Savings | 10,000 | 20,000 | |
| 2 | 23456 | Checking | 5,000 | 15,000 | |
| 3 | 45678 | Savings | 15,000 | 30,000 | |
| 4 | 76543 | Savings | 17,000 | 25,000 | |

**TABLE 1.3**

Logical Representation of Customer and Account Tables

| Explicit Identifiers | | | Quasi-Identifiers | | | Sensitive Data | | | |
|---|---|---|---|---|---|---|---|---|---|
| ID | Name | DOB | Gender | Address | Zip Code | Account Number | Account Type | Account Balance | Credit Limit |
| 1 | Ravi | 1970 | Male | Fourth Street | 66001 | 12345 | Savings | 10,000 | 20,000 |
| 2 | Hari | 1975 | Male | Queen Street | 66011 | 23456 | Checking | 5,000 | 15,000 |
| 3 | John | 1978 | Male | Penn Street | 66003 | 45678 | Savings | 15,000 | 30,000 |
| 4 | Amy | 1980 | Female | Ben Street | 66066 | 76543 | Savings | 17,000 | 25,000 |

The first two data sets, the EI and QI, uniquely identify a record owner and when combined with sensitive data become sensitive or confidential. The data set D is considered as a matrix of m rows and n columns. Matrix D is a vector space where each row and column is a vector

$$D = [D_{EI}] [D_{QI}] [D_{SD}] \qquad (1.1)$$

Each of the data sets, EI, QI, and SD, are matrices with m rows and i, j, and k columns, respectively. We need to keep an eye on the index j (representing QI), which plays a major role in keeping the data confidential.

Apart from assuring their customers' privacy, organizations also have to comply with various regulations in that region/country, as mentioned earlier. Most countries have strong privacy laws to protect citizens' personal data. Organizations that fail to protect the privacy of their customers or do not comply with the regulations face stiff financial penalties, loss of reputation, loss of customers, and legal issues. This is the primary reason organizations pay so much attention to data privacy. They find themselves in a Catch-22 as they have huge amounts of customer data, and there is a compelling need to share these data with specialized data analysis companies. Most often, data protection techniques, such as cryptography and anonymization, are used prior to sharing data. In this book, we focus only on anonymization.

Anonymization is a process of logically separating the identifying information (PII) from sensitive data. Referring to Table 1.3, the anonymization approach ensures that EI and QI are logically separated from SD. As a result, an adversary will not be able to easily identify the record owner from his sensitive data. This is easier said than done. How to effectively anonymize the data? This is the question we explore throughout this book.

## 1.2.2 Privacy and Anonymity: Two Sides of the Same Coin

This brings up the interesting definition of privacy and anonymity. According to Skopek [1], under the condition of privacy, we have knowledge of a person's identity, but not of an associated personal fact, whereas under the condition of anonymity, we have knowledge of a personal fact, but not of the associated person's identity. In this sense, privacy and anonymity are flip sides of the same coin. Tables 1.4 and 1.5 illustrate the fundamental differences between privacy and anonymity.

There is a subtle difference between privacy and anonymity. The word privacy is also used in a generic way to mean anonymity, and there are specific use cases for both of them. Table 1.4 illustrates an anonymized table where PII is protected and sensitive data are left in their original form. Sensitive data should be in original form so that the data can be used to mine useful knowledge.

Anonymization is a two-step process: data masking and de-identification. Data masking is a technique applied to systematically substitute, suppress, or scramble data that call out an individual, such as names, IDs, account numbers, SSNs, etc. Masking techniques are simple techniques that perturb original data. De-identification is applied on QI fields. QI fields such as date

**TABLE 1.4**

Example of Anonymity

| Personal Identity | | | | | | Sensitive Data | | | |
|---|---|---|---|---|---|---|---|---|---|
| SSN | Name | DOB | Gender | Address | Zip Code | Account Number | Account Type | Account Balance | Credit Limit |
| X | X | X | X | X | X | | | | |
| X | X | X | X | X | X | | | | |
| X | X | X | X | X | X | | | | |
| X | X | X | X | X | X | | | | |

*Note:* X, identity is protected.

**TABLE 1.5**

Example of Privacy

| Personal Identity | | | | | | Sensitive Data | | | |
|---|---|---|---|---|---|---|---|---|---|
| SSN | Name | DOB | Gender | Address | Zip Code | Account Number | Account Type | Account Balance | Credit Limit |
| | | | | | | X | X | X | X |
| | | | | | | X | X | X | X |
| | | | | | | X | X | X | X |
| | | | | | | X | X | X | X |

*Note:* X, sensitive data are protected.

of birth, gender, and zip code have the capacity to uniquely identify individuals. Combine that with SD, such as income, and a Warren Buffet or Bill Gates is easily identified in the data set. By de-identifying, the values of QI are modified carefully so that the relationship is till maintained by identities cannot be inferred.

In Equation 1.1, the original data set is D which is anonymized, resulting in data set $D' = T(D)$ or $T([D_{EI}][D_{QI}][D_{SD}])$, where T is the transformation function. As a first step in the anonymization process, EI is completely masked and no longer relevant in $D'$. As mentioned earlier, no transformation is applied on SD and it is left in its original form. This results in $D' = T([D_{QI}])$, which means that transformation is applied only on QI as EI is masked and not considered as part of $D'$ and SD is left in its original form. $D'$ can be shared as QI is transformed and SD is in its original form but it is very difficult to identify the record owner. Coming up with the transformation function is key to the success of anonymization design and this is nontrivial. We spend a lot of time on anonymization design, which is generally applied on static data or data at rest.

The other scenario is protecting SD, as shown in Table 1.5, which is applied on data in motion. The implementation of this is also very challenging.

It is dichotomous as organizations take utmost care in protecting the privacy of their customers' data, but the same customers provide a whole lot of personal information when they register on social network sites like Facebook (of course, many of the fields are not mandatory but most people do provide sufficient personal information), including address, phone numbers, date of birth (DOB), details of education and qualification, work experience, etc. Sweeney [2] reports that zip code, DOB, and gender are sufficient to uniquely identify 83% of population in the United States. With the amount of PII available on social networking sites, a data snooper with some background knowledge could use the publicly available information to re-identify customers in corporate databases.

In the era of social networks, de-identification becomes highly challenging.

## 1.3 Use Cases: Need for Sharing Data

Organizations tend to share customer data as there is much insight to be gained from customer-sensitive data. For example, a healthcare provider's database could contain how patients have reacted to a particular drug or treatment. This information would be useful to a pharmaceutical company. However, these sensitive data cannot be shared or released due to legal, financial, compliance, and moral issues. But for the benefit of the organization and the customer, there is a need to share these data responsibly, which means the data are shared without revealing the PII of the customer. Figure 1.2 sets

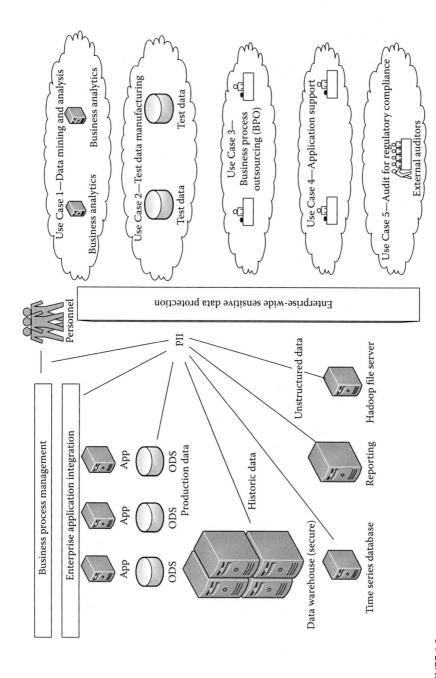

**FIGURE 1.2**
Sensitive data in the enterprise.

the context for this book, which illustrates the importance of enterprise-wide sensitive data protection. PII is found in all layers of architecture like business processes, applications, operational data stores (ODSs), data warehouse for historic data, time series databases, file servers for unstructured data, and reports. Whether data are shared with internal departments or external vendors, it is critical to protect the privacy of customer data. It is important to have an enterprise-wide privacy preservation design strategy to address the heterogeneity in data sources, data structures, and usage scenarios.

What are the relevant use cases for which data are shared by organizations? Let us now explore for what purposes the data are shared and how.

- Data mining and analysis
- Application testing
- Business operation
- Application support
- Auditing and reporting for regulatory compliance

These use cases can be classified under two categories:

1. Privacy protection of sensitive data at rest
2. Privacy protection of sensitive data in motion (at run-time)

The first two use cases fall under the first category and the rest under the second category. One important aspect to note here—without privacy preservation none of these use cases is feasible. Figure 1.3 illustrates this concept. A brief coverage of some of the use cases is provided here, and they are dealt with in detail in dedicated chapters in the book.

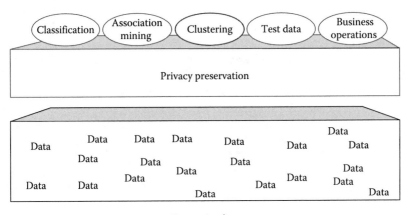

**FIGURE 1.3**
Use cases for privacy preservation.

### 1.3.1 Data Mining and Analysis

Banks would want to understand their customers' credit card usage patterns, a retail company would like to study customers' buying habits, and a healthcare company would like to understand the effectiveness of a drug or treatment provided to their patients. All these patterns are hidden in the massive amounts of data they hold. The intention of the company is to gather comprehensive knowledge from these hidden patterns. Data mining is the technique that is used to gather knowledge and predict outcomes from large quantities of data. The goal of data mining is to extract knowledge, discover patterns, predict, learn, and so on. The key functional blocks in most data mining applications are classification, clustering, and association pattern mining.

Classification is defined as categorizing observations into various classes or groups. Classification is an approach for predicting qualitative discrete response variables—response will be either YES or NO. Many techniques are used for classification—decision trees, random forests, support vector machines, Bayesian classifiers, etc. An example could be that of customers defaulting on mortgage payments. In this case, the intention is to understand "customers in which income bracket will default on payments." For this to work, the classifier needs to work on training data so that it can come up with a model to be used for prediction. Training data contain sensitive customer information. All this needs to be carried out in a way that preserves privacy. Training data are also not directly available. Synthetic data need to be generated to train this model, which will later need testing using some valid test data.

While classification comes under supervised learning where we are interested in predicting an outcome, clustering is an unsupervised learning technique for finding subgroups in the data set. The goal of clustering is exploratory learning rather than prediction. In order to protect the confidentiality of customer data, anonymization techniques are used to prevent identity and attribute disclosure, but the important aspect that needs to be considered is "what is the correct approach to anonymize in cluster analysis?" For example, are perturbative techniques more suitable than nonperturbative techniques for cluster analysis?

Association pattern mining is very similar to clustering and is defined in the context of sparse binary transaction databases where data entries are either 0 or 1. In this context, it should determine all the subsets of columns such that all the values in the columns take on the values of 1. For example, when a customer buys a product A, he will certainly also buy product B—this shows a strong association between A and B. Customers who buy bread may invariably buy butter. Association rule mining is extensively used in retail supermarkets (for positioning their products in store), healthcare, pharmaceuticals, and e-commerce companies. When such data are mined, customers' transactions and their personal information could get compromised. Therefore, it is important to mine association rules or patterns in a way that preserves privacy.

### 1.3.2 Software Application Testing

A number of companies across the globe outsource their application testing. Outsourcing of testing is growing at about 20% every year. Application testing comprises functional requirements and nonfunctional requirements testing. Successful application testing requires high-quality test data. High-quality test data are present in production systems and this is sensitive customer data, which must be anonymized before sharing with testers. A high-level process of test data manufacturing is shown in Figure 1.4. How to ensure the privacy of test data and at the same time make it useful for testing is examined in detail in Chapter 6.

### 1.3.3 Business Operations

Many large companies across the globe outsource their business operations to business process outsourcing (BPO) companies in countries like India, China, and Brazil. For example, a financial services company outsources its business operations to a BPO company in India. Then that BPO company will assist customers of the financial services company in their business operations such as securities trading, managing their financial transactions, and so on.

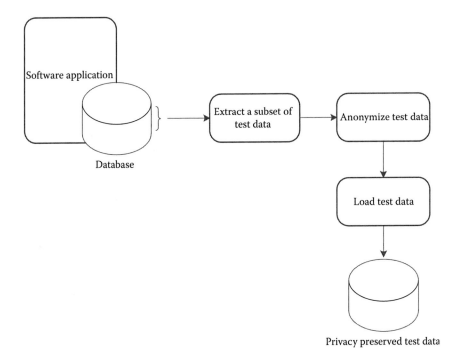

**FIGURE 1.4**
Privacy preserving test data manufacturing.

But access to a customer's trade account during these processes would expose a lot of sensitive information and this is not acceptable to the customer, and the regulation in the country will not permit such access. Therefore, these data have to be protected. But the question is how and what data are to be protected? A technique known as tokenization is used here wherein the sensitive data that should not be seen by the BPO employee are replaced with a token. This token has no relationship with the original data, and outside the context of the application the token has no meaning at all. All these are executed during run-time. Like privacy preserving data mining and test data management, protection of sensitive data is a subject in itself and is covered in depth in this book.

## 1.4 Methods of Protecting Data

One of the most daunting tasks in information security is protecting sensitive data in enterprise applications, which are often complex and distributed. What methods are available to protect sensitive data? Some of the methods available are cryptography, anonymization, and tokenization, which are briefly discussed in this section, and a detailed coverage is provided in the other chapters in the book. Of course, there are other one-way functions like hashing.

Cryptographic techniques are probably one of the oldest known techniques for data protection. When done right, they are probably one of the safest techniques to protect data in motion and at rest. Encrypted data have high protection, but are not readable, so how can we use such data? Another issue associated with cryptography is key management. Any compromise of key means complete loss of privacy. For the use cases discussed in this book, cryptographic techniques are not used widely. Of course, there are techniques like secure multiparty computation (MPC) and zero-knowledge proof (ZKP), which are discussed in detail in Duan and Canny [3].

Anonymization is a set of techniques used to modify the original data in such a manner that it does not resemble the original value but maintains the semantics and syntax. Regulatory compliance and ethical issues drive the need for anonymization. The intent is that anonymized data can be shared freely with other parties, who can perform their own analysis on the data. Anonymization is an optimization problem, in that when the original data are modified they lose some of its utility. But modification of the data is required to protect it. An anonymization design is a balancing act between data privacy and utility. Privacy goals are set by the data owners, and utility goals are set by data users. Now, is it really possible to optimally achieve this balance between privacy and utility? We will explore this throughout this book.

Tokenization is a data protection technique that has been extensively used in the credit card industry but is currently being adopted in other domains as well.

Tokenization is a technique that replaces the original sensitive data with non-sensitive placeholders referred to as tokens. The fundamental difference between tokenization and the other techniques is that in tokenization, the original data are completely replaced by a surrogate that has no connection to the original data. Tokens have the same format as the original data. As tokens are not derived from the original data, they exhibit very powerful data protection features. Another interesting point of tokens is, although the token is usable within its native application environment, it is completely useless elsewhere. Therefore, tokenization is ideal to protect sensitive identifying information.

## 1.5 Importance of Balancing Data Privacy and Utility

In the introductory section, we looked at how an enterprise provisions data for purposes like application testing, knowledge discovery, and data analysis. We also emphasized the importance of privacy preservation of customer data before publishing them. Privacy preservation should also ensure utility of data. In other words, the provisioned data should protect the individual's privacy and at the same time ensure that the anonymized data are useful for knowledge discovery. By anonymizing the data, EI are completely masked out, QI is de-identified by applying a transformation function, and SD is left in its original form. There is a strong correlation between QI and SD fields. So, as part of privacy preservation, this correlation between QI fields and SD fields should not be lost. If the correlation is lost, then the resulting data set is not useful for any purpose.

As a transformation function is applied on QI, it is obvious that the correlation between QI fields and SD fields is affected or weakened, and this indicates how useful the transformed data are for the given purpose. Let us take an example from the healthcare domain to illustrate this important relationship between privacy and utility. HIPAA states that if any of the data elements are associated with health information, it makes that information personally identifiable. HIPAA defines 18 attributes as PII that include name, SSN, geographic information, demographic information telephone number, admission date, etc. [4]. Therefore, in any privacy preserving data analysis of health data, it should be ensured that any of these 18 attributes, if present, should be completely anonymized. If so much information is stripped off, then how can the remaining data be useful for the analysis? Let us take an example of a patient getting admitted to a hospital. According to the HIPAA privacy rules, the admission date is part of the patient's PII and therefore should be anonymized. The healthcare provider can share the patient's medical data to external partners for the analysis, but it will be impossible to analyze the efficacy of the treatment as the date of admission is anonymized as per HIPAA privacy laws. HIPAA's intention is to protect patient privacy, but it impacts medical research in the process. Therefore, it is extremely important to ensure the utility of the data while preserving privacy. In other words, there needs to be a balance between privacy and utility of anonymized data. Figure 1.5 provides a map of privacy versus utility.

In the previous section, we looked at different mechanisms to protect data. Cryptographic mechanism provides low utility (0) and high privacy (1) when data are encrypted and it provides high utility (1) and low privacy (0) when data are decrypted. The privacy or utility in a cryptographic mechanism is either black (0) or white (1), whereas in anonymization methods, it is "shades of gray," meaning that is possible to control the levels of privacy or utility. Anonymization can be viewed as constrained optimization—produce a data set with smallest distortion that also satisfies the given set of privacy requirements. But how do you balance the two contrasting features—privacy and utility?

Anonymized data are utilized in many areas of an organization like data mining, analysis, or creating test data. An important point to remember here is each type of requirement or analysis warrants a different anonymization design. This means that there is no single privacy versus utility measure. To understand privacy versus utility trade-off, let us take the original data given in Table 1.6.

1. Original data table with no privacy but high utility
2. High correlation between QI and SD (attributes fields)

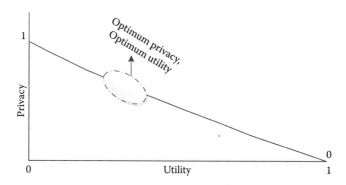

**FIGURE 1.5**
Privacy versus utility map.

**TABLE 1.6**

Original Table with Strong Correlation between QI and SD

| Name | Zip Code | Gender | Income |
|------|----------|--------|--------|
| Chen | 56001 | Male | 25K |
| Jenny | 56015 | Female | 8K |
| Alice | 56001 | Female | 30K |
| Ram | 56011 | Male | 5K |

Table 1.6 shows four individuals. Although many rows have not been shown here, let us assume that the ZIP CODE and INCOME are correlated, in that the ZIP CODE 56001 primarily consists of high-income individuals. Table 1.7 is a modified version of Table 1.6. Let us not worry about the techniques used to anonymize data, but focus just on the results. We can see that the names have been changed, the original ZIP CODES have been replaced with different values and INCOME values are unchanged.

Let us assess gains and losses for this anonymization design.

Privacy gain: Names are substituted (hence protected), financial standing is not attributed to another zip code, and geographical location is anonymized. Utility loss: Gender information is preserved, names are substituted while preserving demographic clues, correlation is preserved but the zip code is different.

Another design can have just "XXXX" for all names, 56001 for all zip codes, and "Male" for all gender values. We can agree that this anonymization design scores well in terms of privacy, but utility is pathetic. Privacy gain: Names are completely suppressed, financial standing cannot be inferred, and geographical location is not compromised. Utility loss: Presence of females in the population, meaningless names lose demographic clues, flat value of zip code annuls the correlation.

This shows that anonymization design drives the extent of privacy and utility, which are always opposed to each other. The two designs also show that privacy or utility need not be 0 and 1 as in encryption; rather, both are shades of gray as stated earlier. A good design can achieve a balance between them and achieve both goals to a reasonable extent.

One way to quantify privacy is on the basis of how much information an adversary can obtain about the SD of an individual from different dimensions in the data set [5–8]. These references state that SD fields can be identified (or estimated/deduced) using QI fields. This is a very simple way to quantify privacy. In fact, this model does not capture many important dimensions, such as background knowledge of the adversary, adversary's knowledge of some of the sensitive data, the complexity of the data structure, etc. We discuss this in sufficient detail in Chapter 4.

The utility loss of a particular anonymization technique is measured against the utility provided by the original data set. A measure of utility

**TABLE 1.7**

Anonymized Table with Generalized Values—Correlation between QI and SD Is Broken

| Name | Zip Code | Gender | Income |
|------|----------|--------|--------|
| Yang | 56000 | Male | 25K |
| Emma | 56010 | Female | 8K |
| Olivia | 56000 | Female | 30K |
| Krishna | 56010 | Male | 5K |

is also the correlation between QI and SD preserved in the anonymized data. There are many anonymization techniques in use today, which can be broadly classified into perturbative and nonperturbative techniques. Each of these techniques provides its own privacy versus utility model. The core goals of these anonymization techniques are (1) to prevent an adversary from identifying SD fields and (2) to ensure minimal utility loss in the anonymized data set by ensuring high correlation between the QI and SD fields. This is easier said than done. These are extremely difficult goals to meet. To address this complex set of problem patterns, we have defined a rich set of anonymization design principles in Appendix A.

### 1.5.1 Measuring Privacy of Anonymized Data

Given a data set D, a data anonymizer can create different anonymized data sets $D_1'$, $D_2'$,..., $D_n'$ based on different anonymization algorithm combinations for each attribute. Each of these anonymized data sets will have different privacy versus utility trade-offs. Privacy is a relative measure. This means that the privacy of $D_1'$ is measured against another anonymized data set $D_2'$. There are multiple ways to measure the difference in privacy. These approaches are broadly classified into statistical and probabilistic methods. Some statistical approaches measure privacy in terms of the difference or variation in perturbed variables. The larger the variance, the better the privacy of the perturbed data. This technique is generally used for statistical databases.

Probabilistic methods measure privacy loss when an adversary has knowledge of the distribution of the data in the original data set and background information about some tuples in the data set. For example, consider the simple example in Table 1.8.

Bob is the adversary and has some background information about Alice as she is his neighbor. Bob knows that Alice smokes heavily but does not really know what disease she is suffering from. However, he has knowledge about the distribution of the sensitive fields in a table containing medical records of a hospital that he has noticed Alice visiting. Bob then uses the knowledge of the distribution of SD fields and background information about Alice to identify her illness, which is cancer.

**TABLE 1.8**

Background Knowledge of the Adversary about the Distribution of SD Fields

| Name | Zip Code | Gender | Disease |
|---|---|---|---|
| John Smith | 46001 | Male | Hypertension |
| Tom Henry | 46005 | Male | Gastritis |
| Alice Williams | 46001 | Female | Cancer |
| Little Wood | 46011 | Male | Asthma |

### 1.5.2 Measuring Utility of Anonymized Data

Assume that in the original data D, QI, and SD are highly correlated. An example could be the correlation between demographic and geographic information, such as year of birth, country of birth, locality code, and income [10]. Data set D contains the truth about the relationship between demographic and geographic information and income. While anonymizing D, the truth should be preserved for the data to be useful. When D is anonymized to D' using a transformation function T, D' = T(D), the QI fields are distorted to some extent in D'. Now, how true is D'? Does the correlation between QI and SD fields in D' still exist? Each anonymization function will provide different levels of distortion. If Q is the distribution of QI fields in D and Q' is the distribution of QI fields in D', then the statistical distance measure of Q and Q' provides an indication of the utility of D' [11]. This reference provides a number of approaches to measure utility.

In Chapter 6, we show that the quality of anonymized test data sets is one of the drivers for test coverage. The higher the quality of test data, the higher will be the test coverage. High-quality test data are present in production systems and contain PII. Privacy preservation results in poor test data quality or utility. Reduced utility reflects lower test coverage. We examine different anonymization approaches and resulting utility.

## 1.6 Introduction to Anonymization Design Principles

Anonymization design is not straightforward. As we saw in Section 1.5, achieving a balance between privacy and utility has many dependencies. So, what are the drivers for anonymization design? Factors that drive anonymization design for a given requirement are illustrated in Figure 1.6.

When there is a need for data privacy, organizations generally use either a commercial or a home-grown product for anonymizing data. It is critical to ensure that an organization's data anonymization program is not limited by the features of the product. Many organizations fail to maintain a balance between privacy and utility. It is generally difficult to determine how much anonymization is required, which results in either loss of information or the anonymized data set becoming unusable. Even with adoption of the best of breed data anonymization products, an organization's anonymization program may not be successful. In addition to this, the pressures of regulatory compliance force many organizations to be very defensive and adopt very high privacy standards that will render the data unusable for any research. Take, for example, HIPAA or Swiss Data Protection Act, which are highly restrictive with an intention to protect the privacy of an individual. If enough care is not taken, then the anonymized data could

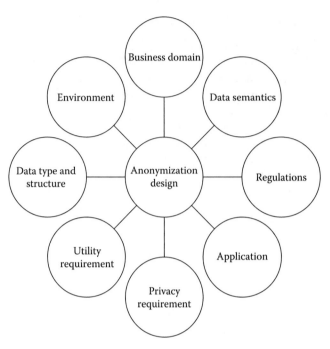

**FIGURE 1.6**
Drivers for anonymization design.

have very little utility. In this context, irrespective of which tool an organization uses, there is a need for a mechanism to monitor privacy versus utility for various privacy requirements. Unfortunately, quantifying privacy and utility is nontrivial. Therefore, it is critical to provide assurance of high quality of data anonymization during the initial phase of the anonymization life cycle. To support this, we felt it is necessary to define a set of design principles. These principles will provide the required guidelines for the data anonymizer to adopt the correct design for a given anonymization requirement.

As software architects, we start the architecting process by following a set of architecture principles that will guide us to come up with the correct design for the system. We base our work here on a similar approach. In [12], the authors classify principles into two broad types—scientific and normative. Scientific principles are laws of nature and form the fundamental truths that one can build upon. Normative principles act as a guide and need to be enforced. Similarly, a data anonymizer needs guidance, and the anonymization design principles should be enforced to ensure proper anonymization design. These principles are fundamental in nature and are applicable to all aspects of anonymization. They connect the high-level privacy and utility requirements to low-level implementation.

In this book, all principles are explained in the following form:

- Principle Name
- Rationale
- Implications

These anonymization principles can be found in Appendix A.

## 1.7 Nature of Data in the Enterprise

### 1.7.1 Multidimensional Data

Multidimensional data also referred to as relational data are the most common format of data available today in many enterprises. In a relational table, each row is a vector that represents an entity. The columns represent the attributes of the entity. As relational data are the most common data format, a lot of attention has been paid to privacy preservation of relational data [2,13,14]. As described earlier, a row of data in a relational table is classified into explicit identifiers, quasi-identifiers, sensitive data, and nonsensitive data. Both perturbative and nonperturbative techniques could be used to protect the data. As a rule, EI are completely masked out, QI are anonymized, and SD are left in their original form. (These terms are explained in detail in Chapter 2.) Depending on the sensitivity of data, appropriate data protection techniques can be applied. The fundamental differences between anonymizing multidimensional data and other data structures are as follows:

- In a multidimensional data table, each record or row is independent of others; therefore, anonymizing a few of the records will not affect other records.
- Anonymizing a tuple in a record will not affect other tuples in the record.

Other complex data structures, such as graph, longitudinal, or time series data, cannot be viewed in this way. Privacy preservation for multidimensional data can be classified into (1) random perturbation methods and (2) group anonymization techniques, such as k-anonymity or *l*-diversity. These techniques are used to prevent identity disclosure and attribute disclosure.

### *1.7.1.1 Challenges in Privacy Preservation of Multidimensional Data*

The challenges in this kind of data preservation are as follows:

1. Difficulty in identifying the boundary between QI and SD in the presence of background knowledge of the adversary
2. High dimensionality of data poses a big challenge to privacy preservation
3. Clusters in sensitive data set
4. Difficulty in achieving realistic balance between privacy and utility

### 1.7.2 Transaction Data

Transaction data are a classic example of sparse high-dimensional data. A transaction database holds transactions of a customer at a supermarket or it can be used to hold the diagnosis codes of a patient in a hospital. Privacy of transaction data is very critical as an adversary who has access to this database can obtain the shopping preferences of customers and exploit that information. But the problem with transaction database is that it is of very high dimensionality and sparsely filled. A supermarket will have thousands of products contributing to the high dimensionality of the transaction database. Moreover, the transactional data contained in the database are binary—either 0 or 1. An event of a transaction is represented by 1; otherwise, it would be a 0 (Table 1.9).

In this table, $P_1$–$P_n$ represents the products in the supermarket. The customer Hari has made a transaction on $P_3$ and $P_6$, which means his shopping cart contains product $P_3$ and $P_6$, say bread and cheese. There is nothing sensitive about a customer buying bread and cheese. But if the product happens to be a blood glucose or blood pressure monitor, then that transaction is sensitive from the customer's perspective as he would not want others to know that he is diabetic. It is the sensitivity of the transaction that needs to be protected. Privacy preservation techniques used in the case of relational data table will not be applicable here.

**TABLE 1.9**

Sample Sparse High-Dimensional Transaction Database
in a Supermarket

| Name | $P_1$ | $P_2$ | $P_3$ | $P_4$ | $P_5$ | $P_6$ | $P_n$ |
|------|------|------|------|------|------|------|------|
| Hari |      |      | 1    |      |      | 1    |      |
| Nancy | 1   |      |      | 1    |      |      |      |
| Jim  |      | 1    |      |      |      |      | 1    |

### 1.7.2.1 Challenges in Privacy Preservation of Transaction Data

Some of the challenges in privacy preservation of transaction data are as follows:

1. High dimensionality.
2. Sparsity.
3. Conventional privacy preservation techniques used for relational tables that have fixed schema are not applicable on transaction data.

## 1.7.3 Longitudinal Data

Longitudinal studies are carried out extensively in the healthcare domain. An example would be the study of the effects of a treatment or medicine on an individual over a period of time. The measurement of the effects is repeatedly taken over that period of time on the same individual. The goal of longitudinal study is to characterize the response of the individual to the treatment. Longitudinal studies also help in understanding the factors that influence the changes in response. Consider the following table that illustrates the effect of treatment for hypertension in a patient (Table 1.10).

The table contains a longitudinal set D, which has three disjoint sets of data—EI, QI, and SD. A few important characteristics of the data set D that must be considered while designing an anonymization approach are as follows:

- Data are clustered—composed of repeated measurements obtained from a single individual at different points in time.
- The data within the cluster are correlated.
- The data within the cluster have a temporal order, which means the first measurement will be followed by the second and so on [15].

**TABLE 1.10**

Sample Longitudinal Data Set in the Healthcare Domain

| ID | Name | DOB | ZIP | Service Date | Diseases | Systolic (mmHg) | Diastolic (mmHg) |
|----|------|-----|-----|--------------|----------|-----------------|------------------|
| 1 | Bob | 1976 | 56711 | 30/05/2012 | Hypertension | 180 | 95 |
| 2 | Bob | 1976 | 56711 | 31/05/2012 | Hypertension | 160 | 90 |
| 3 | Bob | 1976 | 56711 | 01/06/2012 | Hypertension | 140 | 85 |
| 4 | Bob | 1976 | 56711 | 02/06/2012 | Hypertension | 130 | 90 |
| 5 | Bob | 1976 | 56711 | 03/06/2012 | Hypertension | 125 | 85 |
| 6 | Bob | 1976 | 56711 | 04/06/2012 | Hypertension | 120 | 80 |
| 7 | Alice | 1969 | 56812 | 31/03/2012 | Hypertension | 160 | 90 |

These are to be noted because the anonymization design should ensure that these characteristics of D are preserved in the anonymized data set D', otherwise, the truth in the data will be lost.

### 1.7.3.1 Challenges in Anonymizing Longitudinal Data

Anonymization design for longitudinal data should consider two aspects:

1. The characteristics of longitudinal data in the anonymized data set D' should be maintained.
2. Anonymization designs aim to prevent identity and attribute disclosure.

Consider the longitudinal data set D, which has three disjoint sets of data (EI, QI, and SD). EI are completely masked to prevent identification. QI are anonymized using generalization and suppression to prevent identity disclosure. In the case of longitudinal data, anonymizing identity attributes alone is not sufficient to prevent an adversary from re-identifying the patient. An adversary can still link some of the sensitive attributes to the publicly available data, that is, medical records. Now comes the need to prevent attributes disclosure. For longitudinal data, an anonymization design that prevents identity as well as attributes disclosure is required [16]. There are a number of techniques to prevent identity disclosure, such as perturbative and nonperturbative techniques. Effective anonymization techniques are required to prevent attributes disclosure, but these techniques should also ensure that they preserve the characteristics of longitudinal data.

### 1.7.4 Graph Data

Graph data are interesting and found in many domains like social networks, Electronics, Transportation, Software, and Telecom. A graph G = (V,E) consists of a set of vertices together with a set of vertex pairs or edges. Graphs are interesting as they model almost any relationship. This is especially relevant in modeling networks like financial networks and also social networks like Facebook, LinkedIn, and Twitter. It is in these types of applications, we see the need for privacy preservation of graph data. Social networks have many users and contain a lot of personal information, such as network of friends and personal preferences. Social network data analytics is a rich source of information for many companies that want to understand how their products are received by the customers. For example, a bank would like to get feedback from their customers about the various financial products and services they offer. The bank can have its own page on, say, Facebook where its customers provide their views and feedback. Publishing these data for mining and analysis will compromise the privacy of the customers. Therefore, it is required to anonymize the data before provisioning it for analytics. However, graph data are complex in nature. The more complex the data structure, the easier it is to identify entities [17].

Due to the complexity of graph data, the anonymization design applied is different compared to that applied to relational data tables. In the case of relational data tables, each row is treated as an entity and its QI are anonymized to prevent identity disclosure. The attack model in relational data is also straightforward. An adversary will use an external data source to identify an individual via the QI. Graph data are more complex, and because of their complexity they provide more avenues for re-identification. Consider the network shown in Figures 1.7 and 1.8.

Figure 1.7 depicts a network with original data of users. The same has been anonymized in Figure 1.8. Will this anonymization be enough to thwart an adversary's attempt to re-identify the users? The simple answer is no. The many challenges in anonymizing graph data are discussed next.

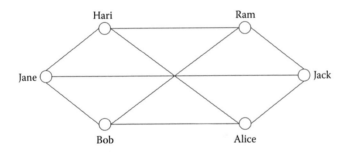

**FIGURE 1.7**
Graph network with original data.

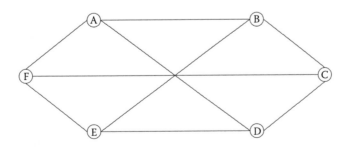

**FIGURE 1.8**
Modified graph network.

### 1.7.4.1 Challenges in Anonymizing Graph Data

Privacy of graph data can be classified into three categories [18]:

1. Identity disclosure
2. Link disclosure
3. Content/attribute disclosure

Apart from these, graph metrics such as betweenness, closeness, reachability, path length, and centrality can also be used to breach the privacy of target individuals in a graph network.

*Identity disclosure*: Identity disclosure occurs when it is possible to identify the users in the network.

*Content disclosure*: Just as in relational table, sensitive content is associated with each node (entity). This sensitive content is classified into explicit identifiers like name, SSN, and QI, such as demographics, gender, date of birth, and other sensitive data such as preferences and relationships.

*Link disclosure*: Links between users are highly sensitive and can be used to identify relationships between users.

It is very challenging to anonymize graph data as it is difficult to devise an anonymizing design. For the graph to maintain privacy and utility after anonymization, the techniques need to alter the graph, but just enough to prevent identity, content, and link disclosure. At the same time, changing the nodes or labels could affect other nodes in the network and could potentially alter the structure of the network itself. Meanwhile, there are multiple avenues to identify a user in a graph network since it is difficult to model the adversary's background knowledge. How to provision graph data in a privacy preserving way for mining and analysis? What anonymization techniques are available for graph data?

### 1.7.5 Time Series Data

Time series data result from taking measurements at regular intervals of time from a process. An example of this could be temperature measurement from a sensor or daily values of a stock, the net asset value of a fund taken on a daily basis, or blood pressure measurements of a patient taken on a weekly basis. We looked at longitudinal data where we considered the response of a patient to blood pressure medication. The measurements have a temporal order. So, what is the difference between longitudinal data and time series data? Longitudinal data are extensively used in the healthcare domain, especially in clinical trials. Longitudinal data represent repeated measurements taken on a person. These measurements are responses to a treatment or drug, and there is a strong correlation among these measurements. A univariate time series is a set of long measurements of a single variable taken at regular

**TABLE 1.11**

Sample Time Series Data Table Showing Weekly Sales of Companies

| ID | Company Name | Address | Week 1 | Week 2 | Week 3 | Week 4 | Week 5 |
|----|------|---------|--------|--------|--------|--------|--------|
| 1 | ABC | Park Street, 56001 | 10,000 | 12,000 | 17,000 | 8,000 | 11,000 |
| 2 | ACME | Kings Street, 56003 | 15,000 | 17,000 | 18,000 | 20,000 | 21,000 |
| 3 | XYZ | Main Street, 56022 | 20,000 | 23,000 | 25,000 | 26,000 | 30,000 |
| 4 | PQR | Queen Street, 56021 | 14,000 | 18,000 | 19,000 | 19,500 | 21,000 |

intervals, say, blood pressure measurements of a patient taken over a period of time. These measurements need not necessarily be a response to a drug or treatment. Longitudinal data have very small dimensions compared to time series data that have high dimensional and keep growing. Sample time series data showing weekly sales of their products are given in Table 1.11.

It can be observed from the table that each record has three disjoint sets of data—EI, QI, and SD. This is very similar to the structure of multidimensional data. But that is where the similarity ends. In multidimensional data, each record is independent of the others and can be anonymized without affecting other records. The tuples in each record can be anonymized without affecting other tuples in the record. But this approach cannot be used with time series data because of its large size, high dimensionality, and pattern. This makes privacy preservation rather challenging.

### 1.7.5.1 Challenges in Privacy Preservation of Time Series Data

Some of the challenges in privacy preservation of the time series data are as follows:

- High dimensionality
- Retaining the statistical properties of the original time series data like mean, variance, and so on
- Supporting various types of queries like range query or pattern matching query
- Preventing identity disclosure and linkage attacks

## References

1. J.M. Skopek, Anonymity: The production of goods and institutional design, *Fordham Law Review*, 82(4), 1751–1809, 2014, http://ir.lawnet.fordham.edu/flr/vol82/iss4/4/.
2. L. Sweeney, k-Anonymity: A model for protecting privacy, *International Journal of Uncertainty, Fuzziness and Knowledge Based Systems*, 10 (5), 557–570, 2002.

3. Y. Duan and J. Canny, Practical distributed privacy-preserving data analysis at large scale, in *Large Scale Data Analytics*, A. Gkoulalas-Divanis, A. Labbi (eds.), 2014 Springer.

4. Summary of the HIPAA Privacy Rule, http://www.hhs.gov/ocr/privacy/hipaa/understanding/summary/index.html. Accessed October, 2015

5. A. Machanavajjhala et al., l-Diversity: Privacy beyond k-Anonymity, in *Proceedings of the 22nd International Conference Data Engineering (ICDE 2006)*, Atlanta, GA, 2006, p. 24.

6. T. Li and N. Li, On the trade-off between privacy and utility in data publishing, in *Proceedings of the 15th ACM SIGKDD International Conference on Knowledge Discovery and Data Mining*, ACM, Paris, France, June 28–July 1, 2009, pp. 517–525.

7. N. Li, T. Li, and S. Venkatasubramanian, t-closeness: Privacy beyond k-anonymity and l-diversity, in *Proceedings of the IEEE International Conference Data Engineering (ICDE 2007)*, 2007, Istanbul, Turkey, pp. 106–115.

8. R.C.-W. Wong, J. Li, A.W.-C. Fu, and K. Wang, ($\alpha$, k)-anonymity: An enhanced k-anonymity model for privacy preserving data publishing, in *Proceedings of the 12th International Conference on Knowledge Discovery and Data Mining*, 2006, Philadelphia, PA, pp. 754–759.

9. X. Xiao and Y. Tao, Anatomy: Simple and effective privacy preservation, in *Proceedings of the 32nd International Conference on Very Large Data Bases (VLDB 2006)*, Seoul, South Korea, 2006, pp. 139–150.

10. N. Shlomo, Accessing microdata via the internet, Joint UN/ECE and Eurostat work session on statistical data confidentiality, Luxembourg, April 7–9, 2003.

11. D. Kifer and J. Gehrke, Injecting utility into anonymized datasets, in *Proceedings of the ACM SIGMOD International Conference on Management of Data (SIGMOD 2006)*, Chicago, IL, June 27–29, 2006.

12. D. Greefhorst and E. Proper, *Architecture Principles: The Cornerstone of Enterprise Architecture*, Springer, Berlin, Heidelberg, 2011.

13. P. Samarati, Protecting respondents identities in micro data release, in *IEEE Transactions on Knowledge Data Engineering*, 2001, pp. 1010–1027.

14. C.C. Aggarwal, On k-anonymity and curse of dimensionality, in *Proceedings of the Very Large Data Base*, Trondheim, Norway, 2005, pp. 901–909.

15. G.M. Fitzmaurice, N.M. Laird, and J.H. Ware, *Applied Longitudinal Analysis*, 2nd edn., Wiley, August 30, 2011.

16. M. Sehatkar and S. Matwin, HALT: Hybrid anonymization of longitudinal transaction, in *11th Annual Conference on Privacy, Security and Trust (PST)*, IEEE, 2013, Tarragona, Spain, pp. 127–137.

17. M.L. Maag, L. Denoyer, and P. Gallinari, Graph anonymization using machine learning, in *The 28th IEEE International Conference on Advanced Information Networking Application*, 2014, Victoria, BC, Canada, pp. 1111–1118.

18. E. Zheleva and L. Getoor, Preserving the privacy of sensitive relationships in graph data, in *Proceedings of the First ACM SIGKDD International Workshop in Privacy, Security and Trust*, 2007, San Jose, CA.

19. B.E. Burke, Information protection and control survey: Data loss prevention and encryption trends. IDC Special Study, Doc. # 211109, 2008.

# 2

# *Static Data Anonymization Part I: Multidimensional Data*

## 2.1 Introduction

In Chapter 1, we looked at various data structures such as multidimensional data, graph data, longitudinal data, transactional data, and time series data. We also understood what attributes in these data structures are to be anonymized. In this chapter, we look at how to effectively anonymize data, anonymization algorithms, quality aspects of algorithms, and privacy versus utility features. This book deals with two main applications of static data anonymization—privacy preserving data mining (PPDM) and privacy preserving test data management (PPTDM)—while the focus is on the study of various anonymization techniques in these application areas.

Static data anonymization deals with protecting identities and preventing breaches on data that are at rest. In this chapter, we focus on multidimensional or relational data, while the next chapter introduces anonymization techniques in complex data structures. Relational data also known as multidimensional data are the easiest format in which data are represented today. Multidimensional data are both easy to work upon and understand, the latter making it an easy target for privacy attacks. This chapter will take us through the classification of data, protection mechanisms of each class, and a look at some popular group anonymization techniques that are in use today.

## 2.2 Classification of Privacy Preserving Methods

A multidimensional data set D consists of four disjoint sets of data: explicit identifiers (EI), quasi-identifiers (QI), sensitive data (SD), and nonsensitive data (NSD). EI consist of identification numbers such as SSN and vehicle identification numbers (VIN), and names (first, last, and middle), or, in other words, any identifier that can directly identify a record owner. QI consist of identifiers such as age, data of birth, address, phone numbers, and so on. These identifiers are categorical attributes, mainly categorical nominal. No arithmetic operations are possible on nominal values, but their finite value range needs to be used while designing anonymization methods.

Sensitive data sets consist of numerical data or strings. Usually, SD are left in their original form to enable the utility of data. But there are exceptional scenarios where it is necessary to protect SD also to some extent.

Data protection methods can be classified into two groups, as shown in Figure 2.1.

To effectively anonymize data, more than one technique needs to be used. Consider a multidimensional data set D shown in Table 2.1.

Data Table D is classified into three disjoint sets of data. This is the first critical step in anonymization design.

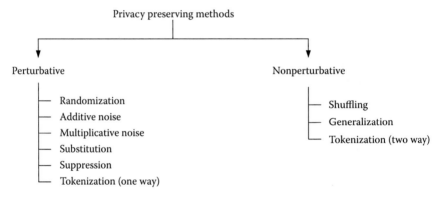

**FIGURE 2.1**
Classification of privacy preserving methods.

**TABLE 2.1**

Sample Salary Data Table

| EI | | | QI | | | SD | | | |
|---|---|---|---|---|---|---|---|---|---|
| ID | Name | Gender | Age | Address | Zip | Basic | HRA | Med | All |
| 12345 | John | M | 25 | 1, 4th St. | 560001 | 10,000 | 5,000 | 1000 | 6,000 |
| 56789 | Harry | M | 36 | 358, A dr. | 560068 | 20,000 | 10,000 | 1000 | 12,000 |
| 52131 | Hari | M | 21 | 3, Stone Ct | 560055 | 12,000 | 6,000 | 1000 | 7,200 |
| 85438 | Mary | F | 28 | 51, Elm st. | 560003 | 16,000 | 8,000 | 1000 | 9,600 |
| 91281 | Srini | M | 40 | 9, Ode Rd | 560001 | 14,000 | 7,000 | 1000 | 8,400 |
| 11253 | Chan | M | 35 | 3, 9th Ave | 560051 | 8,000 | 4,000 | 1000 | 4,800 |

## 2.3 Classification of Data in a Multidimensional Data Set

Classify the data set D as per Principle (1) into EI, QI, SD, and NSD with clear boundaries between them.

### 2.3.1 Protecting Explicit Identifiers

A multidimensional database consists of attributes of different data types, such as numeric, strings, and so on. Data anonymization methods should focus on the semantics of the data and not the syntax.

Principle (8): Understand the semantics of the data in the context of the application so as to apply the correct/appropriate anonymization technique on the data.

Example: EI identify a record owner explicitly and as such should be completely masked. Consider Table 2.1. There are two identifiers that are EI: ID and Name (Table 2.2).

EI generally include identifying fields such as SSN, VIN, driver's license number, tax number, and so on. In a multidimensional database, which is also represented as a relational database, identifying fields, such as SSN, are very commonly used as a primary key in a relational data model design. Whether this is a good practice or not is debatable, but this is often the case. Moreover, these identifying fields are commonly found in downstream and

**TABLE 2.2**

Tokenizing ID and Substituting Name

| ID | Name | ID | Name |
|----|------|----|------|
| (a) Original EI | | (b) Masked EI | |
| 12345 | John | 40011 | Jack |
| 56789 | Harry | 81100 | Sammy |
| 52131 | Hari | 62410 | Mark |
| 85438 | Mary | 79820 | Jane |
| 91281 | Srini | 14532 | Singh |
| 11253 | Chan | 22244 | Khan |

Tokenization (one way) algorithm

Name Database

upstream applications in the enterprise. Therefore, while masking these fields, it is critical to take care of two aspects.

1. Referential integrity
2. Consistently masking across databases

Principle (4): Ensure consistency in masking data across applications in a domain.

To preserve the format of identifying attributes and also bring in consistency across applications in a domain, we suggest a tokenization (one-way)-based algorithm.

The tokenization method generates a unique token for a given input. For example,

Input data: 12345 → TOKENIZE → output token: 40011

So, whenever the input data are 12345, the tokenization algorithm will always generate the same unique token, for example, 40011. The main advantage of tokenization is that it is highly secure, that is, tokens generated have no relationships with the original input data. The token 40011 has no meaning outside the context of the application or domain. The other advantage is that the tokenization algorithm preserves the format of the input data. Moreover, tokenization is not restricted to numeric data types and can be used for other data types, such as strings.

Tokenization is a special form of randomization. In randomization, the transformed data are related to the original data via the randomization function, whereas a tokenized value has no relationship to the original data. The tokenization function generates the tokenized value that is independent of the original data and thus provides a much stronger data protection mechanism. Randomization, however, is weaker when compared to tokenization as prior knowledge of the randomization method will help in identifying the original data.

Tokenization has two variants

1. One-way tokenization
2. Two-way tokenization

One-way tokenization generates unique tokens from which the original data cannot be identified. In two-way tokenization, every input data are mapped to a unique token. The tokens replace the original input data. During a transaction, the original input data are recovered as the mapping between the input data and token is available. Two-way tokenization is extensively used in the credit card industry and is now adopted across other industry verticals. As an example, consider a credit card number that has 16 digits.

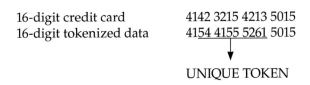

| 16-digit credit card | 4142 3215 4213 5015 |
| 16-digit tokenized data | 41<u>54 4155 5261</u> 5015 |

UNIQUE TOKEN

It is impossible to re-identify the original credit card number from the tokenized data (Figure 2.2)

Two-way tokenization is generally used during run-time or dynamically to address privacy issues. We cover two-way tokenization in sufficient detail in Chapter 8.

Protecting name fields is very important as any disclosure will lead to complete loss of privacy. The best way to protect names of the record owner is to remove them from the published data and substitute them with fictitious names from lookup databases. Substitution is a mechanism by which the original data are replaced or substituted with alternative data values. Figure 2.3 illustrates how substitution works with name fields.

Figure 2.3 illustrates an example of the substitution method, in which the names in the original data table for the North American region are substituted with similar names obtained from an external data source. On the Internet, we can get name databases pertaining to different countries and regions. For example, one can obtain a database containing Spanish names, English names, or Indian Names. As their names are fictitious, they could be safely substituted in place of original names, thus protecting the privacy of the record owner.

EI normally consist of identifying attributes, such as SSN, VIN, passport number, driver's license number, tax number, and names (first, middle, and last). What we have shown here is how to effectively mask them to protect the identity of the record owner. But certain attributes such as record owner's phone number, mobile number, and e-mail IDs are difficult to classify into EI or QI. Residential landline number of the record owner directly identifies

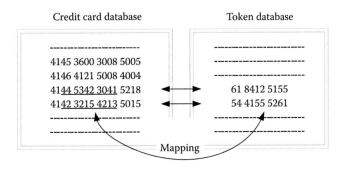

**FIGURE 2.2**
Example of two-way tokenization.

| First Name | Last Name | Gender |
|---|---|---|
| Mark | Anthony | M |
| Lina | Roy | F |
| Larry | Rowe | M |
| Roy | Fred | M |
| Lara | Dow | F |

(a)

Lookup data table
(North American names)

(b)

| | | |
|---|---|---|
| David | Anderson | M |
| Jane | Croft | F |
| Clive | Richards | M |
| Prill | James | M |
| Mary | Thomas | F |

(c)

**FIGURE 2.3**
(a) Original data table, (b) lookup table, and (c) substituted data table.

him, but his office board number does not directly identify him. If the adversary has knowledge of the record owner's phone number and e-mail ID, then it is a violation of the record owner's privacy. So, under which group, EI or QI, do you place the record owner's phone number (residence, landline, office number, mobile number)?

## 2.3.2 Protecting Quasi-Identifiers

In the previous section, we saw that EI are primarily identifiers and names that could directly identify a record owner and hence are completely masked out. By masking EI completely, they are rendered completely unusable but provide high privacy. However, masking EI alone is not sufficient, as an adversary can still use QI to re-identify a record owner, as was demonstrated by Latanya Sweeney where she re-identified the Governor of Massachusetts by linking a health/hospital database with a voters database. This linking is called record linkage where a record from a database is linked with a record in an external data source. This is depicted in Figure 2.4.

| ID | First Name | Last Name | Gender | Address | DOB | Zip | Disease |
|---|---|---|---|---|---|---|---|
| — | — | — | — | — | — | — | — |
| 12432 | | | M | MA | 21/02/1946 | 01880 | Cancer |
| — | — | — | — | — | — | — | — |

(a)

| Voter ID | First Name | Last Name | Gender | Address | DOB | Zip |
|---|---|---|---|---|---|---|
| — | — | — | — | — | — | — |
| 893423 | | Weld | M | MA | 21/02/1946 | 01880 |
| — | — | — | — | — | — | — |

(b)

**FIGURE 2.4**
Record linkage using QIs. (a) Hospital records and (b) voters list captions.

As seen in Figure 2.4, naïve masking of only EI by the hospital is not sufficient as it was linked to an external voters database and the identity of the governor was revealed and so was the disease he was suffering from. Sweeney used just three attributes—gender, date of birth, and zip code—to link records from two databases. A large population in the United States can be identified using these three attributes. Therefore, it is imperative that QI are also protected. QI attributes are categorical nominal, which means no arithmetic operations are possible on them. The finite range of these categorical nominal values needs to be considered while coming up with the anonymization approach. There are two important aspects that need to be considered while anonymizing QI:

- The analytical utility of QI needs to be preserved
- The correlation of QI attributes with sensitive data needs to be maintained to support the utility of anonymized data

So, how to anonymize QI and what methods are available? Let us consider the data Table 2.3 with more dimensions.

QI are defined as those identifiers of a record owner that are also available in external data sources, such as voters database. In Chapter 1, we mentioned that apart from external databases such as a voters list, a lot of information about the record owner is also available on social networking sites, which makes it very difficult to draw a boundary on QI.

### 2.3.2.1 Challenges in Protecting QI

Protection of QI is key to the success of any anonymization program, especially with respect to multidimensional data.

**TABLE 2.3**

Sample Employee Salary Table

| ID | Gender | Day | Month | Year | Address | City | Zip Code | Education | Years of Experience | Salary |
|----|--------|-----|-------|------|---------|------|----------|-----------|---------------------|--------|
| 1 | M | 20 | 08 | 1968 | 5, K G Rd | BLR | 560002 | Doctorate | 20 | 34,000 |
| 2 | M | 23 | 01 | 1970 | 1, M G Rd | BLR | 560001 | Postgraduate | 19 | 24,000 |
| 3 | M | 15 | 12 | 1967 | 8, Park Rd | BLR | 560033 | Doctorate | 22 | 36,000 |
| 4 | F | 16 | 02 | 1985 | 15, Canton Rd | BLR | 560004 | Graduate | 10 | 14,000 |
| 5 | F | 03 | 09 | 1982 | 12, Hosur Rd | BLR | 560068 | Postgraduate | 12 | 16,000 |
| 6 | M | 17 | 10 | 1970 | 6, Cubbon Rd | BLR | 560001 | Postgraduate | 18 | 22,000 |

Identifying the boundary between QI and SD and anonymizing the QI is probably the toughest problem to solve in privacy preservation. The main challenges in anonymizing QI attributes are

- High dimensionality
- Background knowledge of the adversary
- Availability of external knowledge
- Correlation with SD to ensure utility
- Maintaining analytical utility

High dimensionality is a major challenge in anonymization of relational data [1,2]. Consider a personal loan application in a bank. It has over two hundred fields that need to be filled in by the applicant. Most of these fields happen to be QI. Such a high number of fields in QI proves a major challenge for anonymization. PPDM is exploratory in nature, and irrespective of which anonymization technique is used, there is bound to be high information loss or low utility. With high-dimensional data, it becomes difficult to define a clear boundary between QI and SD as we do not know how much background knowledge an adversary has. A good example is that you can never hide an employee database from a disgruntled human resources employee as she will have sufficient background information of the employees in the organization. Whether it is PPDM or PPTDM, high dimensionality coupled with the background knowledge of the adversary, which is not known in advance, makes anonymization design very ineffective.

With reference to the example of the personal loan application, which is highly dimensional, how can we anonymize data effectively and provision it for either PPDM or PPTDM? There are no effective anonymization methods for high dimensionality plus the complexity of adversary's background knowledge. Principle (6) offers guidance in this area.

One approach can be based on an assumption that the user has no background knowledge. This will help in identifying a boundary between QI and SD and also reduce the problem to some extent but will not eliminate it. We discuss this situation in further detail in Chapter 4.

Apart from high dimensionality and background knowledge of an adversary, the amount of external information available about a record owner makes the anonymization of QI attributes more difficult. With proliferation of social networking sites, such as Facebook, Google+, LinkedIn, Twitter, and so on, it is very difficult to say how much information is published on their sites by the record owner. Not everyone is discreet about sharing personal information on these sites. Many are naïve and share a lot of personal information and do not really use or are unaware of the privacy controls available on these sites. Only time will tell how their publicly available personal information is exploited by adversaries.

Another important aspect to consider while anonymizing QI attributes is that the correlation between QI and SD attributes must be maintained. For example, in a life insurance application, the age of a policy holder and the premium she pays for a particular insurance product are correlated. Higher the age, higher the premium. Here, AGE is a QI attribute and PREMIUM is an SD attribute. Therefore, as part of the anonymization, it is important to maintain this relationship between QI and SD attributes wherever applicable.

Another aspect that needs to be looked into is the analytical utility of anonymized QI attributes. Different anonymization techniques will result in different privacy levels and corresponding utility. Utility is a highly relative measure and depends on the application and the context in which it is used. Based on application context, the anonymized QI attributes should support all the different queries that the original data set supported. With reference to Tables 2.4 and 2.5, which data set will support the following query?

- How many employees with EDUCATION = "Doctorate" are part of this company?

Data set in Table 2.4 will answer this query at the cost of some privacy loss. Data set in Table 2.5 will not support this query but provides higher levels of privacy at the cost of utility.

In Tables 2.4 and 2.5, we have used perturbative masking techniques to preserve privacy. But the use of perturbative masking techniques reduces the utility of data by eliminating the truth in the data, whereas nonperturbative techniques such as generalization transform the data into semantically similar values and preserve the utility of the data.

Perturbative techniques are generally referred to as masking and nonperturbative techniques as anonymization. QI attributes are generally composed of a record owner's demographics, which are available in external data sources, such as a voters database. It is indeed a challenge to anonymize QI attributes especially in the presence of external data sources, protect outlier records, and provide high utility. Principle (13) comes into play here.

One of the techniques suggested is group-based anonymization where data are anonymized in a group-specific manner. This technique is called k-anonymization, which we discuss in Section 2.4.1.

### 2.3.3 Protecting Sensitive Data (SD)

Data protection design ensures that EI are completely masked and QI are anonymized, leaving out SD in original form as it is required for analysis or as test data. As EI are completely masked, the transformed data make no sense and are not useful for re-identification, and properly anonymized QI also prevent

**TABLE 2.4**

Anonymized Employees' Salary Table—Suppression and Randomization

| ID | Gender | Day | Month | Year | Address | City | Zip Code | Education | Years of Experience | Salary |
|----|--------|-----|-------|------|---------|------|----------|-----------|---------------------|--------|
| 1 | M | — | — | 1968 | 512, —— | BLR | 560002 | Doctorate | 20 | 34,000 |
| 2 | M | — | — | 1970 | 115, —— | BLR | 560001 | Postgraduate | 19 | 24,000 |
| 3 | M | — | — | 1967 | 188, —— | BLR | 560033 | Doctorate | 22 | 36,000 |
| 4 | F | — | — | 1985 | 157, —— | BLR | 560004 | Graduate | 10 | 14,000 |
| 5 | F | — | — | 1982 | 121, —— | BLR | 560068 | Postgraduate | 12 | 16,000 |
| 6 | M | — | — | 1970 | 610, —— | BLR | 560001 | Postgraduate | 18 | 22,000 |

**TABLE 2.5**

Anonymized Employees' Salary Table—Suppression, Randomization, and Generalization

| ID | Gender | Day | Month | Year | Address | City | Zip Code | Education | Years of Experience | Salary |
|----|--------|-----|-------|------|---------|------|----------|-----------|---------------------|--------|
| 1 | M | — | — | 1968 | 512, ------- | BLR | 560001 | Graduate | 20 | 34,000 |
| 2 | M | — | — | 1970 | 115, ------- | BLR | 560004 | Graduate | 19 | 24,000 |
| 3 | M | — | — | 1967 | 188, ------- | BLR | 560068 | Graduate | 22 | 36,000 |
| 4 | F | — | — | 1985 | 157, ------- | BLR | 560001 | Graduate | 10 | 14,000 |
| 5 | F | — | — | 1982 | 121, ------- | BLR | 560033 | Graduate | 12 | 16,000 |
| 6 | M | — | — | 1970 | 610, ------- | BLR | 560002 | Graduate | 18 | 22,000 |

re-identification. If sensitive data are in original form, then it provides a channel for re-identification. Take an example of an employees' salary database. Here, the SD is the salaries of the employees, which are numerical in nature. Numerical data provide an easy avenue for re-identification to an adversary with background knowledge. Consider Table 2.6 with original salary data values and Table 2.7 with randomly perturbed salary data.

In Table 2.7, the data have been perturbed by adding noise. If you notice, random perturbation disturbs the original data. Even though the data have been randomly perturbed, they have been ensured that the mean and covariance of the original table and perturbed tables are the same. This means that the transformed table is still valid for analysis rendering the data to be useful at the same time maintaining the privacy of the data.

**TABLE 2.6**

Employees' Salary Table—Original Data

| Base Salary | Allowance | Medicals | Perks | Total |
|---|---|---|---|---|
| 10,000 | 5000 | 1000 | 6000 | 22,000 |
| 12,000 | 6000 | 1000 | 7200 | 26,200 |
| 9,000 | 4500 | 1000 | 5000 | 19,000 |
| 14,000 | 7000 | 1000 | 8400 | 30,400 |
| 13,000 | 6500 | 1000 | 7800 | 28,300 |
| 11,000 | 5500 | 1000 | 6600 | 24,100 |
| 15,000 | 7500 | 1000 | 9000 | 32,500 |
| 10,500 | 5250 | 1000 | 6300 | 23,050 |
| 12,500 | 6250 | 1000 | 7500 | 27,250 |
| 9,500 | 4750 | 1000 | 5700 | 20,950 |

**TABLE 2.7**

Employees' Salary Table—Randomly Perturbed Data

| Base Salary | Allowance | Medicals | Perks | Total |
|---|---|---|---|---|
| 10,500 | 5250 | 1000 | 6300 | 23,050 |
| 12,800 | 6400 | 1000 | 7680 | 27,880 |
| 9,760 | 4880 | 1000 | 5856 | 21,496 |
| 11,950 | 5975 | 1000 | 7170 | 26,095 |
| 14,000 | 7000 | 1000 | 8400 | 30,400 |
| 10,250 | 5125 | 1000 | 6150 | 22,525 |
| 13,830 | 6915 | 1000 | 8298 | 30,043 |
| 10,500 | 5250 | 1000 | 6300 | 23,050 |
| 12,200 | 6100 | 1000 | 7320 | 26,620 |
| 10,700 | 5350 | 1000 | 6420 | 23,470 |

## 2.4 Group-Based Anonymization

In this section, we will cover techniques that are useful to anonymize QI. The majority of this section is devoted to k-anonymization as this is one of the foremost techniques used today to anonymize data and release it for consumption. Later, we also cover *l*-diversity and t-closeness in brief.

### 2.4.1 k-Anonymity

#### 2.4.1.1 Why k-Anonymization?

In the previous sections, we looked at different data protection techniques and how they are used with respect to EI, QI, and SD. Using naïve masking techniques on QI, as shown in Tables 2.4 and 2.5, renders data unusable. Therefore, there is a need for effective anonymization techniques for QI that satisfy the following criteria:

- Record linkage: As most QI attributes are also present in external data sources, such as a voters database, the anonymization technique should prevent the linking of a record owner's QI attribute to these external data sources.

- Utility of the transformed data: Naïve perturbation of QI attributes renders the data unusable. Nonperturbative techniques, such as generalization, preserve the truth in the data table.

- Protection of outlier records: It is difficult to mask outlier records. When techniques such as additive noise are used to transform the data, outlier values still show up. For example, when the distribution (statistical) is computed, one cannot hide the net worth of Warren Buffet or Bill Gates!

- The correlation/association between QI and SD must be preserved and protected.

k-Anonymization is used to address these requirements. k-Anonymization is a technique for preserving individual identification. It makes each record of a table identical to at least k-1 other records, over a set of attributes called quasi-identifiers. k-Anonymization works on the principle of indistinguishability. Consider an example data table similar to the one shown in Table 2.8.

Table 2.9 has QI (GENDER, DATE OF BIRTH, ZIP CODE, ADDRESS, CITY) of which the identifiers GENDER, DATE OF BIRTH, and ZIP CODE uniquely identify the record owner in Table 2.8. Therefore, an adversary can link the QI from an external table to re-identify the record owner. So, how to prevent record linkage? One approach is to mask the QI in data Table 2.8. But that would reduce the utility of the data. What is the alternative? An approach called k-anonymity is proposed by Sweeney [3].

**TABLE 2.8**

Employees' Salary Data Table

| ID | Gender | Day | Month | Year | Address | City | Zip Code | Education | Years of Experience | Salary |
|----|--------|-----|-------|------|---------|------|----------|-----------|---------------------|--------|
| 1 | M | 15 | 07 | 1973 | | BLR | 560001 | Doctorate | 20 | 35,000 |
| 2 | M | 20 | 11 | 1975 | | BLR | 560045 | Masters | 17 | 28,000 |
| 3 | F | 12 | 12 | 1977 | | BLR | 560033 | Graduate | 18 | 15,000 |
| 4 | F | 08 | 07 | 1974 | | BLR | 560041 | Doctorate | 20 | 38,000 |
| 5 | F | 17 | 06 | 1985 | | BLR | 560003 | Graduate | 12 | 10,000 |
| 6 | M | 05 | 07 | 1980 | | BLR | 560002 | Graduate | 10 | 9,000 |
| 7 | F | 01 | 02 | 1977 | | BLR | 560044 | Masters | 15 | 18,000 |
| 8 | M | 03 | 01 | 1978 | | BLR | 560001 | Masters | 18 | 22,000 |
| 9 | M | 10 | 11 | 1980 | | BLR | 560042 | Graduate | 20 | 15,000 |
| 10 | F | 18 | 12 | 1982 | | BLR | 560031 | Doctorate | 15 | 32,000 |
| 11 | M | 22 | 10 | 1980 | | BLR | 560035 | Masters | 12 | 14,000 |
| 12 | M | 25 | 11 | 1979 | | BLR | 560033 | Masters | 14 | 16,000 |

**TABLE 2.9**

External Data Source (Publicly Available Voters Database)

| Name | Gender | Date of Birth | Address | City | Zip |
|------|--------|---------------|---------|------|-----|
| Hari | M | 05/07/1980 | | Bangalore | 560002 |

In Tables 2.10 and 2.11, we see that education values have been overgeneralized to such an extent that we have lost all the utility in the data. Is there a better way of generalization?

| Education | Education (4-Anonymous) |
|-----------|-------------------------|
| Doctorate | Grad school |
| Masters | Grad school |
| Bachelors | Bachelors |
| Doctorate | Grad school |
| Bachelors | Bachelors |
| Bachelors | Bachelors |
| Masters | Masters |
| Masters | Masters |
| Bachelors | Bachelors |
| Doctorate | Grad school |
| Masters | Masters |
| Masters | Masters |

The values in EDUCATION have been generalized and at the same time retain some utility. These data can be further generalized by mapping Masters → Grad school.

So how does k-anonymity protect against linking attack or record linkage attacks? A linking attack occurs when an adversary links the QI to an external table with the QI in the private table (PT), which is released. Consider PT where QI are denoted by $QI_{PT}$ ($q_1$, $q_2$, .... $q_m$). PT is partitioned into graphs, and the tables in each group are made identical with respect to $QI_{PT}$. This is pictorially represented in Table 2.12.

The advantage of k-anonymity is that it protects against record linkage by making k records indistinguishable from each other, and thus, the probability of linking to the original record based on QI is not more than 1/k.

Here, the value of k defines the privacy. Higher the value of k, higher the privacy, but at the cost of lower utility of the transformed data. This is apparent from Tables 2.10 and 2.11.

Though k-anonymity protects against linking attacks, it fails when it becomes difficult to model the background knowledge of the adversary. The boundary between QI and SD is not strictly defined. In Tables 2.10 and 2.11, even though QI are k-anonymous, it is difficult to protect these tables from an internal human resource employee who will have knowledge of the employees in the organization.

**TABLE 2.10**

4-Anonymous Table

| ID | Gender | Day | Month | Year | Address | City | Zip Code | Education | Years of Experience | Salary |
|----|--------|-----|-------|------|---------|------|----------|-----------|---------------------|--------|
| 1  | Any Sex | — | — | 1973 | — | BLR | 560000 | Any_Degree | 20 | 35,000 |
| 2  | Any Sex | — | — | 1975 | — | BLR | 560040 | Any_Degree | 17 | 28,000 |
| 3  | Any Sex | — | — | 1977 | — | BLR | 560030 | Any_Degree | 18 | 15,000 |
| 4  | Any Sex | — | — | 1974 | — | BLR | 560040 | Any_Degree | 20 | 38,000 |
| 5  | Any Sex | — | — | 1985 | — | BLR | 560000 | Any_Degree | 12 | 10,000 |
| 6  | Any Sex | — | — | 1980 | — | BLR | 560000 | Any_Degree | 10 | 9,000 |
| 7  | Any Sex | — | — | 1977 | — | BLR | 560040 | Any_Degree | 15 | 18,000 |
| 8  | Any Sex | — | — | 1978 | — | BLR | 560000 | Any_Degree | 18 | 22,000 |
| 9  | Any Sex | — | — | 1980 | — | BLR | 560040 | Any_Degree | 20 | 15,000 |
| 10 | Any Sex | — | — | 1982 | — | BLR | 560030 | Any_Degree | 15 | 32,000 |
| 11 | Any Sex | — | — | 1980 | — | BLR | 560030 | Any_Degree | 12 | 14,000 |
| 12 | Any Sex | — | — | 1979 | — | BLR | 560030 | Any_Degree | 14 | 16,000 |

**TABLE 2.11**

2-Anonymous Table

| ID | Gender | Day | Month | Year | Address | City | Zip Code | Education | Years of Experience | Salary |
|---|---|---|---|---|---|---|---|---|---|---|
| 1 | Any Sex | — | — | 1973 | — | BLR | 560010 | Any_Degree | 20 | 35,000 |
| 2 | Any Sex | — | — | 1975 | — | BLR | 560050 | Any_Degree | 17 | 28,000 |
| 3 | Any Sex | — | — | 1977 | — | BLR | 560040 | Any_Degree | 18 | 15,000 |
| 4 | Any Sex | — | — | 1974 | — | BLR | 560040 | Any_Degree | 20 | 38,000 |
| 5 | Any Sex | — | — | 1985 | — | BLR | 560010 | Any_Degree | 12 | 10,000 |
| 6 | Any Sex | — | — | 1980 | — | BLR | 560010 | Any_Degree | 10 | 9,000 |
| 7 | Any Sex | — | — | 1977 | — | BLR | 560050 | Any_Degree | 15 | 18,000 |
| 8 | Any Sex | — | — | 1978 | — | BLR | 560000 | Any_Degree | 18 | 22,000 |
| 9 | Any Sex | — | — | 1980 | — | BLR | 560030 | Any_Degree | 20 | 15,000 |
| 10 | Any Sex | — | — | 1982 | — | BLR | 560030 | Any_Degree | 15 | 32,000 |
| 11 | Any Sex | — | — | 1980 | — | BLR | 560040 | Any_Degree | 12 | 14,000 |
| 12 | Any Sex | — | — | 1979 | — | BLR | 560040 | Any_Degree | 14 | 16,000 |

**TABLE 2.12**

k-Anonymity Illustrated

| ← | $QI_{PT}$ | → | | |
|:---:|:---:|:---:|:---:|:---:|
| $q_1$ | $q_2$ | .... | .... | $q_m$ |
| Y | Y | Y | | Records are |
| Y | Y | Y | | indistinguishable |
| Y | Y | Y | | from each other |

(left side braced with k)

If we notice in both Tables 2.10 and 2.11, we have used the techniques of generalization and suppression to anonymize QI. Generalization and suppression are used together to anonymize QI and also ensure the utility of the data. Of course, other techniques such as shuffling or scrambling can also be used.

### 2.4.1.2 How to Generalize Data?

Generalization is a technique of replacing more specific values with generic and semantically similar values. Syntactically, it should be the same, as the storage requirement would also be the same for the transformed data. Generalization can be applied at cell or tuple or attribute levels. Generalization uses the concept of domain generalization and value generalization. Each attribute in a multidimensional database is a domain. If you refer to Table 2.8, you will notice that there are domains such as address, zip code, education, and so on. The value generalization hierarchy associates a value in domain $D_i$ to a unique value in the general domain $D_j$.

Consider the following attributes from Table 2.10 or 2.11: DATE OF BIRTH, GENDER, ADDRESS, ZIP CODE, EDUCATION. Among these attributes, DATE OF BIRTH and ADDRESS are suppressed. The remaining attributes are {GENDER, ZIP CODE, EDUCATION}. These attributes are classified as QI as they are also available in public databases, such as a voters database. Of course, EDUCATION will not be part of a voters database; so, should this attribute be considered as QI? The education level of many users is available in external social network sources, such as Facebook, LinkedIn, Twitter, and so on. The attributes {GENDER, ZIP CODE, EDUCATION} can be generalized in different ways.

Consider Table 2.8 as $D_i$ and Table 2.10 as $D_j$, the generalized domain table. Table 2.8 is transformed to 4-anonymous table, that is, the value of k is set to 4. We have used the techniques of suppression and generalization. The DATE OF BIRTH (day and month) and ADDRESS fields are suppressed. Generalization is applied on the GENDER, ZIP CODE, and EDUCATION fields. Figure 2.5 illustrates the method of domain and value generalization.

Table 2.11 is 2-anonymous and in this case also we have used generalization and suppression. Suppression is a technique of removing a data field from the table. In Tables 2.10 and 2.11, some of the fields such as ADDRESS,

DAY, and MONTH are suppressed. If you notice, generalization as a technique is difficult to design and implement. It is really a tough task to generalize all fields in QI and more so when the dimensions are high. Added to this is the presence of outliers, which require high levels of generalization that would result in loss of information or low utility.

Returning to Table 2.13, the data here have been transformed to Table 2.14 using a technique called full domain generalization. In this approach, the value for each attribute is generalized to a generic value, which is at the same

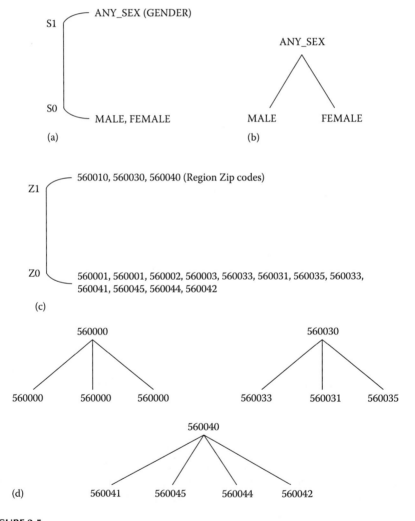

**FIGURE 2.5**
Example of substitution method. (a) GENDER—Domain Generalization; (b) Value Generalization; (c) Zip code—Domain Generalization; (d) Zip code—Value Generalization.

(*Continued*)

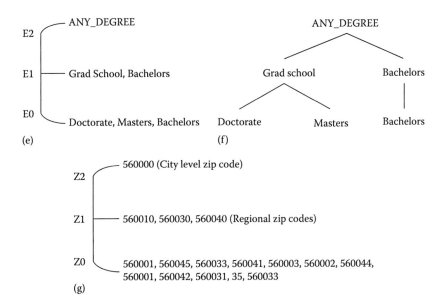

**FIGURE 2.5 (*Continued*)**
Example of substitution method. (e) Education—Domain Generalization; (f) Value Generalization; (g) Full Domain Generalization.

level in the taxonomy. The domain generalization hierarchy for ZIP CODE is shown in Figure 2.5g.

An alternative approach called local recoding is shown in Figure 2.5c for zip codes. Using local recoding, the zip code 560001 → 560010, where 560010 can be a region code. The difference between full domain generalization and local recoding is that in full domain generalization, some

**TABLE 2.13**

Original Table

| Gender | Zip Code | Education |
|--------|----------|-----------|
| M | 560001 | Doctorate |
| M | 560045 | Masters |
| F | 560033 | Bachelors |
| F | 560041 | Doctorate |
| F | 560003 | Bachelors |
| M | 560002 | Masters |
| F | 560044 | Masters |
| M | 560001 | Bachelors |
| M | 560042 | Doctorate |
| F | 560031 | Masters |
| M | 560035 | Masters |
| M | 560033 | Doctorate |

**TABLE 2.14**

Full Domain Generalized Table

| Gender | Zip Code | Education |
|--------|----------|-----------|
| ANY_SEX | 560000 | ANY_DEGREE |
| ANY_SEX | 560000 | ANY_DEGREE |
| ANY_SEX | 560000 | ANY_DEGREE |
| ANY_SEX | 560000 | ANY_DEGREE |
| ANY_SEX | 560000 | ANY_DEGREE |
| ANY_SEX | 560000 | ANY_DEGREE |
| ANY_SEX | 560000 | ANY_DEGREE |
| ANY_SEX | 560000 | ANY_DEGREE |
| ANY_SEX | 560000 | ANY_DEGREE |
| ANY_SEX | 560000 | ANY_DEGREE |
| ANY_SEX | 560000 | ANY_DEGREE |
| ANY_SEX | 560000 | ANY_DEGREE |

truth in the data is retained. In other words, when zip code 560001 → 560000, the mapping is to a city code, which retains some truth in the data, whereas in local recoding, when 560001 → 560010, it becomes incorrect mapping and the truth is complexly lost.

In Tables 2.10 and 2.11, the zip codes were all from the same city and full domain generalization of the ZIP CODE attribute results in the same values for the entire column. To illustrate generalization, let us consider another example where the zip codes are from different cities/states. Table 2.15 is similar to Tables 2.10 and 2.11 except that the values are different.

**TABLE 2.15**

Original Data

| Gender | Zip Code | Education |
|--------|----------|-----------|
| M | 500011 | Doctorate |
| M | 600018 | Masters |
| F | 560033 | Bachelors |
| F | 560041 | Doctorate |
| F | 600022 | Bachelors |
| M | 500012 | Masters |
| F | 560044 | Masters |
| M | 600021 | Bachelors |
| M | 560042 | Doctorate |
| F | 500013 | Masters |
| M | 500014 | Masters |
| M | 600020 | Doctorate |

In this context, suppression helps in reducing the level of generalization as a high level of generalization renders data of low utility.

To summarize, higher value of k means higher levels of privacy and lower levels of utility of the transformed data. Similarly, higher levels of generalization result in higher levels of privacy but with lower levels of utility. Both these aspects are evident in Tables 2.10 and 2.11. So, what is the optimum level of generalization? What should be the value of k? And how to implement k-anonymization?

Tables 2.16 and 2.17 show both full domain generalization and local recoding, respectively. A point to note: As part of the generalization process, the

**TABLE 2.16**

Full Domain Generalization

| Gender | Zip Code | Education |
|--------|----------|-----------|
| ANY_SEX | 500000 | ANY_DEGREE |
| ANY_SEX | 600000 | ANY_DEGREE |
| ANY_SEX | 560000 | ANY_DEGREE |
| ANY_SEX | 560000 | ANY_DEGREE |
| ANY_SEX | 600000 | ANY_DEGREE |
| ANY_SEX | 500000 | ANY_DEGREE |
| ANY_SEX | 560000 | ANY_DEGREE |
| ANY_SEX | 600000 | ANY_DEGREE |
| ANY_SEX | 560000 | ANY_DEGREE |
| ANY_SEX | 500000 | ANY_DEGREE |
| ANY_SEX | 500000 | ANY_DEGREE |
| ANY_SEX | 600000 | ANY_DEGREE |

**TABLE 2.17**

Local Recoding

| Gender | Zip Code | Education |
|--------|----------|-----------|
| ANY_SEX | 500010 | Grad School |
| ANY_SEX | 600010 | Grad School |
| ANY_SEX | 560040 | ANY_DEGREE |
| ANY_SEX | 560040 | Grad School |
| ANY_SEX | 600020 | ANY_DEGREE |
| ANY_SEX | 500010 | Grad School |
| ANY_SEX | 560040 | Grad School |
| ANY_SEX | 600020 | ANY_DEGREE |
| ANY_SEX | 560040 | Grad School |
| ANY_SEX | 500010 | Grad School |
| ANY_SEX | 500010 | Grad School |
| ANY_SEX | 600020 | Grad School |

generalized values in the target (anonymized) database will have the same syntax, semantics, and storage features as the original data.

To generalize the zip codes, the leftmost digit is replaced at level $Z_1$ and at level $Z_2$. The second digit from left is replaced with a 0. At level $Z_2$, the state level code is reached, which can be considered as the highest level of generalization for zip codes.

Tables 2.16 and 2.17, that is, full domain generalization and local recoding, do not preserve the statistical properties of the original data set, which means that there is a degradation in the utility of generalized data. Local recoding means to give better utility when EDUCATION attribute is considered but gives very incorrect results when ZIP CODE attribute is considered. At the same time, full domain generalization provides some truthful data when ZIP CODE attribute is considered but absolutely useless results are obtained on education attribute.

### 2.4.1.3 Implementing k-Anonymization

A number of algorithms have been proposed for implementing k-anonymity [4–8]. Most of the algorithms proposed use the approach of domain generalization hierarchy (DGH). The algorithms used both generalization and suppression. Using only generalization without suppression will render data with no utility as such an approach would require a very high level of generalization. Another class of algorithms based on clustering has been proposed to implement k-anonymity [9].

#### 2.4.1.3.1 Samarati's Approach

Samarati's algorithm is based on domain generalization hierarchy (DGH). Samarati's algorithm uses the technique of AG-TS (attribute generalization–tuple suppression). Figures 2.5 and 2.6 illustrate domain generalization of individual QI attributes such as ZIP CODE and EDUCATION. It is also possible to use combinations of attributes to define domain generalization. Samarati's algorithm approach is to determine the minimum level of generalization that is required to preserve k-anonymity. Taking the combination of zip code and education from Tables 2.13 and 2.14, what would be the minimum level of generalization required to preserve k-anonymity?

The goal of minimal generalization is to determine the node $<Q_i, Q_j>$ that is closest to the most specific node in the lattice structure that satisfies k-anonymity. For example, in Figure 2.7 the node $<Z_0, E_0>$ is the most specific node in the lattice structure and the node $<Z_1, E_1>$ is a generic node that is closest to it that satisfies k-anonymity. Of course, one could consider nodes at a higher level in the lattice structure, such as $<Z_1, E_2>$, but a higher node in the lattice structure indicates higher generalization at the cost of information loss. Samarati's algorithm uses a search mechanism to identify the generalized node in the lattice structure that satisfies k-anonymity and is at the least distance from the most specific node. If h is the maximum height of the

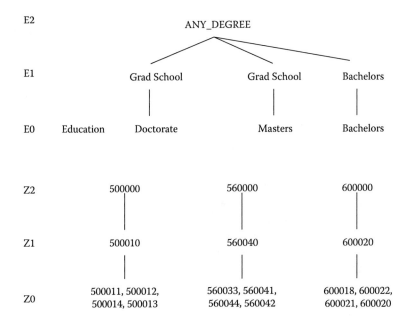

**FIGURE 2.6**
Full domain generalization of zip codes and education.

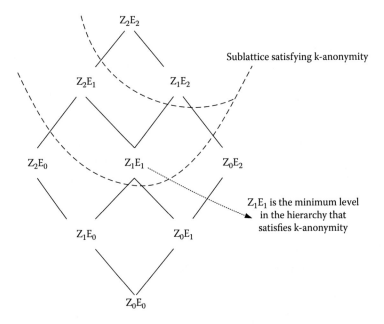

**FIGURE 2.7**
Domain generalization hierarchy over a pair of attributes to determine minimal generalization that satisfies k-anonymity.

lattice from the most specific node, then the algorithm searches at h, h/2, h/4, and so on until it finds a minimal generalization that satisfies k-anonymity.

### 2.4.1.4 How Do You Select the Value of k?

Anonymization of data is an exercise in optimization. A balance between privacy and utility needs to be achieved. There are many forces that decide the level of privacy, such as the record owner's perception of privacy and his requirement, adherence to regulatory compliance, intended use of anonymized data, complexity of the underlying data structure, and so on. Many of these forces are completely opposed to each other. For example, the record owner expects complete protection or privacy for his data, whereas the users of anonymized data expect high utility of data, which means low privacy. Therefore, there is always a need to have balance between privacy and utility.

k-Anonymization is used to prevent identity disclosure by making k records indistinguishable from each other. This is achieved by generalizing and suppressing attribute values in QI. Given a multidimensional data table of size m × n and k < m, given the size of m (number of records in the data table), what should be the size of k for optimum privacy and utility?

k-Anonymization is achieved by generalizing and suppressing over QI fields. Without suppression, the level of generalization required will be very high, and the resultant data set will have very low utility. Therefore, generalization and suppression techniques are used together to achieve k-anonymity. Consider Table 2.13. Generalization is applied over fields {GENDER, ZIP CODE, EDUCATION}, and it is observed that in Table 2.14 the number of equivalence classes created can be greater than 4 with the highest level of generalization. This means that k<=4; so, k can take a value of 4 or 2 and cannot be greater than 4. It is intuitive that k = m (number of rows) when QI attributes are generalized to a very generic value. Take, for example, Tables 2.13 and 2.14. If all QI attributes are generalized to a generic value, then k will take a value of 12, which is the number of records. But such a table will have no utility. Currently, the value of k is chosen arbitrarily. There are no analytical approaches to determine the value of k [10]. The complexity in choosing an optimal value of k stems from conflicting requirements. The value of k depends on many parameters:

$$k = f\left(P_R, U_R, C_R, G_L, C\right) \tag{2.1}$$

where
   $P_R$ is the privacy requirement of the data owner
   $U_R$ is the utility requirement of users of anonymized data
   $C_R$ is the compliance requirement of privacy of data
   $G_L$ is the generalization level
   C refers to the constraints

This is a complex problem to solve, and more research is required to come up with a practical approach to determine an optimal value of k.

### 2.4.1.5 Challenges in Implementing k-Anonymization

A number of privacy preserving algorithms are used to protect customer information while mining data. It is important to evaluate or assess the quality aspects of the algorithms. In this section, an assessment framework to capture the quality aspects of the algorithms is presented. To start with, the quality aspects of k-anonymization are assessed in the following dimensions

- Provable privacy
- Efficiency and performance of the algorithm (computational complexity)
- Scalability
- Robustness
- Utility/data quality

#### 2.4.1.5.1 Provable Privacy

k-Anonymity is satisfied when each tuple in a table D having attributes D $(a_1, \ldots, a_n)$ and attributes $a_i$, i = 1,..., n is a QI and is indistinguishable from other k-1 tuples in D. This means that k tuples form an equivalence class and the records in the class are indistinguishable from each other.

Identity disclosure occurs through QI when an adversary is able to link the QI in table D to an external database, for example, a voters database. k-Anonymization is meant to prevent identity disclosure as the probability of linking an individual to an external record based on QI is no more than 1/k. This means that the value of k controls privacy level and also affects the utility of the anonymized data. A higher value of k means higher levels of privacy.

#### 2.4.1.5.2 Computational Complexity

k-Anonymization is a complex algorithm. Implementing an optimal k-anonymization is NP-hard.

#### 2.4.1.5.3 Scalability of the k-Anonymization Algorithm

There are two kinds of scaling in question:

1. Horizontal scaling—higher number of dimensions
2. Vertical scaling—increase in number of records

There are two issues that affect the dimensions of data:

1. Unable to clearly define a boundary for QI attributes
2. Increased dimensionality of QI data set—too many attributes

k-Anonymization algorithm has an inherent problem with high-dimensional data [1,2] and has a scalability issue with very high numbers of records.

### 2.4.1.5.4 Robustness

k-Anonymization is meant to prevent identity disclosure, and it is effective against linkage attacks but is susceptible to homogeneity attacks.

In k-anonymization, generalization is applied over QI attributes, which results in equivalence classes. k-Anonymization transforms QI attributes and leaves the sensitive data set in its original form. If there is a cluster of similar values of sensitive data in the equivalence classes, then an adversary who has background knowledge can use it to easily re-identify the record owner. This is referred to as a homogeneity attack. To illustrate this, consider Tables 2.15 through 2.17, which implements full domain generalization.

In Table 2.18, the equivalence class consists of four tuples, that is, k = 4, and full domain generalization is implemented to all the QI attributes. The sensitive attribute SALARY contains a cluster of similar values that can be used by an adversary having some background knowledge to infer and identify the record owner. The purpose of k-anonymization is to prevent identity disclosure through record linkage and is not robust enough as it does not protect the sensitive data set and is susceptible to homogeneity attacks.

### 2.4.1.5.5 Utility/Data Quality

The utility of anonymized data is always measured/assessed with respect to the utility provided by the original data. The utility of anonymized data is a function of the anonymization algorithm and the intended use of anonymized data. Therefore, utility measure should be determined in the context of the application and the anonymization technique used.

With respect to k-anonymization, some of the utility/data quality metrics are

- Information loss metric (LM) [7]
- Classification Metric (CM) [7]

**TABLE 2.18**

Example of Homogeneity Attack

| Gender | Zip Code | Education | Salary |
|--------|----------|-----------|--------|
| ANY_SEX | 560000 | ANY_DEGREE | 15,000 |
| ANY_SEX | 560000 | ANY_DEGREE | 20,000 |
| ANY_SEX | 560000 | ANY_DEGREE | 20,000 |
| ANY_SEX | 560000 | ANY_DEGREE | 20,000 |

Classification metric (CM) is defined as the sum of the individual penalties for each row in the table normalized by the total number of rows N

$$CM = \frac{\displaystyle\sum_{\text{All Rows}} \text{penalty}(\text{row r})}{N} \qquad (2.2)$$

A row r is penalized if it is suppressed or if its class label class(r) is not the majority class label (G) of its group G.

$$\text{Penalty}(\text{row r}) = \begin{cases} 1 & \text{if r suppressed} \\ 1 & \text{if class}(r) \neq \text{majority}\,(G(r)) \\ 0 & \text{otherwise} \end{cases}$$

### 2.4.1.6 What Are the Drawbacks of k-Anonymization?

As stated earlier, k-anonymization is primarily meant to prevent identity disclosure. The k-anonymization approach has a number of drawbacks:

a. It is not robust enough to prevent homogeneity attacks.

b. Optimal k-anonymization is NP-hard—computationally very hard.

c. It has an inherent problem with high-dimensional data and large record sizes.

d. It is difficult to balance or optimize privacy versus utility, as higher levels of k provide high privacy and low utility and vice versa. No scientific method is available to determine an optimal value of k.

e. The techniques of generalization and suppression are used in implementing k-anonymization. The use of suppression leads to high information loss or low utility and using only generalization leads to a highly generic table having very low utility.

In spite of all its issues, k-anonymization is one of the widely used and researched algorithms. One of the most important advantages of k-anonymity is that no additional noise is added to the original data. All of the tuples in the anonymized data remain trustworthy [2,11].

To address some of the drawbacks of k-anonymization, other techniques have been proposed:

- *l*-Diversity
- t-Closeness

## 2.4.2 *l*-Diversity

In k-anonymization, a higher value of k will result in higher levels of privacy. The equivalence class will have more records. But in spite of a higher value of k if the sensitive data in the equivalence class do not exhibit diversity, then the data set lends itself to homogeneity attacks.

Hence, the need arises to counter this risk. In [12], the authors point out and demonstrate homogeneity attacks that arise out of k-anonymized data sets when the adversary has acute background knowledge of the record owner. The example stated in their work is that of a patient whose record is 4-anonymized within an inpatient data set. A hostile neighbor with the knowledge of location and approximate age of the record owner can easily infer the disease. If we revisit Table 2.18, it becomes clear that if the education values were left as is, then it would most definitely be possible for a neighbor to know which record among these would belong to his or her neighbor who holds a bachelor's degree.

Consider the example of the patient data in Table 2.19. If we apply k-anonymization here, with a value of k = 4 while suppressing CITY, then the resulting data will be as shown in Table 2.20.

*l*-Diversity works on the SD values of a data set to introduce sufficient number of dissimilar values in the set so as to prevent the re-identification of the record owner by an adversary with background knowledge. Thus, the equivalence class will contain *l* well-represented values for each sensitive attribute. The number of values that are changed is based on a model designed based on various parameters that contribute to background knowledge of the adversary.

In Table 2.20, for the records with age <40, all four record owners are suffering from bronchitis. A homogeneity attack will help the adversary ascertain their target's disease. Now let us apply *l*-diversity to this data set.

**TABLE 2.19**

Original Data Set

| Age | Zip Code | City | Disease |
|-----|----------|------|---------|
| 52 | 560001 | Bangalore | Sinus |
| 59 | 560002 | Bangalore | Flu |
| 23 | 540020 | Chennai | Bronchitis |
| 29 | 540013 | Chennai | Bronchitis |
| 68 | 560003 | Bangalore | Diabetes |
| 28 | 540023 | Chennai | Bronchitis |
| 27 | 540018 | Chennai | Bronchitis |
| 82 | 560004 | Bangalore | Hernia |

**TABLE 2.20**

4-Anonymized Data Set

| Age | Zip Code | City | Disease |
|-----|----------|------|---------|
| <85 | 560001 | ********* | Sinus |
| <85 | 560001 | ********* | Flu |
| <85 | 560001 | ********* | Diabetes |
| <85 | 560001 | ********* | Hernia |
| <40 | 540020 | ********* | Bronchitis |
| <40 | 540020 | ********* | Bronchitis |
| <40 | 540020 | ********* | Bronchitis |
| <40 | 540020 | ********* | Bronchitis |

In Table 2.21, the 4-anonymous table is transformed into a 3-diverse table. The patients from Chennai, all of whom suffer from bronchitis, are protected from homogeneity attack. We do not delve deep into the reasoning behind choosing the number 3 for $l$ as it is beyond the scope of this discussion.

### 2.4.2.1  Drawbacks of l-Diversity

A drawback of $l$-diversity is the impact it has on the utility of the data set. The inference drawn from a data set containing a high number of patients from the same geographical region suffering from the same disease is that there could be a local health hazard or environmental factor causing it. The 3-diverse data set, though, does not give such an impression. Whenever sensitive data are changed from a data set, the analysis yields a different result. Besides the utility impact, in Li et al. [13], the authors also highlight other problems such as skewness attack, similarity attack, and $l$-diversity's inability to deal with a pair of data values of which one is sensitive and

**TABLE 2.21**

$l$-Diversity Applied to 4-Anonymized Data Set

| Age | Zip Code | City | Disease |
|-----|----------|------|---------|
| <85 | 560001 | ********* | Sinus |
| <85 | 560001 | ********* | Flu |
| <85 | 560001 | ********* | Diabetes |
| <85 | 560001 | ********* | Hernia |
| <40 | 540020 | ********* | Sinus |
| <40 | 540020 | ********* | Diabetes |
| <40 | 540020 | ********* | Bronchitis |
| <40 | 540020 | ********* | Bronchitis |

the other is not (e.g., positive and negative results of an HIV test). Finally, *l*-diversity does not ensure semantic closeness of the new value, which replaces the original value of SD.

### 2.4.3 t-Closeness

An equivalence class is said to have t-closeness if the distance between the distribution of a sensitive attribute in this class and the distribution of the attribute in the whole table is no more than a threshold t. A table is said to have t-closeness if all equivalence classes have t-closeness [13]. The primary argument for t-closeness originates from the inadequacies observed in *l*-diversity. So, what is t-closeness?

#### 2.4.3.1 What is t-Closeness?

The explanation of t-closeness is as follows:

$B_0$ is the belief of an observer about an individual's sensitive attribute.

$B_1$ is the belief after observing the distribution Q of the entire set.

$B_2$ is the belief after observing the distribution P of the equivalence class.

The larger the difference between $B_0$ and $B_1$ is, the more valuable the data are. Besides, the intention of retaining the SD as is, it should be made available for the analysis. Ideally, $B_1$ to $B_2$ should be limited as this is the insight gained after the anonymization effort is made. Thus, if $B_1$ and $B_2$ are to be close, then P should be designed in such a way that it is close to Q as well. The closeness is governed by the parameter t that controls the balance between privacy and utility. The distance between the two distributions is denoted by D[P,Q].

As SD could be either numerical or categorical in nature, one needs to decide on a distance function to calculate the distance. For numerical values, ordered distance can be used, while for categorical data equal distance or hierarchical distance can be used. A good classification hierarchy based on the relevant domain will help assess the distance between the original and the replaced categorical attribute value. While assessing the distance, the value of *t* can be fixed so that the closeness is ensured.

Overall, t-closeness is a good measure that operates on maintaining both privacy and utility in sensitive data. When used in combination with k-anonymization, the two can yield a good-quality data set for many application domains, such as test data creation and data mining.

### 2.4.4 Algorithm Comparison

In Tables 2.22 and 2.23, we assess the algorithms discussed in this chapter.

**TABLE 2.22**

Assessment of Privacy Preserving Algorithms—Privacy and Utility

| Algorithms | Utility Measure | | | Privacy | | |
| | Query | Classification | Distribution | Provable Privacy | Robustness | |
| --- | --- | --- | --- | --- | --- |
| Randomization (additive) | Gaussian noise perturbs the data with a range. Hence, the impact on the data values is minimal. If the maximum and minimum of data values are within the query range, then it will support that kind of querying | Additive Gaussian noise will support classification | Gaussian noise maintains distributions | Poor | Poor |
| k-Anonymity | k-Anonymity supports queries, depending on the level of generalization | k-Anonymity supports classification if the equivalence classes are within the entropy | k-Anonymity maintains the distribution | 1/k as the probability of identification is 1 in k records | k-Anonymity is robust but fails with homogeneous SD data |
| l-Diversity | l-Diversity does not support querying | l-Diversity does not support classification as it may introduce values that are not part of the classifiers | l-Diversity changes the distribution in search of better privacy | Supports | Not robust |
| t-Closeness | Querying is possible | Supports classification | Supports | Does not guarantee high privacy | Not robust |

**TABLE 2.23**

Assessment of Privacy Preserving Algorithms—Complexity

| | Complexity | | |
|---|---|---|---|
| **Algorithms** | **Computation** | **High Dimensionality** | **Vertical Scaling** |
| Randomization (additive) | Gaussian noise is not expensive | High dimensionality affects randomization. | Supports |
| k-Anonymity | Expensive | High dimensionality affects k-anonymization | Affects k-anonymization |
| *l*-Diversity | Expensive | High dimensionality affects *l*-diversity | Affects *l*-diversity |
| t-Closeness | Not expensive | High dimensionality does not affect t-closeness | Affects t-closeness |

## 2.5 Summary

In this chapter, we have understood that data are classified into four categories: explicit identifiers (EI), quasi-identifiers (QI), sensitive data (SD), and nonsensitive data (NSD). The first three categories require privacy preservation. EI are too important from a privacy perspective and hence require to be masked. QI are most vulnerable to attacks due to their illusion of not being helpful for re-identification. We now know that when combined with background knowledge and external data sources, QI can be used to easily identify record owners. Sensitive data are facts in the data containing vital trends and patterns that are useful to the researcher or application consuming it. Intuitively, these are kept as is, barring some special scenarios. One such scenario is the presence of outliers that threaten to point to the record owner's identity. We also discussed the challenges faced while anonymizing each of these categories of data.

In the second half of this chapter, we looked at group anonymization techniques. k-Anonymization works exclusively on QI to make a set of k records indistinguishable from each other so that the adversary has just a 1 in k probability (1/k) to identify a record owner uniquely. k-Anonymity is generally used in conjunction with suppression to achieve provable privacy. Generalization in k-anonymity can be of two kinds: domain generalization and value generalization. The degree of generalization will decide the extent of balance we can achieve between privacy and utility of data. The failure of k-anonymization in the face of homogeneity attacks makes the case for *l*-diversity. *l*-Diversity introduces different values into the SD equivalence class in order to prevent homogeneity attacks. However, it does have drawbacks, as pointed out in our discussion on t-closeness, the most important being that *l*-diversity does not pick a semantically close value for the replacement of original data. t-closeness focuses on maintaining the utility of SD by assessing the closeness of the replacement value with a threshold t.

Finally, we presented our assessment of all anonymization techniques discussed in this chapter that should help the reader make informed choices while using these techniques.

## References

1. C.C. Aggarwal, Privacy and the dimensionality curse, Springer US, pp. 433–460.
2. C.C. Aggarwal and P.S. Yu (ed.), *Privacy Preserving Data Mining: Models and Algorithms*, Springer US, 2008.
3. L. Sweeney, Achieving k-anonymity privacy protection using generalization and suppression, *International Journal on Uncertainty, Fuzzy and Knowledge Based Systems*, 10(5), 571–588, 2002.
4. L. Sweeney, Guaranteeing anonymity when sharing medical data, The datafly system, in *Proceedings of the Journal of American Medical Informatics Association*, Hanley and Belfus Inc, Nashville, TN, 1997.
5. P. Samaraty, Protecting respondents' identifies in microdata release, *IEEE Transactions on Knowledge and Data Engineering*, 13(6), 1010–1027, 2001.
6. K. LeFevre, D. DeWitt, and R. Ramakrishnan, Incognito: Efficient full domain k-anonymity, in *Proceedings of the 2005 ACM SIGMOD International Conference on Management of Data*, Baltimore, MD, June 13–16, 2005.
7. V. Iyengar, Transforming data to satisfy privacy constraints, in *Proceedings of the Eighth ACM SIGKDD International Conference on Knowledge Discovery and Data Mining*, Edmonton, AB, 2002.
8. R. Bayardo and R. Agarwal, Data privacy through optimal k-anonymization, in *Proceedings of the 21st International Conference in Data Engineering*, Tokyo, Japan, 2005.
9. M. Ercan Nergiz and C. Clifton, Thoughts on k-anonymization, in *ICDEW'06: Proceedings of the 22nd International Conference on Data Engineering Workshops*, IEEE Computer Society, Atlanta, GA, 2006, p. 96.
10. R. Dewri, I. Roy, and D. Whitley, On the optimal section of k in the k-anonymity problem, in *ICDE*, IEEE, Cancun, Mexico, 2008.
11. M. Hua and J. Pei, A survey of Utility based Privacy preserving data transformation methods, in *Privacy-Preserving Data Mining*, Springer US, 2008, pp. 207–237.
12. A. Machanavajjhala, D. Kifer, J. Gehrke, and M. Venkitasubramaniam, *l*-Diversity: Privacy beyond k-anonymity, *ACM Transactions on Knowledge Discovery from Data*, 1(1), Article 3, Publication date: March 2007.
13. N. Li, T. Li, and S. Venkatasubramanian, t-Closeness Privacy beyond k-anonymity and *l*-diversity, in *ICDE Data Engineering*, Istanbul, Turkey, 2007.

# 3

## Static Data Anonymization Part II: Complex Data Structures

## 3.1 Introduction

In Chapter 2, we covered privacy preservation of multidimensional data, which is the most common form of data structure found in any enterprise. As seen in Chapter 2, a rich set of privacy preserving algorithms are currently in use. Emphasis on deriving knowledge from data along with the rapid evolution of digital platforms in enterprises have resulted in more and more complex data structures being analyzed. Nowadays, it is common to find complex data structures such as graph data, time series data, longitudinal data, transaction data, and spatiotemporal data in many enterprises. Mining these complex data results in a lot of useful insights that can benefit businesses. But these complex data structures contain personally identifiable information that must be anonymized before they can be mined. Multidimensional data, which were studied in the previous chapters, are much simpler in their structure, and traditional anonymization techniques can be used on such data. But these techniques cannot be used for complex data structures. The more complex the data structure, the more the avenues are to be re-identified. Therefore, anonymization techniques that address the various dimensions of a data structure are required. In this part, we examine the anonymization techniques for graph data, time series data, longitudinal data, and transaction data.

The data are complex and so are anonymization techniques. Anonymization techniques used on multidimensional data are not applicable to such complex data structures. Anonymization design for these complex data structures is an emerging area. A survey of research literature in this field reveals the growing traction in this subject. Here, we provide a systematic review of the work carried out in this area and cover briefly graph, longitudinal, time series, and transaction data structures.

## 3.2 Privacy Preserving Graph Data

Graph data structure is very common across many business domains such as healthcare, finance, electronics, software, social networks, and so on. Graph data analysis has attracted a lot of attention of late, as social networks such as Facebook, Twitter, and LinkedIn are involved in it. Social network data analysis is widely carried out by companies to understand how customers use and feel about their products. For example, a company offering mutual fund products and having a page on social network sites such as Facebook would like to understand how their products are received by its customers. For this, the company should analyze the posts of its customers. The company may use a third party to analyze these data. But the data contain customers' sensitive information. So, how will the company share these data with the customers' privacy preserved? Before getting into the subject of the anonymization of graph data, let us understand the structure of graph data and the challenges they pose to anonymization design.

### 3.2.1 Structure of Graph Data

It is very important to understand the structure of the data before deciding on an anonymization design. A graph G (V, E) consists of a set of vertices V together with a set of vertex pairs or edges or links. Graphs are interesting as they model any relationship. Consider the simple graph in Figure 3.1 showing the relationship between entities.

Even this simple graph is quite complex and has many aspects that need to be considered while analyzing and deciding on an anonymization approach. The graph G has the following aspects:

- Vertex properties
- Vertex labels
- Link relationships
- Graph metrics

Structural information such as vertex degree, neighborhoods, embedded subgraphs, and graph metrics such as betweenness, closeness, centrality, path length, and reachability should be considered while choosing an anonymization design for graph data.

Relational data have fixed schema and each record represents an entity. Each record or tuple can be transformed independent of each other. Because of its simple structure, it is easier to prevent both identity and attribute disclosure; but with graph data, there are more dimensions to be taken care of.

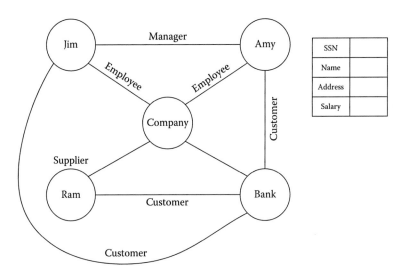

**FIGURE 3.1**
A simple graph.

## 3.2.2 Privacy Model for Graph Data

Consider Figure 3.1, which illustrates a simple graph. There are multiple dimensions in this network that need to be factored in while choosing an anonymization design—vertices, edges, relationships, labels, structural information, and graph metrics. An adversary could gain knowledge of the graph through any of these dimensions. Zheleva and Getoor [1] categorize the privacy model into three dimensions: identity, content, and link. Our proposition is to include one more dimension to the model—graph metrics, which is very similar to the one proposed by Zhou et al. [2]. Therefore, to protect the graph, a privacy model is defined (Figure 3.2).

A graph is a highly interconnected structure, and any change in the nodes or edges affects the characteristics of the graph and also the utility of the anonymized graph. The usage of the anonymized data should be considered when deciding on an anonymization approach. So, how to protect graph data and what are the available methods? Broadly, anonymization methods for graph data can be classified into three approaches: naïve anonymization, random perturbation, and clustering. Naïve anonymization is generally easier to implement but not the recommended approach. It is effective when the adversary has absolutely no background knowledge of the network on the entities and relationship in the network, which is usually not the case. Adversaries generally plan an attack using some background knowledge such as structural information.

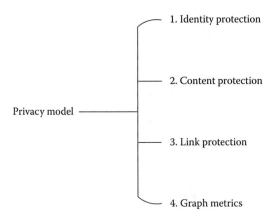

**FIGURE 3.2**
Privacy model for graph data.

### 3.2.2.1 Identity Protection

As mentioned, there are three approaches to identity protection (Figure 3.3).

#### 3.2.2.1.1 Naïve Anonymization

In the case of relational data, removing or masking just the identifiers is not sufficient to protect the record owner. Even when EIs were removed, Latanya Sweeney demonstrated that it is possible to re-identify the record owner by using a record linkage technique. This holds good for graph data also. In a social network, vertices represent entities or individuals in the network, and edges represent the relationships between vertices or nodes. Every node has a number of attributes both sensitive and nonsensitive and

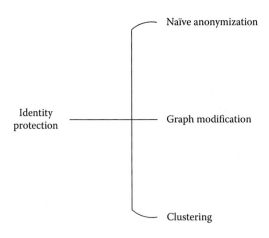

**FIGURE 3.3**
Identity protection methods.

a unique identifier. In naïve anonymization, this unique identifier is replaced by a random number and the anonymized network is published. Such a network is high in utility but low in privacy, especially when adversaries have some form of structural information of the network.

### 3.2.2.1.2 Graph Modification

The naïve anonymization technique wherein node identifiers are replaced with a pseudonym does not guarantee privacy. According to Liu and Terzi [3], the degree of a node in a graph, among other structural characteristics, can, to a large extent, distinguish the node from other nodes and thus can reveal the identities of individuals. They propose a graph anonymization approach where a graph is k-degree anonymous if for every node v, there exists at least k-1 other nodes in the graph with the same degree as v. This definition of anonymity presents the re-identification of individuals by adversaries having background knowledge of the degree of certain nodes. In this approach, for a given graph G (V, E), a modified graph is constructed G′ (V, E).

### 3.2.2.1.3 Clustering

To resist re-identification attacks, Hay et al. [10] proposed a novel algorithm that anonymizes a graph by partitioning nodes and then describing the graph at the level of partitions. The output is a generalized graph, which consists of a set of supernodes—one for each partition—and a set of superedges—which report the density of edges (in the original graph) between the partitions they connect. The generalized graph can be used to study graph properties by randomly sampling a graph that is consistent with the generalized graph description and then performing a standard analysis on this synthetic graph. These sampled graphs retain key properties of the original—degree distribution, path lengths, and transitivity—allowing complex analyses.

### 3.2.2.2 Content Protection

Content protection in a graph is very similar to that of relational data. Anonymization techniques such as randomization, k-anonymity, l-diversity, and t-closeness are applicable to protect identity and prevent attribute disclosures.

### 3.2.2.3 Link Protection

A graph has multiple dimensions such as vertices, its properties, and their interconnections via edges or links. Protecting vertices or identities alone is not sufficient as re-identification can be done using links. Links in a graph are considered sensitive as they can provide a lot of information about the individuals in a network. Graphs are found almost in all the domains, and in that sense, they are ubiquitous and more commonly used in domains where they model interconnectedness or links between entities or nodes. One of the key tasks of a graph data mining is link prediction—is it possible to predict whether two entities that are not connected currently will connect in future based on their current networks? In this context, the existing links of nodes are considered sensitive and could be exploited by an adversary. Therefore, while publishing graph data, it is necessary to protect the links.

Similar to node protection, link protection methods can be classified into three categories (Figure 3.4).

### 3.2.2.3.1 Naïve Anonymization

Links or edges connect nodes in a graph. Consider a graph G (V, E) where V are vertices and E are edges, $E(E_1, E_2, ..., E_n)$. In this set of edges, there is a set of sensitive edges $E_s$. Naïve anonymization techniques remove these sensitive edges $E_s$ from the set of edges in the graph. Though this technique is simple, there is always a possibility for link re-identification through other edges.

### 3.2.2.3.2 Random Perturbation

Random perturbation or randomized edge construction method proposed by Hay [4] method constructs an anonymized graph G' from the original graph G through a sequence of m edge deletions followed by m edge insertions. Edges deleted are chosen at random from the set of all existent edges in G, while edges inserted are chosen at random from the set of all non-existent edges of the interim graph. Vertices are not changed. This approach provides high privacy at the cost of utility. High privacy is achieved because an adversary must consider the set of possible worlds implied by anonymized graphs G' along with m random edge insertions and m deletions.

### 3.2.2.3.3 Clustering Method

Clustering means grouping similar objects. In the case of graphs, there are different clustering approaches—vertex clustering, edge clustering, and

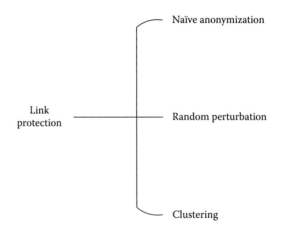

**FIGURE 3.4**
Link protection methods.

vertex–edge clustering [2]. One of the approaches to preventing re-identification is clustering of nodes having the same degree. This clustering forms equivalence classes (ECs). The edges connecting these equivalence classes can also be clustered to prevent link disclosure.

### 3.2.2.4 Graph Metrics

A graph is characterized by many properties called metrics. These metrics describe a graph in multiple ways [11]. These can be considered the graph equivalent of the statistical properties that we often discuss with respect to relational data. Therefore, these properties represent the facts about a graph data set. Let us understand some of them.

*Centrality*: Centrality of a node is a property that indicates its importance in a graph. Importance has many meanings, each giving birth to a new measure of centrality.

*Betweenness*: A flavor of centrality, betweenness of a node v is the number of shortest paths from two other vertices a and b that pass through v.

*Closeness*: Another flavor of centrality, closeness of a node v is the sum of the metric distances of v from all its neighboring nodes.

*Reachability*: This property is that of an undirected graph, where there exists a sequence of nodes to reach from node *a* to node *b* which starts with *a* and ends with *b*.

Apart from these, there are many other metrics of a graph. When anonymizing graph data using random perturbation or clustering, what is the effect on these metrics?

### 3.2.2.4.1 Effects of Anonymization

Random perturbation introduces new edges and deletes the same number of edges, doing both of these randomly. This changes reachability, closeness, and centrality of a graph. Clustering a graph using vertex or edge clustering changes neighboring nodes, which in turn affects metrics such as betweenness and closeness. Although they preserve privacy, such modifications result in loss of utility, because they alter the facts in the graph data set. Any analysis using modified graph data yields orthogonal results compared to those achieved using the original graph data set.

## 3.3 Privacy Preserving Time Series Data

A sequence of observations indexed by the time of each observation is called a time series. A time series could represent financial data such as stock prices, bond, and interest rates, or in healthcare, it represents health parameters such as blood pressure and blood glucose of a patient over a period of time. A few other examples are a net asset value of a fund over a period of time, stock prices, interest rates, etc. Time series data are interesting because they are generally used for forecasting. Forecasting helps in understanding how, for example, a fund will perform in future based on the past performance. An example from healthcare is how a patient's health parameters vary over time. Another good example is the study of vehicular traffic in specific routes over a period of time so that better traffic control can be put in place.

Table 3.1 provides blood sugar levels of patients over a period of time. Similarly, one can have the financial performance of industries in a specific sector and region as shown in Table 3.2.

These data sets are very useful as they can be mined and used for prediction. For example, it is possible to understand how a group of patients respond to a treatment or how a specific industry in a region performs. Though it is beneficial to mine and understand how patients respond to a treatment over a period of time, the patients would not want to be associated with the data as it could be a breach of their privacy. So, how to share these data in a privacy preserving way? And what are the challenges in privacy preservation of time series data?

Time series data are complex and have the following characteristics:

1. Time series can be univariate or multivariate. Univariate data are single dependent variable varying with time, whereas multivariate data have multiple variables with respect to time. This chapter covers univariate data only, which as shown in Tables 3.1 and 3.2, have large number of points in time, which mean high dimensionality. Time series data by nature are highly dimensional.

**TABLE 3.1**

Time Series Data of Patients' Blood Sugar Level

| ID | Name | Address | Week 1 | Week 2 | Week 3 | ... | Week n |
|----|------|---------|--------|--------|--------|-----|--------|
| 12345 | Hari | Bangalore | 90 | 100 | 110 | | 140 |
| 34567 | Jay | Bangalore | 140 | 160 | 110 | | 180 |
| 23456 | Jane | Bangalore | 95 | 90 | 95 | | 100 |
| 13579 | Ash | Bangalore | 90 | 95 | 90 | | 95 |

**TABLE 3.2**

Financial Time Series Data of Companies in a Specific Sector and Region

| ID | Name | Address | Week 1 | Week 2 | Week 3 | ... | Week n |
|----|------|---------|--------|--------|--------|-----|--------|
| 9876 | ACME | Bangalore | 10,000 | 12,000 | 14,000 | | 22,000 |
| 6842 | ABC | Bangalore | 20,000 | 24,000 | 26,000 | | 40,000 |

2. Time series data are represented in both time domain and frequency domain.

3. Time series data represent data that change in time, which means that as time increases, new data stream will be appended representing newer values and patterns.

   The structure of time series data and classification is shown below

| EI | | | QI | | | | SD | |
|----|----|----|----|----|----|----|----|----|
| ID | Name | Address | Gender | $A_1$ | ... | $A_N$ | $A_{S1}$ | $A_{S2}$ |

The data set contains three disjoint sets of data:

a. Explicit Identifiers (EI) such as SSN and names.

b. Quasi-identifiers (QIs) contain a series of time-related data $(A_1,..., A_N)$.

c. Sensitive attributes are a series of time-related data that are considered sensitive and should not be altered.

4. Time series has values at consecutive time instants, and the series itself exhibits a pattern.

By contrasting these properties of time series data with those of multidimensional data, it is easy to conclude that anonymization techniques designed for multidimensional data cannot be applied to time series data. Tuples in multidimensional data can be anonymized/transformed independent of other tuples. Data in a tuple can be transformed without affecting other data values in the tuple. But these approaches will not work on time series data. So, what are the effective anonymization techniques for time series data? What are the challenges in preserving the privacy of time series data?

### 3.3.1 Challenges in Privacy Preservation of Time Series Data

Time series data have a very complex structure. They are used for various purposes such as forecasting or prediction, study of underlying processes, industrial applications, pattern discovery, and so on. Therefore, when transforming/anonymizing time series data, the anonymized data should be useful and provide accurate results in these applications. Because of the complexity of time series data structure, anonymization is rather challenging as there are too many aspects to be taken care of. Some of the key challenges in privacy preservation of time series data are as follows.

#### 3.3.1.1 High Dimensionality

Univariate time series data of 500 values have 500 dimensions to choose from. Protecting high-dimensional data is a problem that does not have an effective solution. Moreover, high-dimensional data coupled with the unknown background knowledge of the adversary make their privacy protection a major challenge.

### 3.3.1.2 Background Knowledge of the Adversary

Modeling background knowledge of the adversary is not possible, which makes it difficult to decide which data to protect or anonymize. Because of this, the data protection method may lead to high protection or low protection, thus resulting in poor utility (Figure 3.5).

### 3.3.1.3 Pattern Preservation

Time series data have both instant values and a pattern.

Figure 3.6 shows time series data, for example, the sales figure of a company, which has peak sales every quarter when the company announces a discount sale and a trough or periods of low sales. Any privacy preserving method should ensure that the patterns in the anonymized data set should be preserved as much as possible.

### 3.3.1.4 Preservation of Statistical Properties

Time series data exhibit certain statistical properties such as mean, variance, and so on. Any privacy preservation method should ensure that these properties are maintained in the anonymized data set (Figure 3.7).

The mean of a discrete time series data is given by

$$\mu = \frac{1}{n} \sum_{i=0}^{n} X_i \tag{3.1}$$

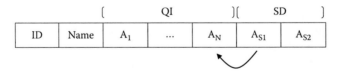

Classify as QI or SD? – Boundary between QI ans
SD is "blurred" when dimensions are high. Because
of the unknown background knowledge of the adversary,
it is difficult to classify the attributes as QI or SD

**FIGURE 3.5**
Effect of high dimensionality and unknown background knowledge of the adversary in privacy preservation methodology.

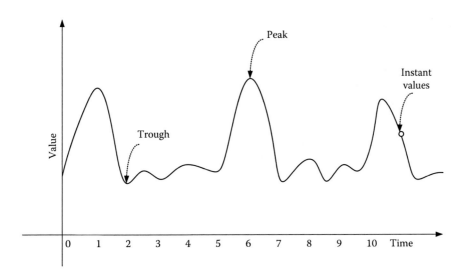

**FIGURE 3.6**
Patterns in time series data.

### 3.3.1.5 Preservation of Frequency-Domain Properties

Time-domain data have a frequency-domain representation. The frequency domain represents the various frequencies in the time series data and provides the spectrum of frequencies in the time-domain signal (Figure 3.8).

Consider, for example, the time domain represents the stock price of a company over a period of time. The frequency-domain representation will provide the frequencies.

### 3.3.2 Time Series Data Protection Methods

Time series data can be classified into three sets—identifying fields (EIs), QIs, and SD. EIs are completely masked, and sensitive data set is left in its original format so that it is useful for analysis. This leaves QIs. But QI data set can be used to re-identify the record owner by linking to external data. However, anonymizing QI data set and maintaining the utility of the entire data set are nontrivial. Anonymization techniques for time series data fall in two broad categories.

1. Perturbative methods—additive random noise
2. Generalization—k-anonymization

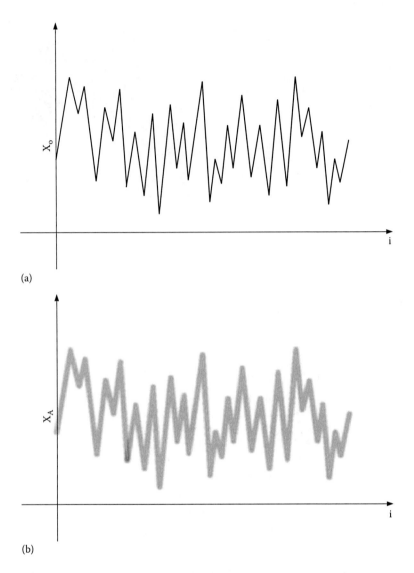

**FIGURE 3.7**
(a) Original time series. (b) Time series + white noise.

### 3.3.2.1 Additive Random Noise

There are two approaches to perturbation of time series data with additive noise:

1. Perturbation of time series data with white noise
2. Perturbation of time series data with correlated noise

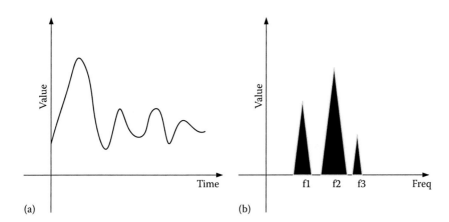

**FIGURE 3.8**
(a) and (b) Time-domain signal and frequency-domain representation.

### 3.3.2.1.1 Perturbation of Time Series Data with White Noise

This approach of adding white noise to time series data is probably the simplest but at the same time the weakest method from a privacy perspective (Figure 3.9).

In this approach, white noise that is at high frequency is added to time series data, which results in perturbation of values in the original time series data. This approach protects the data by perturbing the values of the original time series data.

The benefits of perturbing time series data with white noise are that the utility of the anonymized data set is better when compared with other methods. This is because the transformed data retain most of the statistical properties of the original time series data set, preserve the pattern, retain frequency-domain properties, and so on. But the drawback is poor privacy level.

Re-identification of time series data perturbed by random noise can be achieved by

- Filtering
- Regression

Filtering is a technique that can be used when additive noise is not correlated with the original time series data. White noise, which is at higher frequencies compared to the original time series data, can be filtered out using a low-pass filter.

Regression as a technique is ineffective when independent noise is added to time series data.

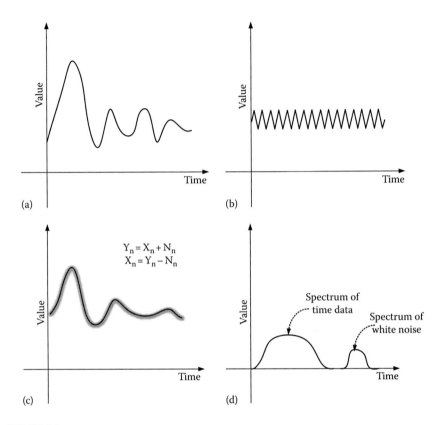

**FIGURE 3.9**
Time series data perturbation with white noise and their representation in frequency domain.
(a) Time series data $(X_n)$, (b) random noise $N_n$ (white noise), (c) perturbation with white noise
$(Y_n)$, and (d) frequency spectrum of original time series.

### 3.3.2.1.2 *Perturbation of Time Series Data with Correlated Noise*

To avoid filtering attacks, time series data can be perturbed with correlated noise as shown in Figure 3.10.

Perturbation with correlated noise changes the values of time series data: the pattern and the frequency. This affects the utility of data but provides higher privacy.

Re-identification of time series data perturbed by correlated noise is possible with a regression model. An adversary can use his background knowledge to implement linear regression model to protect the values.

### 3.3.2.2 *Perturbation of Time Series Data Using Generalization: k-Anonymization*

k-Anonymization is used to prevent linkage attacks, where QI attributes in a record are generalized to be identical with k-1 records. k-Anonymization

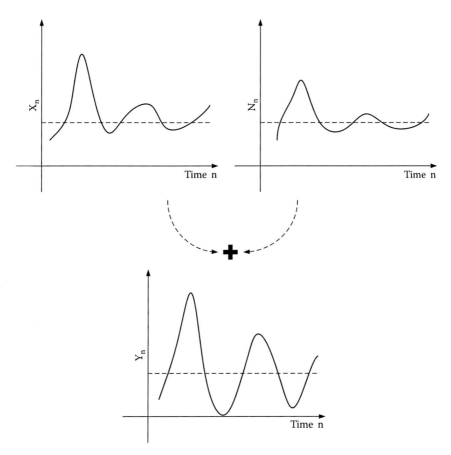

**FIGURE 3.10**
Time series data perturbation using correlated noise.

is covered in detail earlier, and the same approach applies also to time series data. The issue with this approach is that with higher levels of generalization, the pattern of the anonymized data set could get distorted.

Apart from the basic anonymization techniques discussed here, there are a few other studies that discuss more advanced techniques that build on these basic approaches.

## 3.4 Privacy Preservation of Longitudinal Data

Longitudinal data are most commonly found in healthcare domain. They are used to represent a series of measurements taken from a patient or patients who are treated for a particular disease or a problem. For example, a patient is undergoing a treatment for diabetes; he is administered medicines, and every week his blood glucose level is measured. Such a set of measurements are shown in Table 3.3.

How to publish this table in a privacy preserving way? What challenges do longitudinal data present? What are the characteristics of longitudinal data?

## 3.4.1 Characteristics of Longitudinal Data

Longitudinal data are very similar to time series data, but there are a few differences. Table 3.3 shows the measurements of a patient over a period of time. Each measurement is a result of a treatment provided to the patient. The following is observed from the table:

- The data are clustered and comprise repeated measurements obtained from a single patient at different points in time.
- The record in the table is classified into EI, QI, and SD. There is a relationship between the patient and his health parameters, and there is a strong correlation among the records in the cluster.
- Data within the cluster have a temporal order, which means that there is a pattern in the data. This pattern is important as it reflects how the patient is responding to a drug or treatment.

### 3.4.1.1 Challenges in Anonymizing Longitudinal Data

All these characteristics pose some serious challenges to the anonymization design that should address the following:

- Identity disclosure—prevent record linkage.
- Attribute disclosure—prevent sensitive data linkage.
- Correlation in the cluster.
- Pattern in the clustered data set.
- Take into account that the records in the clustered data set cannot be treated independent of each other as in the case of multidimensional data (relational data).
- Unknown background knowledge of the adversary.

**TABLE 3.3**

Sample Longitudinal Data

| ID | Name | Age | Gender | Address | Admin Date | Disease | Reading |
|----|------|-----|--------|---------|-----------|---------|---------|
| 123 | John | 34 | M | Bangalore | 12/12/2011 | Diabetes | 180 |
| 123 | John | 34 | M | Bangalore | 19/12/2011 | Diabetes | 160 |
| 123 | John | 34 | M | Bangalore | 26/12/2011 | Diabetes | 150 |
| 123 | John | 34 | M | Bangalore | 02/01/2011 | Diabetes | 140 |

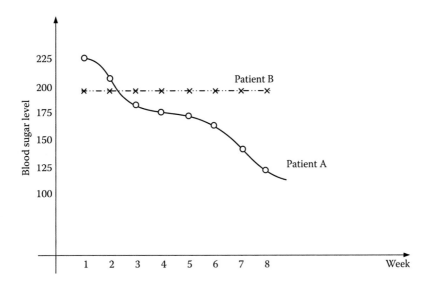

**FIGURE 3.11**
Responses of two patients to the treatment for diabetes.

There are not many anonymization methods currently to publish longitudinal data in a privacy preserving way. In fact, the anonymization of longitudinal data is still nascent. A few relevant studies on longitudinal data protection are reported in the literature. Two papers [5, 6] focus on the prevention of identity disclosure and [7] on the prevention of both identity and attribute disclosure.

Longitudinal data are very complex. The data in the records are correlated, and the records in the cluster are also correlated. Because of this strong correlation, it is very difficult to create an optimized anonymization design. Let us take, for example, the sensitive data values of a patient treated for diabetes.

Figure 3.11 shows responses of two patients to the treatment of diabetes. Patient A responds to the treatment, whereas patient B hardly responds to the treatment. There is a pattern in the data set, and it cannot be disturbed by the anonymization method. If it is disturbed, then the truth in the data is lost and it leads to poor utility. The risk of not anonymizing the sensitive attributes is that an adversary can use his background knowledge to re-identify. Based on the requirements, an anonymization design needs to provide an appropriate trade-off between privacy and utility.

## 3.5 Privacy Preservation of Transaction Data

Transaction data are complex, which are attributed to their high dimensionality and sparsity. Transaction data are used extensively in retail domain. They are a log of transactions a customer does in a retail store or on an e-commerce website. A retail store or an e-commerce website sells thousands of products. Whenever a customer buys a product, a value of 1 is updated in the log data or the transaction data. Otherwise, it would be 0. These data are of high interest to retail companies as they help to understand customers' shopping patterns. Companies would be interested in finding association or correlation among the transactions of a customer. For example, when a customer buys bread, he is likely to buy cheese, or butter, or milk. If a large number of customers buy bread and milk together more often, the retail store will place these products close to each other. This analysis helps both companies and their customers, but there is one catch—many customers would not want some of the sensitive transactions to be revealed. For example, a customer's purchase of very expensive products, specific medicines, or gadgets such as sex toys is considered to be sensitive. Therefore, this sensitivity involved in such transactions should be protected before releasing the data for analysis. But that is easier said than done as transaction data are more complex in nature. To understand this, consider Table 3.4.

There are a few aspects that are to be noted in this table:

- EI such as ID and names are not part of the transaction data table. They are shown here for completeness.
- The table is sparse; very few cells have entries in this high-dimensional space.
- There are few sensitive transactions that are classified as sensitive data (shown in bold). There is no fixed length for QIs and SD.
- A large set of transactions considered nonsensitive data form the QI data set. QIs have very high dimensions.
- The sensitivity in the transaction needs to be protected.

So, how does one protect the privacy of sensitive data and at the same time support utility?

Privacy preserving algorithms such as generalization or *l*-diversity are mainly focused on fixed schema tables and when applied to transaction data result in very high information loss. For relational tables, there are well-established privacy protection methods such as k-anonymity, *l*-diversity,

**TABLE 3.4**

A Sample Transaction Data Table

| ID | Name | $P_1$ | $P_2$ | $P_3$ | — | — | — | — | $P_{n-2}$ | $P_{n-1}$ | $P_n$ |
|----|------|-------|-------|-------|---|---|---|---|-----------|-----------|-------|
| 123 | Jane | 1 | | | | 1 | | | **1** | | |
| 567 | Mary | | | 1 | 1 | | | | | | |
| 891 | Hari | | | | | | | 1 | | 1 | |
| 987 | Ram | | 1 | | | | **1** | | | | |

and randomization, but for transaction data, very few approaches have been reported [8,9] in the literature.

## 3.6 Summary

After discussing privacy preservation of multidimensional data in Chapter 2, we took up complex data structures and discussed four complex data structures in this chapter: graph, time series, longitudinal, and transaction data. Graph data, being a popular social networking data format today, contain data about entities and their relationships in the form of edges and vertices, respectively. Attributes that need to be protected include identity, content, and link protections, all of which have been discussed in this chapter. We have discussed many studies that focus on graph modification, random perturbation, and clustering. Each of these has altered the structure of the graph, impacting utility to a certain degree.

Privacy preservation of time series data is a complex data structure as it is primarily used for making predictions by analyzing patterns hidden in the data. In time series data, tuples are not unrelated to previous tuples unlike multidimensional data, thus making anonymization a highly complex task. In addition to this, high dimensionality, background knowledge and pattern preservation of time series data poses a huge challenge to privacy preservation. We have discussed these challenges at length and also provided techniques that can be applied for privacy preservation.

Longitudinal data is data that is recorded at regular intervals and is especially the data of patients' response to a treatment. We have shown that each value in longitudinal data is correlated to previous values. Privacy preserving algorithms also need to preserve the utility of data, which is of high significance while conducting clinical trials. We have also discussed the challenges of preserving privacy in longitudinal data.

Finally, we have introduced privacy preservation techniques in sparse high-dimensional transaction data sets. These highly correlated data sets can be anonymized using some specialized techniques cited in this chapter.

## References

1. E. Zheleva and L. Getoor, Preserving the privacy of sensitive relationships in graph data, in *Proceedings of the First ACM SIGKDD Workshop on Privacy, Security and Trust in KDD*, (*PinKDD 2007*), Springer-Verlag Berlin, Heidelberg, 2007, pp. 153–171.
2. B. Zhou, J. Pei, and W.-S. Luk, A brief survey on anonymization techniques for Privacy Preserving Publishing of Social Network data, *SIGKDD Explorations*, 10(2), 12–22, 2009.

3. K. Liu and E. Terzi, Towards identity anonymization on graphs, in *Proceedings of the 2008 ACM SIGMOD International Conference on Management of Data (SIGMOD'08)*, ACM Press, New York, 2008, pp. 93–106.
4. M. Hay, Anonymizing social networks, Technical Report 07–19, University of Massachusetts Amherst, Amherst, MA, 2007.
5. G. Loukides, A.G. Koulalas-Divanis, and B. Malen, Anonymization of electronic medical records for validating genome-wide associateion studies, *Proceedings of the National Academy Sciences*, 107(17), 7898–7903, 2010.
6. A. Tamerroy, G. Loukides, M. E. Nergiz, Y. Saygin, and B. Malin, Anonymization of longitudinal electronic medical records, *IEEE Transactions on Information Technology in Biomedicine*, 16, 413–423, 2012.
7. M. Sehatkar and S. Matwin, HALT: Hybrid anonymization of longitudinal transactions, in *11th Annual Conference on Privacy, Security and Trust (PSI)*, IEEE, 2013, Tarragona, Spain, pp. 127–134.
8. Y. Xu, K. Wang, A.W.C. Fu, and P.S. Yu, Anonymizing transaction databases for publication, in *Proceedings of the 14th ACM SIGKDD International Conference on Knowledge Discovery and Data Mining (KDD'08)*, ACM, Las Vegas, NV, August 2008.
9. G. Ghinita, Y. Tao, and P. Kalnis, On the anonymization of sparse high dimensional data, in *2008 IEEE 24th International Conference on Data Engineering*, Cancun, Mexico, April 7–12, 2008, pp. 715–724.
10. M. Hay, G. Miklau, D. Jensen, D. Towsley, and P. Weis, Resisting structural re-identification anonymized social networks, *Proceedings of VLDB Endowment*, 1, 102–114, 2008, Computer Science Department Faculty Publication Series, Paper 179. http://scholarworks.umass.edu/cs_faculty_pubs/179.
11. S.P. Borgatti, Centrality and network flow, in *Sunbelt International Social Networks Conference*, New Orleans, LA, 2002.

# 4

## Static Data Anonymization Part III: Threats to Anonymized Data

### 4.1 Threats to Anonymized Data

Threat modeling helps in identifying possible threats to the system. Identifying threats is key to building an appropriate protection mechanism. So, what are the possible threats and where are the vulnerabilities in an enterprise's anonymization design? Anonymized data sets are released by an enterprise as test data or for purposes such as analysis and knowledge discovery. Is it possible to identify the record owner and his or her sensitive data? Threat models include a broad range of de-anonymization attacks.

We examine threats at the following levels:

- Location and user complexity (adversary)—This includes background and external knowledge. Background and external knowledge are a function of the location.
- Data structure complexity—This includes dimensionality, sparsity, and clusters.
- Anonymization algorithm.

Consider the data given in Table 4.1, which contain the original values.

Table 4.2 is an anonymized version of Table 4.1, which is generally released for analysis or other purposes. An attacker or data snooper who has access to Table 4.2 will try and de-anonymize to identify the record owner and his sensitive data, which is the goal of the attacker. So, how does he accomplish the task of re-identification? There is an old saying: "The way to a man's heart is through his stomach." There is only one way or path a woman can use. But in the case of anonymized data, an attacker can use many ways to re-identify.

When data are anonymized, the analytical utility of the data should be maintained. Therefore, it is very important to understand the threats to anonymized data. One more way of looking at this is the surface area of attack.

**TABLE 4.1**

Account Table of a Record Owner

| Statistical Properties of Quasi-Identifiers | | | Correlation between QI and SD Fields | Clusters of Sensitive Data | | Statistical Properties of SD Data Set or Individual Sensitive Attribute | |
|---|---|---|---|---|---|---|---|
| SSN | Name | DOB | ZIP | Gender | Balance | Credit Limit | Available Balance Credit |
| | John Snow | | | | 10,000 | 20,000 | 15,000 |

**TABLE 4.2**

Anonymized Version of Table 4.1

| SSN | Name | DOB | ZIP | Address | Gender | Balance | Credit Limit | Available Balance Credit |
|---|---|---|---|---|---|---|---|---|
| | Jack Samy | | | | | 10,000 | 20,000 | 15,000 |

"Surface area" means what aspects of anonymized data are compromised. The more the surface area, the more the data available for re-identification.

In anonymization, the problem lies in determining the level of anonymization required in the given context or environment.

> PRINCIPLE (8): Understand the sensitivity of data and disclosure risk for a given environment and setting.

So, where are the threats? What information or knowledge does an adversary or attacker use to gain information about a record owner and his sensitive data? Figure 4.1 illustrates the different dimensions of background and external knowledge of an adversary.

In [1], the authors present the model of the external knowledge of an adversary. Here, we make a point that an adversary has multiple dimensions of information that he or she can use to re-identify such as external knowledge and background knowledge. External knowledge is acquired from external sources such as public databases or social networking sites like Facebook. When an organization such as a bank loses customer-specific data to a hacker, the customers either move to a different bank or sometimes sue the bank for loss of privacy. But the same customers post a whole lot of their personal information on social networking sites. So, it is rather very difficult to create an anonymization design when so much of personal information is available in an external data source.

Is it not a good idea to come up with a new approach of collecting personal information about customers? Instead of collecting personal data such as address, zip code, gender, and date of birth, one could consider

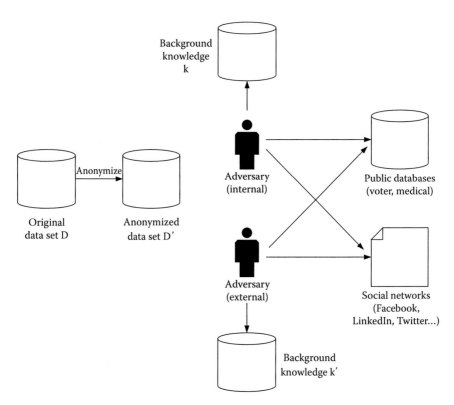

**FIGURE 4.1**
Dimensions of background knowledge and external knowledge.

collecting the biometric data of customers, which makes it very difficult for a hacker—just a thought!

We make a distinction between external knowledge and background knowledge. External knowledge is obtained from external sources, but background knowledge is the information an adversary has about an individual or individuals in the data set. Background information could include the distribution (statistical) of quasi-identifiers; for example, it could be the number of Asians in the database or the statistical properties of sensitive data, clusters of sensitive data, and so on. Another important aspect to consider about background information is who the adversary is—is he external or internal to the organization?

The background information an internal adversary possesses will be higher than an external adversary does. For example, an internal human resource (HR) personnel has more access to the employee database, even though it is anonymized, compared with an external adversary. Therefore, it is important to know whom you are trying to protect the data from. It is clear that an internal adversary has more background information than an external adversary.

Quasi-identifiers are defined as a data set that is also available in a public database such as a voters list and medical databases. But in today's world of social networks, one can find a mix of personal information and sensitive data. Many users of social networks post their current coordinates, their preferences, and so on. Many users of matrimonial sites and advertisements in India post their salary details, place of work, and health issues, if any. If one is able to connect the publicly available information with what is available on social network sites, then it becomes very difficult to draw a clear boundary between quasi-identifiers and sensitive data.

So, how do you anonymize the data set D to protect it from two different adversaries who have different background knowledge? This problem gets accentuated when companies start offshoring or outsourcing their work. So, it is necessary to understand the effect of the location, background knowledge, and external knowledge of an adversary.

Companies do have some options in this regard. They may choose to carry out data mining, analysis, and testing either in-house by their own employees or have it done by an offshore arm of the same company but in a different geographical location. Companies may also outsource to third party providers who are either in the same geographical location or outside.

Most of the published research work focuses on the strength of anonymization algorithms such as randomizations or k-anonymization and how they can be attacked. Our focus is on the internal versus external adversary and their location, which is critical to identifying where the intensity of threats lies and how to protect data, which is illustrated in Table 4.3 (Figure 4.2).

From the table and diagram, it is evident that an anonymization design should take into account the location and actor (adversary) complexity.

In the next section, we examine the various threats or attacks on different types of data structures in an enterprise.

**TABLE 4.3**

Effect of an Adversary's Location on an Anonymization Design

| Location | Background Knowledge | External Knowledge | Threat Level |
|---|---|---|---|
| In-house (internal) | High | High | High |
| Offshore (internal)—same company but in a different geographical location | High | High | High |
| Outsourced (same geography) | Medium | Medium | Medium |
| Outsourced (outside the geographical boundary) | Low | Low | Low |

Cannot link; no context

## 4.2 Threats to Data Structures

In the first chapter, we mentioned that an enterprise's data contain different data structures. For example, a healthcare organization's data have data structures such as relational or multidimensional data, text, time series data, longitudinal data, graph data, and so on. A patient's electronic medical records contain various health issues such as blood sugar, blood pressure, and other parameters that are measured over a period of time. These type of data can be represented by time series data, and repeated measurement of a patient's response to a drug taken over a period of time is represented as longitudinal data. Data structures such as time series data, longitudinal data, and graph data are complex. Privacy preservation of complex data structures is a challenge as they provide an adversary with more avenues for attack. To understand this further, consider the tables in Figure 4.3.

Compared to Figure 4.3c, which represents multidimensional data, Figure 4.3d representing a graph structure is more complex and as such provides more avenues for an adversary, as more information is available. The "surface area" available in the case of graph data for an adversary is high and includes QI, SD, the links between users in the network, the

1  In-house ($I_1$) (internal) Adversary. External Adversary ($I'_1$)

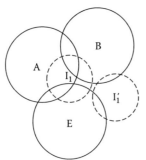

- Adversary (internal) has application context, background and external knowledge
- Adversary's background knowledge is difficult to model and poses significant threat

Background knowledge of the adversary could include

- Identity attributes
- Distribution of identity attributes
- Sensitive data (values of some sensitive data like salary or health issues of some of the users in the dataset
- Distribution of sensitive attribute values like for example, number of patients with HIV in a certain population
- Knowledge of the anonymization algorithm used for data protection
- Outliers in the data
- Associations in the data
- And many more

An external adversary will rely heavily on external knowledge; he may or may not have background knowledge

**FIGURE 4.2**
Venn diagram of an adversary's location and knowledge. A, application and organizational context; B, background knowledge; and E, external knowledge. *(Continued)*

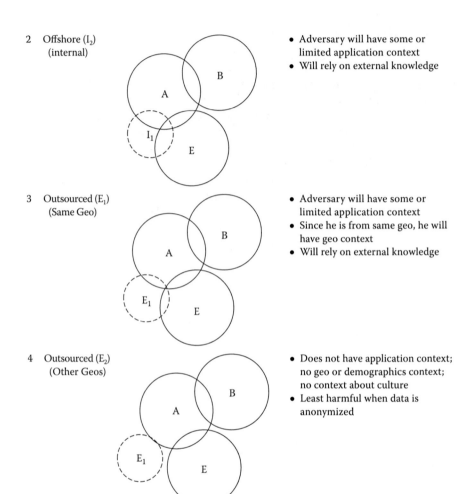

2   Offshore ($I_2$)
    (internal)

- Adversary will have some or limited application context
- Will rely on external knowledge

3   Outsourced ($E_1$)
    (Same Geo)

- Adversary will have some or limited application context
- Since he is from same geo, he will have geo context
- Will rely on external knowledge

4   Outsourced ($E_2$)
    (Other Geos)

- Does not have application context; no geo or demographics context; no context about culture
- Least harmful when data is anonymized

**FIGURE 4.2 (*Continued*)**
Venn diagram of an adversary's location and knowledge. A, application and organizational context; B, background knowledge; and E, external knowledge.

node ID, and the properties of the graph network such as centrality, density, reachability, and so on.

At a structure level, possible threats exist in the following dimensions:

- Complexity of the data structure—complex data structure provides more avenues to an adversary for attack [2].
- Complex data structures make anonymization very difficult.
- High-dimensional data.
- Sparse high-dimensional data—transaction data.
- Clusters in data.

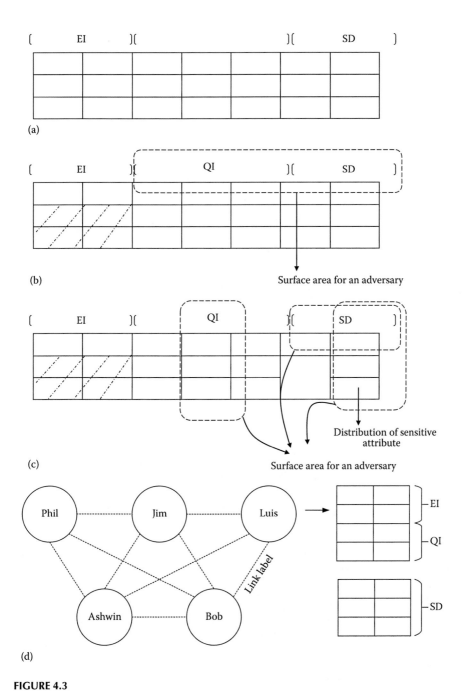

**FIGURE 4.3**
Data structures. (a) Original table, (b) only EI are masked, (c) anonymized table, and (d) graph of interconnected people.

Let us examine various data structures and threats or attacks that can be carried out on them.

## 4.2.1 Multidimensional Data

Multidimensional data set D can be considered as an n × m matrix, where n is the number of records and m is the number of attributes or columns. Relational data represented as multidimensional data are the most widely used data structure. Multidimensional data have three disjoint sets of data: explicit identifiers (EIs), quasi-identifiers (QIs), and sensitive data (SD); in fact, it is four disjoint sets of data that include nonsensitive data, which are not included here. EIs by default are completely masked (perturbed), which leave QIs and SD. QIs are anonymized and SD are left as is to enable analysis. Most of the attacks are directed toward QI (identity disclosure) and SD (attribute disclosur e). Table 4.4 explores the various attacks on multidimensional data structure.

## 4.2.2 Longitudinal Data

Longitudinal data are extensively used in healthcare domain, especially in clinical trials. Longitudinal data are a series of measurements taken over

**TABLE 4.4**

Multidimensional Data and Attack Types

| Target | Attack Type |
|---|---|
| Identity (quasi-identifiers) | Linkage attacks—links to external data sources. This happens when QI attributes can be linked to an external data source. |
| | Background knowledge attacks. |
| | Inference attacks—An adversary knows that the record owner is present in the data set. |
| | Data distribution attack—An adversary has knowledge about the statistical distribution of QI attributes. |
| | Outlier identification, for example, only Asian in the population. |
| | Probabilistic attacks. |
| Attribute (sensitive data) | Homogeneity attacks—Presence of clusters in sensitive data records. |
| | Background knowledge attack—An adversary has knowledge about a record owner's QIs and knows that he or she is in the data set and some aspect of SD and hence can infer. For example, the adversary knows that Alice (record owner) smokes heavily and also some of her QIs. With this background information, the adversary can infer that Alice suffers from lung cancer by referring to the released medical records. |
| | Association attack—An adversary is able to identify shopping patterns of a record owner with the help of background information of the record owner. |
| | Data distribution attacks. |
| | Outlier identification. |

a period of time from a patient in response to medication or treatment. The time period is generally not long as in the case of time series data. The measurements form the sensitive data set. The measurements taken from the patient are correlated with the treatment, and the measurements themselves form a correlated cluster. It is very difficult to anonymize a correlated cluster as any change in the values of the reading will affect the pattern of the response, which will lead to incorrect interpretations about the treatment. Longitudinal data are simple in structure but have innate complexity in correlated cluster of measurements. The threats to longitudinal data occur on both identifying attributes and sensitive data (Table 4.5).

### 4.2.3 Graph Data

Graph data are very complex. A graph G(V,E) has many vertices V, which are all linked through the edges E. There are so many dimensions in a graph that can be exploited by an adversary. A graph has vertices, sensitive vertex labels, relationship, edge labels, edge weights, and graph properties that can be attacked by an adversary. A graph's structural information can be used to attack the graph. Privacy preservation of graph should ensure that the privacy of individuals, including their properties, should be protected in the anonymized graph, but the aggregate property should be available for analytics and learning (Table 4.6).

### 4.2.4 Time Series Data

Time series data are characterized by high dimensionality, pattern, and frequency-domain characteristics. Anonymization techniques should ensure that all these characteristics are preserved in the anonymized data set. Conventional anonymization techniques used in relational data will not directly apply here. Generally, the attacks focus on identity, pattern, and time series values (Table 4.7).

**TABLE 4.5**

Longitudinal Data and Attack Types

| Target | Attack Type |
| --- | --- |
| Identity | Record linkage attacks. |
| | The identity of a record owner can be reidentified using external data if QIs are not anonymized properly. |
| Sensitive data | Background knowledge. |
| | An adversary having background knowledge of a patient such as admission date, disease, and so on can re-identify the record owner. |
| Sensitive data | Probabilistic attack. |

**TABLE 4.6**

Graph of Data and Attack Types

| Target | Attack Type |
|---|---|
| Identity—vertex existence | An adversary can use the vertex degree or node degree to identify the existence of a particular individual in the graph network. |
| Identity—sensitive vertex labels | A vertex represents an individual in a social network. An individual has associated personally identifiable information and sensitive data. The individual can be reidentified using different attack techniques: |
| | Identity disclosure—linkage attacks. |
| | Identity disclosure—background knowledge attacks. |
| | Sensitive attribute disclosure—background knowledge attacks. |
| | Background knowledge consists of both attribute knowledge and structural information—attributes of vertices, specific link relationships between some target individuals, vertex degrees, neighborhoods of some target individuals, embedded subgraphs, and graph metrics. |
| Link relationship | Background knowledge attacks—an adversary who attacks a graph always has some background knowledge of the network and the individuals in the network and some properties of the network without which it is difficult to attack an anonymized network. Re-identifying link relationships is generally based on the knowledge of the individuals in the network. |
| Identity and link relationship identification | Cross-reference attacks—an adversary who wants to identify individuals and their link relationships in an anonymized network $G_{main}$ can use an auxiliary network $G_{aux}$. The adversary has background knowledge that the individuals are also members of the auxiliary network. He uses this information to cross-refer with $G_{main}$ to identify the individuals and their relationships. |
| Identity and link relationship identification | Neighborhoods—an adversary has background knowledge of the neighborhood of a target individual. |
| Identity and link relationship identification | Graph metrics—an adversary uses graph metrics such as closeness, betweenness, degree, centrality, and so on to identify individuals in the network. |

## 4.2.5 Transaction Data

Transaction data are characterized by high dimensionality and sparsity. High dimensionality means that there are too many columns or attributes in the database, and sparsity means that each individual record contains values only for a small percentage of the columns. Sparsity increases the probability that re-identification succeeds, reduces the amount of background knowledge required in the re-identification process, and makes it difficult to effectively anonymize transaction data and balance privacy against utility. In a transaction database, identifying the sensitiveness of the transaction is important to the adversary (Table 4.8). For example, if a

**TABLE 4.7**

Time Series Data and Attack Types

| Target | Attack Type |
| --- | --- |
| Identity | Even though EIs are masked, one could re-identify them using QI attributes. Background information about an entity can be used to re-identify. For example, a patient who has undergone an ECG would not want to reveal or publish his ECG values to others as he feels it is his personal data. But if an adversary knows that the patient has undergone an ECG test, then this is itself a loss of privacy even though the adversary has no knowledge of the ECG values. This is the fundamental difference between anonymity and privacy. |
| Time series patterns | A time series has a pattern. For example, a car rental company will have a maximum sale during the holiday season. An adversary having this kind of background knowledge will be able to re-identify. |
| Time series values | Filtering attacks—time series data perturbed with white noise can be subjected to filtering attacks. Specialized filters can be used to remove the noise and reveal the time series values. |
| Time series values | Regression attacks—time series data perturbed with correlated noise can be subjected to regression attacks. An adversary with some specific values of the time series can build a regression model to predict the values of the time series. |

**TABLE 4.8**

Transaction Data and Attack Types

| Target | Attack Type |
| --- | --- |
| Identity | Removing identification information is not sufficient for anonymity. An adversary having background knowledge of a target individual and her shopping preferences could still be able to re-identify. |
| Sensitive transaction | Background knowledge attacks—an adversary having some background knowledge of a target individual will be able to find the sensitive transaction. |

customer buys bread and milk, the transaction record is of no interest to an adversary, but if a customer buys a special medicine, it attracts the attention of an adversary.

## 4.3 Threats by Anonymization Techniques

Anonymization techniques have weaknesses that adversaries exploit to recover original data. In Chapter 2, we have discussed many techniques that anonymize data. Let us now explore the threats posed by these techniques.

### 4.3.1 Randomization (Additive)

White noise or Gaussian noise, when used on a set of SD, has one weakness, for example, when an adversary knows the original SD value for a few records in a data set. This could be due to background knowledge or external data knowledge. By calculating the offset of anonymized values compared to the original data, an adversary can determine the interval in which the additive white noise is being generated. Although deducing the exact value is not easy, the adversary can certainly expect the deduced value to be close to the original value.

Correlated noise is difficult to attack as the range of anonymized data is different from that of the original. Hence, unless an original value is known, it cannot be attacked easily. However, if the original value is known, using regression, other values can be obtained.

### 4.3.2 k-Anonymization

k-Anonymization provides good privacy for QI attributes but is vulnerable to homogeneity attacks on SD when all values of small equivalence class have the same value.

### 4.3.3 *l*-Diversity

*l*-Diversity is vulnerable to two attacks: skewness attack and similarity attack [3]. When the overall distribution is skewed, satisfying *l*-diversity does not prevent attribute disclosure. When sensitive attribute values in an equivalence class are distinct but semantically similar, an adversary can obtain important information.

### 4.3.4 t-Closeness

Due to its high focus on utility, t-closeness is unable to provide optimum privacy. Besides, it tries to replace original SD with semantically similar ones. If an adversary knows that he or she is looking at a table with t-closeness, then the adversary knows that the data in SD are either the original data or something close to it.

---

## 4.4 Summary

In this chapter, we have discussed the different dimensions of threat model like location of the adversary, the inherent nature of the data structure, and weaknesses in anonymization techniques and so on. We have also explained the dimensions that are at play in background knowledge and external knowledge. The location of an adversary plays a vital role in determining what level of external knowledge and background knowledge are available. Using Venn diagrams, we have explained each scenario involving the application context, background knowledge, and external knowledge. This representation helps in understanding all the possible threats that arise while protecting data. We have also covered the threats prevalent in various data structures and the weaknesses in some anonymization techniques.

---

## References

1. B.-C. Chen, K. LeFevre, and R. Ramakrishnan, Privacy Skyline—Privacy with multidimensional adversarial knowledge, in *Proceedings of 33rd International Conference on Very Large Data Bases* (*VLDB 2007*), July 2007.
2. M.L. Maug, L. Denoyer, and P. Gallinari, Graph anonymization using machine learning, in *IEEE 28th International Conference on Advanced Information Networking and Application*, 2014, pp. 1111–1118.
3. N. Li, T. Li, and S. Venkatasubramanian, t-closeness: Privacy beyond k-anonymity and l-diversity, in *Proceedings of the 21st International Conference on Data Engineering* (*ICDE 2007*), 2007.

# 5

## Privacy Preserving Data Mining

## 5.1 Introduction

Massive amounts of data are being collected by companies from their customers, suppliers, and any other entity that conducts business with them. These data are an asset to the companies, and they are mined to extract knowledge.

Data mining is a process where critical business data are analyzed to gain new insights about customers, businesses, and markets. This new knowledge gained can be used to improve customer relationships and to produce better-quality products and services, which can result in higher revenues and profits. These data are generally in a relational or multidimensional format and stored in companies' central data warehouses. But with the evolution of the enterprise, a diverse set of data structures have come to be used: graph data, which could feed from social network sites; time series data; longitudinal data; semistructured data, such as XML; unstructured data; and big data. There is a need for different data repositories to store all these diverse data. Analytics is carried out on the data in the repositories. Access to these data repositories is strictly controlled by access control rights. Strict security measures are employed to secure the data as they are very sensitive and contain customer-identifying information. In addition to all security measures, companies ensure that the data are anonymized before being used for analytics/mining. More often, companies share their data with specialized analytics firms, and the data need to be protected before sharing.

The goal of data mining is to extract knowledge from the data. Some of the key functions of data mining are as follows:

- *Clustering*: Clustering means partitioning a data set into clusters of similar data.
- *Classification*: Classification is used for prediction. In predictive modeling, a model is built to predict a value of a single variable based on the values of the other variables.

- *Association rule/pattern mining*: Association rule mining is used to find associations between the transactions of a customer.
- *Outliers*: Identifying outlying data, that is, the data whose value is way outside or away from other data values.

The first three functions, clustering, classification, and association rule mining, generate an output that does not contain any customer data but generalized models. Therefore, there is no threat of re-identification, but there are reasons to protect the data. First, data are often shared with third parties for analysis. Second, as described in the earlier chapters, it is not possible to model the background knowledge of a data snooper, and therefore, there is a compelling need to protect the data. Third, there is a need for regulatory compliance.

This chapter explores some relevant anonymization methods and their effects on data mining functions, such as association rule mining and clustering, with reference to multidimensional data. In the earlier chapters, we have discussed most of the anonymization techniques. In data mining, association rule mining, clustering, and classification rely heavily on random perturbation techniques. This chapter gives an overview of privacy preservation of association rule mining and clustering. Many of these methods are also applicable for classification.

## 5.2 Data Mining: Key Functional Areas of Multidimensional Data

### 5.2.1 Association Rule Mining

Super markets and retail chains are keen to understand their customers' buying patterns. This information will help to gain insights into what customers buy, when they buy, how much they buy, and what items they buy together. This will help the stores to strategically place items and offer promotions and discounts. This is referred to as market basket analysis (MBA). Retail stores also offer loyalty cards to customers. Such cards can be tracked by the store to understand customers' buying patterns. MBA can also be used to track what customers are not buying. Closely linked to MBA is association rule mining, which is used to find frequent patterns or correlations among items in the transaction database; for example, customers who buy bread also buy butter or cheese. Therefore, there is an association between bread and butter. Another example of association among items discovered was between baby diapers and beer. Men who bought baby diapers also bought beer. Understanding these patterns helps retailers to provide strategic services to the customers, increase sales, and generate more revenue and profits.

The problem of association rule mining is to find relationships among items in a database. Given a database D, let $I = \{i_1, i_2, ..., i_m\}$ be a set of items. Let $T = \{t_1, t_2, ..., t_n\}$ be a set of transactions on the database D. Each transaction $t_i$ is a set of items such that $t_i \subseteq I$.

$$X \rightarrow Y, \text{ where } X \subset I, Y \subset I, \text{ and } X \cap Y = \varnothing$$

X, Y are a set of items also called item set. A transaction, for example, can be

{Bread, butter, eggs}

where bread and butter are X and eggs are Y; $X \rightarrow Y$.

Therefore, when customers buy bread and butter, they also tend to buy eggs, which means that there is an association between {bread, butter} and {eggs}. Take, for example, the transactions shown in Figure 5.1.

The number of transactions that contain {bread, butter} items (an example) is called support. If the support is too low, then such a transaction rarely occurs, and therefore, a minimum support (minSup) needs to be defined and any association below minSup is not to be considered.

Another measure called confidence is that the percentage of transactions in T that contain X also contain Y. A minimum Confidence (minConf) needs to be defined, and a Confidence below minConf indicates that it is not possible to predict Y from X. The following association rule has Support of 75% and Confidence is 100%. If Support and Confidence is greater than minSup and minConf respectively then the association rule is valid.

{bread, butter} $\rightarrow$ {eggs} (Support = 6/8; Confidence = 4/4)

Customers' transactions are recorded in a transaction database. A store or a supermarket has hundreds of products or items that determine the dimensions of the database. Therefore, a transaction database is of high dimension and is sparsely filled with binary data. The transaction set in Figure 5.1 will have entries in the transaction database as shown in Table 5.1.

Is there a privacy risk in sharing the transaction in Table 5.1? Definitely not. A privacy risk comes only when Table 5.1 is tagged/joined with customer identity data. Table 5.2 shows customers' transactions.

| $t_1$ | Bread, butter, eggs, cheese, chocolates |
| $t_2$ | Chocolates, bread, butter, cheese |
| $t_3$ | Eggs, flour, butter |
| $t_4$ | Bread, butter, eggs |
| $t_5$ | Bread, butter, cheese |
| $t_6$ | Bread, butter, meat, beer |
| $t_7$ | Bread, butter, eggs, milk |
| $t_8$ | Eggs, flour, chocolates |

**FIGURE 5.1**
Transaction set.

**TABLE 5.1**

Sample Transaction Database

| Transaction ID | Bread | | Butter | Eggs | Milk | Chocolate | Cheese | Flour | Beer | Meat |
|---|---|---|---|---|---|---|---|---|---|---|
| | $i_1$ | $i_2$ | | | | | | | | $i_m$ |
| $t_1$ | 1 | | 1 | 1 | | 1 | 1 | | | |
| $t_2$ | 1 | | 1 | 1 | | 1 | | 1 | | |
| $t_3$ | | | 1 | 1 | | | | | | |
| $t_4$ | 1 | | 1 | 1 | | | | | | |
| $t_5$ | 1 | | 1 | | | | 1 | | | |
| $t_6$ | 1 | | 1 | | | | | | 1 | 1 |
| $t_7$ | 1 | | 1 | 1 | 1 | | | 1 | | |
| $t_8$ | | | 1 | | | 1 | | | | |

When a transaction table is associated with customer data, then the table becomes sensitive. The challenges to privacy preservation are high dimensionality, no fixed schema, and Boolean data. Anonymization techniques that use generalization and suppression such as k-anonymity are more suitable for relational data with fixed schema and not suitable here. Anonymization techniques such as *l*-diversity that protect sensitive data are also not suitable as they also focus on relational data with fixed schema.

### *5.2.1.1 Privacy Preserving of Association Rule Mining: Random Perturbation*

There are two approaches to preserving the privacy of association rules— preserving the privacy of the input data and hiding sensitive output rules. In the first approach of input data privacy, a randomization technique is considered. In privacy preserving methods, random data or noise is added to the original data to hide its true value. But with the transaction database, data values are Boolean, and therefore, a random perturbation technique is used. One such technique is MASK (Mining Associations with Secrecy Konstraints) proposed in Rizvi and Haritsa [1]. MASK uses a probabilistic distortion of input data. The distortion technique is to simply flip each 0 or 1 with a parameterized probability p, or to retain as is with a complementary probability 1-p. Another technique called "select-a-size" is proposed in Evfimievski et al. [2]. In this technique, randomization operation is composed of three steps for every customer transaction $t_i$.

1. For customer transaction $t_i$ of length m, a random integer j from [1,m] is first chosen with probability $p_m[j]$.
2. Then j items are uniformly and randomly selected from the original transaction and inserted into the randomized transaction.

**TABLE 5.2**

Customer Transaction Table

| Customer | Transaction ID | Bread i₁ | Bread i₂ | Butter | Eggs | Milk | Chocolate | Cheese | Flour | Beer | Meat |
|---|---|---|---|---|---|---|---|---|---|---|---|
| John | $t_1$ | 1 | | 1 | 1 | | 1 | 1 | | | |
| Hari | $t_2$ | 1 | | 1 | 1 | | 1 | | | | |
| Mary | $t_3$ | | | 1 | 1 | | | | 1 | | |
| Jane | $t_4$ | 1 | | 1 | 1 | | | | | | |
| Jack | $t_5$ | 1 | | 1 | | | | 1 | | | |
| Henry | $t_6$ | 1 | | 1 | | | | | | 1 | |
| Andy | $t_7$ | 1 | | 1 | 1 | 1 | | | 1 | | |
| Prill | $t_8$ | | | 1 | 1 | | 1 | | | | 1 |

3. A uniformly and randomly chosen fraction $p_m$ of the remaining items in the database that are not present in the original transaction is inserted into the randomized transaction.

In summary, the final randomized transaction is composed of a subset of the true items from the original transaction and additional false items from the complementary set of items in the database [3].

Algorithms such as Apriori are used to mine association rules from transaction databases, but when mining association rules from a perturbed database, the Apriori algorithm needs to be modified. Evfimievski et al. [2] provides a modified version of the Apriori algorithm.

## 5.2.2 Clustering

A bank, for example, would want to understand how its customers use their credit cards and what their spending patterns are. Table 5.3 provides an overview of customers' spending patterns during the festive month.

The bank has thousands of credit card customers and wants to explore all of their spending patterns. This is a challenging task. In data mining, clustering is a very important function, which is widely used for exploratory studies. Data clustering is a method of creating groups of objects in such a way that objects in one cluster are very similar and objects in different clusters are quite distinct. Data clustering is also referred to as unsupervised learning. With reference to Table 5.3, many clusters can be defined as shown in Figure 5.2.

Figure 5.2 shows different clusters created based on attributes such as *EDUCATION, INCOME,* and *CREDIT CARD SPENDS (CC. SPENDS).*

**TABLE 5.3**

Sample Table Illustrating Spending Patterns on Credit Card

| Cust ID | Name | Age | Education Level | Income | Credit Card Spends |
|---|---|---|---|---|---|
| 1 | Bob | 25 | Grad | 90,000 | 5,000 |
| 2 | Mary | 35 | Postgrad | 150,000 | 7,000 |
| 3 | Hari | 40 | Doctorate | 300,000 | 15,000 |
| 4 | Swamy | 30 | Grad | 120,000 | 7,000 |
| 5 | Jim | 27 | Grad | 100,000 | 3,000 |
| 6 | Jack | 45 | Doctorate | 350,000 | 20,000 |
| 7 | Bill | 40 | Postgrad | 200,000 | 10,000 |
| 8 | Mark | 50 | Doctorate | 375,000 | 18,000 |
| 9 | Ram | 30 | Grad | 130,000 | 10,000 |
| 10 | Jane | 47 | Grad | 200,000 | 12,000 |
| 11 | Sam | 50 | Doctorate | 400,000 | 25,000 |
| 12 | Mike | 45 | Postgrad | 250,000 | 15,000 |

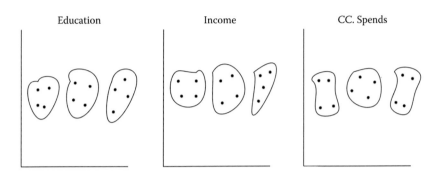

**FIGURE 5.2**
Example of clustering.

Of course, it is possible to cluster by combining the vital attributes of the customer and financial data. As clustering is purely exploratory in nature, there is no right or wrong approach to create clusters. Take, for example, the clusters formed based on income data: low income, middle income, and high income. Each cluster has a mean of 100K, 200K, and 300K, respectively. Note that each of the income clusters is formed around the mean value also referred to as the center of the cluster. The goal of clustering is to find the intrinsic grouping of data for which a distance function is used. Consider that the mean of a group is denoted by $m_i$ and the data in the group is denoted by $x_i$. Then the distance between $x_i$ and $m_i$ in the Euclidean distance

$$\text{dist}\,(x_i, m_i) = \|x_i - m_i\|$$

$$= \left( \sum_i (x_i, m_i)^2 \right)^{1/2} \tag{5.1}$$

Data points similar to one another and also close to the mean come together to form a cluster. This brings up some important aspects of a cluster such as cluster quality, which indicates that similar data points form a cluster and dissimilar points are in different groups of clusters. One of the features of cluster quality is similarity (similarity function). Similar data points constitute a cluster, and dissimilar points are not in the same cluster. A cluster has a center point, and other points in the cluster are close to it (distance measure) and the structure of the cluster. To summarize, cluster quality is controlled by the

- Similarity measure
- Center
- Distance measure
- Structure

These aspects of cluster quality are important when privacy preservation techniques are applied before clustering.

When an organization wants to carry out data mining activities such as clustering, they generally outsource the task to specialized analytics firms. Outsourcing customer data has a major issue: customer data need to be protected before outsourcing.

Given a data table D that needs to be transformed to D' before outsourcing for cluster analysis, what data anonymization techniques can be applied on D that ensures high cluster quality and at the same time preserves the privacy of customer data?

### 5.2.2.1 A Brief Survey of Privacy Preserving Clustering Algorithms

Chapter 2 explored various anonymization techniques such as randomization and group anonymization techniques such as k-anonymization, *l*-diversity, and t-closeness and their inherent strengths and weaknesses. In the case of privacy preserving clustering, some general approaches are considered:

1. Random perturbation
2. Group anonymization
3. Secure multiparty computation (SMC)

Here, the focus will be only on random perturbation techniques.

#### 5.2.2.1.1 Random Perturbation

When Table 5.3 is perturbed with random noise, then cluster quality will be affected in the following dimensions:

- Mean or center
- Distance measure—distance between mean and other points
- Similarity measure—could get affected since a point in one cluster could get pushed to another cluster
- Structure

Cluster quality may get affected if random perturbation is not well designed. The goal of privacy preserving clustering is to ensure that as much cluster quality is maintained as possible without any loss of privacy.

Random perturbation techniques can be classified as shown in Figure 5.3.

*5.2.2.1.1.1 Additive Random Perturbation*   Additive random perturbation, also known as a value-based technique, is probably the easiest technique to implement. In this technique, sensitive values in a user's record are perturbed using a randomized function, which can be either Gaussian or Uniform [4].

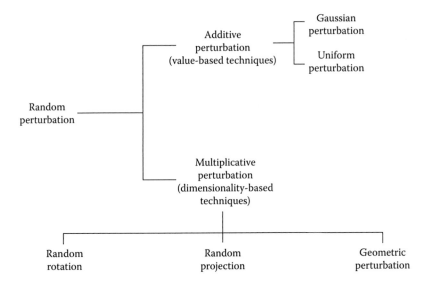

**FIGURE 5.3**
Classification of random perturbation techniques.

Consider $x_i$ as the original data and $n_i$ as the random perturbation. Then the final perturbed data would be $X_i$:

$$X_i = x_i + n_i \tag{5.2}$$

n could be either Gaussian or Uniform perturbation. The use of Gaussian or Uniform perturbation depends on the application [5].

Additive perturbation preserves the privacy of a single attribute or dimension and is not well suited for data mining or distance-based data mining applications such as clustering.

*5.2.2.1.1.2 Multiplicative Random Perturbation*   Some of the multiplicative perturbation techniques are based on the work by Johnson and Lindenstrauss [6]. Multiplicative perturbation is more suitable for data mining applications such as clustering as it preserves the distribution across multiple dimensions, which is not possible with additive perturbations. With regard to clustering, multiple perturbation techniques maintain inter-record distances.

In random projection, data points in a high-dimensional space are projected onto a space of randomly chosen lower-dimensional space. The distance between the data points can be approximately preserved. This technique provides high privacy as high-dimensional data cannot be recovered from low-dimensional data because some information is lost due to the projection. This technique is very useful for privacy preserving clustering. A few other dimension-based techniques are discussed in Oliveira and Zaiane [7].

## 5.3 Summary

This chapter provides an introduction to anonymization in data mining with a brief overview of some techniques used in association rule mining and clustering. The most common techniques used are random perturbation for association rule mining and clustering, which are discussed with examples to show the privacy and utility levels achieved by them.

## References

1. J. Rizvi and J.R. Haritsa, Maintaining data privacy in association rule mining, in *Proceedings of 28th International Conference on Very Large Databases (VLDB)*, Hong Kong, China, August 2002.
2. A. Evfimievski, R. Srikant, R. Agarwal, and J. Gehrke, Privacy preserving mining of association rules, in *Proceedings of Eighth ACM SIGKDD International Conference on Knowledge, Discovery, and Data Mining*, Edmonton, AB, Canada, 2002.
3. J.R. Haritsa, Mining association rules under privacy constraints, in *Privacy Preserving Data Mining: Models and Algorithms*, C. Aggarwal and P.S. Yu (eds.), Springer, New York, 2008.
4. R. Agrawal and R. Srikant, Privacy preserving data mining, in *Proceedings of the 2000 ACM SIGMOD International Conference on Management of Data*, May 2000, Dallas, TX, pp. 439–450.
5. X. Li, Z. Yu, and P. Zhang, A review of privacy preserving data mining, in *IEEE International Conference on Computer and Information Technology*, Xi'an, China, 2014.
6. W. Johnson and J. Lindenstrauss, Extension of Lipshitz mapping into Hilbert space, *Contemporary Mathematics*, 26, 189–206, 1984.
7. S.R.M. Oliveira and O. Zaiane, Privacy preserving clustering by data transformation, in *Proceedings of 18th Brazilian Symposium for Databases*, Brazil, October 2003, pp. 304–318.

# 6

## Privacy Preserving Test Data Manufacturing

## 6.1 Introduction

Testing is an important part of the systems development life cycle (SDLC). The quality of software application depends on the quality of testing. High-quality testing requires high-quality test data. Test data play an important role in ensuring that testing materializes effectively and comprehensively. In this chapter, we concentrate on test data privacy. Test data contain sensitive personally identifiable information (PII), and they should be protected. There is also a mandatory compliance requirement to protect test data. Regulations like the Health Insurance Portability and Accountability Act (HIPAA), the EU Data Protection Act, the Family Educational Rights and Privacy Act (FERPA), the Swiss Data Protection Act, and so on mandate protection of test data. Chapters 2 through 4 focused on static data anonymization, the classification of data, and the techniques that are available. In this chapter, our focus will be to explore the application of the same concepts and techniques with respect to test data.

Software testing is a process, or a series of processes, designed to ensure that computer code does what it was designed to do and that it does not do anything unintended [1]. Defining software testing in this way makes it clear that when data are being created for testing, they should support both the former and the latter clauses. This would define the extent of utility of the test data.

Maintaining privacy in test data is as important as preserving utility. Often, enterprises use portions of production data to compensate for the test data that they are unable to provision. While doing so, the privacy of individuals' data needs to be maintained.

In this chapter, we will discuss the fundamentals of test data, present our view of privacy and utility in a testing setting, define the challenges, and present ways of implementing a good practice of preserving privacy in test data.

## 6.2 Related Work

The need to preserve privacy in test data has risen primarily due to privacy regulations aimed at protecting personal data. Organizations doing business globally have had to abide by laws preventing the usage of data across international boundaries due to various legislations. The UK's Information Commissioner's Office is an independent authority set up to uphold information rights in public interest, promoting openness by public bodies and data privacy for individuals [2]. Similar privacy regulatory bodies exist in other parts of the world. This is primarily due to outsourcing of work by data owners to their business partner entities. Outsourcing, especially to other countries, has become a popular business model today due to its promise of cost reduction, making data sharing across boundaries with business associates unavoidable. A fundamental problem in test outsourcing is how to allow a database-centric application owner to release its private data with guarantees that the entities in these data (e.g., people, organizations) are protected at a certain level while retaining testing efficacy [3]. In Chapter 4, we saw Venn diagrams demonstrating how location- and user-based background knowledge or external knowledge enhances the perspective of adversaries.

Multidimensional data are a commonly found data structure being tested today. Privacy preservation in multidimensional databases has seen a lot of work done on it. Data perturbation using methods such as transformation [4], rotation [5], and noise addition [6] has been proposed. Although perturbative techniques have been used fairly commonly, the use of nonperturbative techniques, such as group anonymization, for example, k-anonymization or t-closeness, has hardly been discussed from a test data perspective.

Test efficacy, specifically of automated test execution for nonfunctional testing, has been measured in Metsa et al. [7] using aspect-oriented techniques. In their work, the authors do talk about test data as one of the important aspects but refrain from demonstrating the importance of test data in system behavior in the larger context of measurement.

In [8], there is a good discussion on privacy preservation and behavior preservation. A *kb*-anonymity model is introduced that focuses on both privacy and utility aspects of test data. The behavioral aspect of *kb*-anonymity tries to maintain the same paths of execution using the test data as that of the original data. *kb*$^e$-anonymity [9] is a technique that has evolved from *kb*-anonymity to handle test data anonymization of evolving programs.

## 6.3 Test Data Fundamentals

Prior to starting a discussion on privacy in test data, we briefly discuss some basic concepts of testing. This section will help the reader get an understanding about testing phases, challenges, test efficacy parameters, and current trends. We will limit our overview to software application testing.

### 6.3.1 Testing

Testing aims at uncovering defects at various levels in a software system. Common testing phases include system testing, system integration testing, performance testing, and security testing. These phases are classified into functional and nonfunctional testing.

#### 6.3.1.1 Functional Testing: System and Integration Testing

System testing is the first phase of testing, where the software system is assessed against the requirements document. Test cases are written based on their respective use cases. The data needed for this testing phase are usually of good volume and high quality to suit all test cases and possess qualities of the original data.

System integration testing is performed after individual modules have already passed system testing. Integration mechanisms like messages cannot be tested directly. Simulations help with virtualizing calls made across modules, thus testing the interactions. Test data required are rarely voluminous, often in the form of files, and usually contain sensitive data.

#### 6.3.1.2 Nonfunctional Testing

A system's nonfunctional characteristics are evaluated by various kinds of testing phases. Stress or load, scalability, responsiveness, reliability, security, etc., look at various nonfunctional characteristics of the software system and assess it against the agreed benchmarks, respectively. Nonfunctional requirements are the foundations of the system's architecture and thus need to be tested thoroughly.

### 6.3.2 Test Data

Data that invoke pieces of code to satisfy successful execution of a test case or test script are called test data. A good test case design takes into account all paths of the program using all possible inputs. However, exhaustive input testing and exhaustive path testing, as discussed in Myers [1], are impracticable. Realistically, test data are limited to the predicates laid out by the testing team. Nevertheless, the motivation is always to maximize test and code coverage. Until today, most of these terms have been used with respect to the code, but it is the data that ultimately make a particular piece of code execute.

Many organizations have realized that optimizing test planning and processes can produce gains. Often, a zero defect result from a testing phase is desired to certify that a software system is ready for production. But finally, it is the quality of test data that determines the success or failure of a test phase and not the defects unearthed. With good-quality test data, more defects will be detected, thus making testing fruitful.

Naturally, the best source of test data is using the production data itself. However, there is one problem—privacy. Original data cannot be used in nonproduction environments directly. The presence of personal data compromises the privacy of its record owners. Thus, privacy preserving test data manufacturing is one of the most important areas of focus today in the SDLC. Speaking of SDLC, let us understand the bathtub curve of reliability.

### 6.3.2.1 Test Data and Reliability

Software reliability, which is often represented by the hzf (hazard function), displays a "bathtub shape," as shown in Figure 6.1.

A theory often traced to the seventeenth century [10], the curve shows that any device has three distinct phases of reliability. Applying this to a software system, we define the three phases as follows:

1. *Early failure*: Software exhibits many defects that are uncovered by initial rounds of testing. Defects are high at this time.

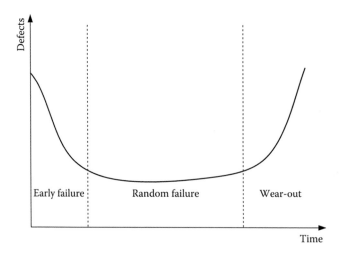

**FIGURE 6.1**
Bathtub curve of reliability.

2. *Random failure*: Past the initial phases, the software stabilizes and exhibits a steady state with random defects that get discovered intermittently, while minor amendments are made to the software system.

3. *Wear-out*: Software system is becoming old and needs updating to keep up with changes in policy/ business/ technology that require numerous amendments. During this phase, again the number of defects begins to increase and continues to do so until the software system is unable to adapt any further and is abandoned.

Test data are an integral ingredient of all the three phases of the bathtub curve. Throughout the life span of the application, various phases of testing will be carried out on it. Each functional and nonfunctional test helps discover defects. One needs to recognize test data as a major influencer than a mere catalyst.

Figure 6.2 gives a big picture of the kind of data essential for each test phase.

### 6.3.2.1.1 Early Failure

The "early failure" phase needs to test all functional aspects of the software system. Data needed to test these are mainly acquired from the

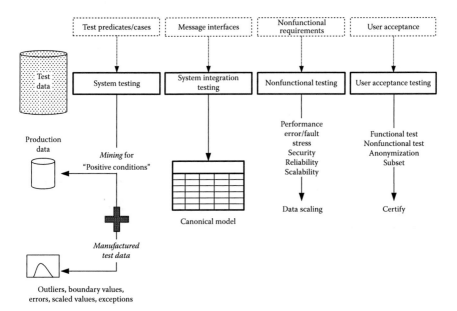

**FIGURE 6.2**
Test Data Design.

production data source. Most positive scenarios get tested with these data, but alternate flows of programs require some manufactured data. Manufactured data are what we call synthetic data. We cover synthetic data generation in Chapter 7.

Integration testing requires message files to be anonymized in a way that no PII is exposed. Masking is an option here, but this requirement is best serviced using synthetic data. In the early failure phase, service virtualization is used to implement this.

Nonfunctional tests are performed to ensure all benchmarks are met and complied with consistently. Data needed for stress or load tests are obtained by scaling the original production data manifolds. Security testing might be carried out by taking a slice of data representing all roles and user groups required during testing.

This test data design yields maximum number of defects and helps stabilize the application and move it into a steady state.

### 6.3.2.1.2 Random Failure

During the steady state, testing is done on a set of incremental features that are introduced. Regression testing is the most common method used in this phase, as system behavior is assessed against the previous version. Regression testing does not require a new data set, but one that is different from the previous data set by a factor of $\delta$, where $\delta$ represents the data needed to test the new functionality $\Delta$ introduced into the software system.

### 6.3.2.1.3 Wear-Out

During the tail end of the software system's existence, a lot of changes need to be made to keep it up to date with the current technology and business scenario. As architectural-level changes are not done, patchy code changes introduce a lot of bugs. Along with these changes, the test data also change drastically to cater to the new test cases that evaluate the evolving software system. This phase resembles the initial "early failure" phase as many defects start coming out of testing. Unless architectural changes are made to the system, the software system reaches a state where further enhancements are not sustainable, and this results in its total abandonment.

### 6.3.2.2 How Are Test Data Created Today?

Companies like IBM and Informatica have been leading the area of test data management (TDM) as per Gartner's Magic Quadrant [11]. The two primary areas bundled under test data management are data masking techniques and the ability to create subsets. Privacy in TDM tools is often limited to their offering of masking algorithms, which include substitution, shuffling, scrambling, randomization, blurring, etc. It is important to observe that although services offered do promise good implementations of the algorithms mentioned earlier, it is left to the discretion of the practitioner to exercise good judgment and use them. The data subset capability is based on the reduction of data based on rows, columns, and relationships. Most companies today are expecting to move toward test case–based test data provisioning, which is not part of the tools available today.

So, what are good-quality test data? We will get to that in a bit.

### 6.3.3 A Note on Subsets

Test environments do not get the same kinds of resources as production. A result of this is the need to reduce the amount of data that can be brought into test. This poses an interesting problem of not only having the correct set of data for testing but also picking a smaller size of the same (Figure 6.3).

> Subsets are samples of data picked from original data in a way that they represent the entire data in syntax, semantics and statistics.

The goal of creating a sample is to ensure that the responses derived from the sample are identical to those derived by using the original data itself. In the context of test data, a subset should assure the tester of comparable test coverage as that expected to be achieved using original production data.

## 6.4 Utility of Test Data: Test Coverage

Coverage is a quality assurance metric that determines how thoroughly a test suite exercises a given program [12]. Test coverage is arguably the most important goal of testing. Often expected to perform exhaustive input testing and exhaustive path testing, which are unattainable, testing tries to achieve the highest levels of test efficacy.

Anonymization of test data is essential in many domains like financial services and healthcare. In this section, we will define what effect anonymized test data will have on one of the key test quality metrics: test coverage. When you test a software application with original data you ensure optimum test coverage. However, when you anonymize the data, it is clear that the coverage will not be as high. The loss of test coverage can be measured using the lines of code that were covered using original and anonymized data.

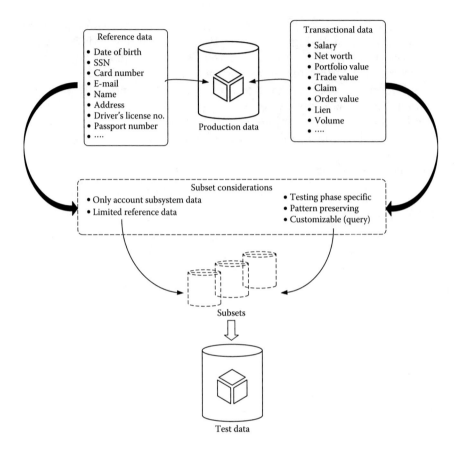

**FIGURE 6.3**
Subset creation.

Further, we show how the pivot keeps fluctuating between privacy and utility with an example. Finally, we lay down guidelines to achieve high test coverage and anonymization using good anonymization designs.

As test coverage is a yardstick to measure test efficacy, an important parameter is the data provisioned for testing. To illustrate the problem, one can envision a software system S with data D. Test phases T are performed on the data.

The test coverage TC for each test phase t, denoted as TC(t), is a summation of the individual test coverage for each test case n as shown in (6.1)

$$TC(t) = \sum_{n=1}^{N} tc_n \tag{6.1}$$

where N is the total number of test cases.

The test coverage of each test case $tc_n$ is a function of the subsystem being tested and the data provisioned from the same as shown in (6.2)

$$tc_n = f(S_n, d_n) \tag{6.2}$$

Section 6.4.3 will discuss a concrete measure for test coverage.

### 6.4.1 Privacy versus Utility

In Chapter 1, we introduced the disproportionate relationship between privacy and utility. The privacy versus utility map (Figure 1.5) shows that there is a region where one could expect to balance the loss of privacy and loss of utility. Test data utility is defined by the usability of test data to execute test cases effectively. We measure test data utility by analyzing three qualities of data (Figure 6.4).

In the increasing order of basicity, syntax, semantics, and statistics are three pillars on which the quality of test data can be evaluated. We discuss these qualities later in this chapter.

Test data anonymization always begins with the classification of PII. Using the principle of classification (1), all data must first be classified into the four categories of explicit identifiers (EI), quasi-identifiers (QI), sensitive data (SD), and nonsensitive data (NSD). Figure 6.5 shows the classification.

The principle of concealment states that EI should be masked. Most EI do not have any functionality built around them and hence can be easily replaced with masked values. Besides, the semantics or statistics of EI are irrelevant for the utility of test data.

Similarly, the principles of utilization (5) and contextual anonymization (8) show that the application scenario and the context play key roles in the classification of the data into EI, QI, and SD. For example, the color of hair eye

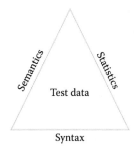

**FIGURE 6.4**
Qualities of test data.

| A logical row of data | Explicit identifiers (EI) | Quasi-identifiers (QI) | Sensitive data (SD) | Non-sensitive data (NSD) |
|---|---|---|---|---|

| Explicit identifiers (EI) | First Name, Last Name, Social Security Number, Account Number, Driver's License Number, Passport Number etc. |
|---|---|
| Quasi-identifiers (QI) | Gender, Date of Birth, Postal Code, Color of Eyes/Hair, Address Lines 1, Address Line 2, Landline Number, Zip, City, State etc. |
| Sensitive data (SD) | Income/Salary, Account balance, Order total, Trade amount, Date of purchase, Address of Mortgaged Property |
| Non-sensitive data (NSD) | Everything Else |

**FIGURE 6.5**
Classification of test data.

can be easily classified as QI in any loan, mortgage, or DMV database. When it comes to a cosmetologist, these data are part of a patient's private data and could be part of a procedure the individual has undergone. Similar examples exist in mortgage domain too where property address would be classified as SD rather than as QI.

The reason we discuss these situations is because in testing, SD represent the facts in a software system. It projects the current state of the system, whereas EI and QI are details around the current state.

The transactional data represent system behavior and contain truth and behavioral trends, load information, correlations, and other statistical facts that help test all possible conditions and branching handles that a tester is looking for. The reference data, on the other hand, describe actors and their identities. Thus, a tester would always like to have the transactions maintained as is.

### 6.4.2 Outliers

Outliers have significance in test data. They are important since they tend to invoke parts of code that do not execute often. Numerical outliers in SD are generally beyond $3\sigma$ distance from the mean value, where $\sigma$ is the standard deviation. Outliers in categorical data appear in the form of rare occurrences, like a rare disease in a healthcare database.

The best way to deal with outliers from a privacy perspective is to suppress them as they have potential to reveal identities on their own. For a test manager, removal of outliers does not help test coverage. The context and importance of testing exceptional situations should be factored in when outliers are encountered in test data, since it is critical to attain a balance between privacy and utility of test data. The next section discusses a measure for utility in test data.

### 6.4.3 Measuring Test Coverage against Privacy

Test coverage is generally measured in terms of the line of code (LOC) tested. Let

D → Production data set
T → Optimal subset of D
f → Anonymization function applied on T
L → LOC tested
T′ → Anonymized test data subset
L′ → LOC tested with T′
T = Subset (D)
T′ = f(T)

$$\text{Utility } U = 1 - \left[ \frac{L - L'}{L} \right] \qquad (6.3)$$

Test data subset T, which is derived from the production data D, can be used to test only the "happy" conditions or "positive" flows in the application. L is the number of LOC tested using T. When T is anonymized, the number of LOC tested is L′, which is lesser than L:

$$L' < L \qquad (6.4)$$

In certain conditions, where we are able to balance privacy and utility, L′ = L, thus making the utility U to 1. Although it appears to be a tall order to achieve this, later in this chapter, we will show how a good anonymization design can increase the value of L′.

We consider various anonymization options and examine their effects on test coverage in the next section.

## 6.5 Privacy Preservation of Test Data

The first step in privacy preservation of test data is to clearly classify the metadata. The principle of classification (1) is applicable in test data (Table 6.1).

### 6.5.1 Protecting Explicit Identifiers

In test data, EI play a small role in governing test coverage. As part of the three qualities of test data, syntax is most important in case of EI. While privacy preserving of EI can be achieved using masking, there are some basic principles to be followed.

**TABLE 6.1**

Sample Salary Data Table

| EI | | QI | | | | SD | | | |
|---|---|---|---|---|---|---|---|---|---|
| ID | Name | Gender | Age | Address | Zip | Basic | HRA | Med | All |
| 12345 | John | M | 25 | 1, 4th St. | 560001 | 10,000 | 5,000 | 1000 | 6,000 |
| 56789 | Harry | M | 36 | 358, A dr. | 560068 | 20,000 | 10,000 | 1000 | 12,000 |
| 52131 | Hari | M | 21 | 3, Stone Ct | 560055 | 12,000 | 6,000 | 1000 | 7,200 |
| 85438 | Mary | F | 28 | 51, Elm st. | 560003 | 16,000 | 8,000 | 1000 | 9,600 |
| 91281 | Srini | M | 40 | 9, Ode Rd | 560001 | 14,000 | 7,000 | 1000 | 8,400 |
| 11253 | Chan | M | 35 | 3, 9th Ave | 560051 | 8,000 | 4,000 | 1000 | 4,800 |

### 6.5.1.1 Essentials of Protecting EI

There are two important aspects when it comes to protecting EI in a test data setting: Referential Integrity and Consistency.

Table 6.2 shows the primary key relationship the employee salary table has with the HR information table, which are linked to each other by the ID. There are cases where these primary keys appear as foreign keys in other tables. Hence, while masking any key field, care should be taken to propagate the same masked value to all respective rows of tables where this field appears. This is essential to preserve data integrity. As discussed in Chapter 2, referential integrity is all the more important in the case of test data, as the absence of it can affect application functionality adversely (Table 6.3).

Often, fields are related to each other in some way. In a credit card application form, it is common to find separate fields for FIRST NAME, LAST NAME, and MIDDLE NAME. While processing, the application logic uses the UI fields concatenated to populate the FULL NAME field. As test data are prepared off-line, the luxury of automatic population of concatenated data not available. Therefore, this logic needs to be embedded into the masking logic. As Table 6.2 shows, it is important to maintain the relationship between such fields for data to be meaningful. This is a good application of the principle of consistent masking (4).

**TABLE 6.2**

Referential Integrity

| ID | Name | ID | Designation |
|---|---|---|---|
| 12345 | John | 12345 | Project Manager |
| 56789 | Harry | 56789 | Architect |
| 52131 | Hari | 52131 | Developer II |
| 85438 | Mary | 85438 | Program Mgr |
| 91281 | Srini | 91281 | Tester I |
| 11253 | Chan | 11253 | Consultant |

**TABLE 6.3**

Consistency

| ID | First Name | .... | .... | Full Name |
|----|-----------|------|------|-----------|
| 12345 | John | .... | .... | John Bailey |
| 56789 | Harry | .... | .... | Harry Wagner |
| 52131 | Hari | .... | .... | Hari Krishna |
| 85438 | Mary | .... | .... | Mary Allen |
| 91281 | Srini | .... | .... | Srini Iyengar |
| 11253 | Chan | .... | .... | Chan Nair |

Another example of consistency is shown in Table 6.4.

A field such as FIRST NAME also indicates gender. It is important to ensure that gender consistency is maintained when FIRST NAME fields are being masked. In the case tokenization is used, then the token will not be a valid name and hence does not matter. If substitution is used, it is important to substitute a name from the correct gender's name set.

### 6.5.1.2 What Do Tools Offer?

The industry has been able to conquer the problem of masking EI. There are several tools today that offer masking as a basic feature. Apart from a wide repertoire of masking techniques, the tools also consider referential integrity and consistency. Some of the techniques used in the industry are given in Table 6.5.

### 6.5.1.3 How Do Masking Techniques Affect Testing?

EI play a relatively smaller role when it comes to application functionality. It is generally observed that EI are either just displayed, edited, or deleted. Therefore, masking of EI appears to be quite straightforward. In this section, we examine the impact masking techniques have on the utility of data with examples.

Let us now look at each of the techniques and analyze their effects on testing.

**TABLE 6.4**

Semantic Consistency

| ID | First Name | ID | First Name |
|----|-----------|----|-----------|
| 12345 | John | 12345 | Jack |
| 56789 | Harry | 56789 | Paul |
| 52131 | Hari | 52131 | Ralf |
| 85438 | Mary ———— | 85438 ————▶ | *George* |
| 91281 | Srini | 91281 | Jerry |
| 11253 | Chan | 11253 | Vijay |

**TABLE 6.5**

Masking Techniques

| Masking Technique | Brief Explanation |
|---|---|
| Substitution | Prepopulated sets of data are created, for example, first name, last name, and middle name, which are directly substituted in place of original data. Substitution is difficult to implement when consistency is a requirement due to the randomness involved in picking the replacement. |
| Scrambling | Original data are replaced with a set of characters that do not have any relation with the original data. Some implementations maintain the length of the original data for syntactic reasons. |
| Shuffling | Name fields are shuffled within the column resulting in the reassignment of the same name set to different row IDs. |
| Suppression | The entire field is replaced with XXX or is just emptied. |
| Credit card, social security number, Aadhaar card number | Format is preserved while replacing original digits and characters with authentic-looking data. |
| E-mail address | Based on standards being followed, either e-mail addresses are generated for entire record set uniquely or a common e-mail address is assigned to each row. |
| Mobile phone numbers | Mobile numbers are very personal as opposed to landline numbers, which may correspond to offices, hence they are EI. Customized implementations can choose to keep certain parts of the original number while randomizing the rest. |
| Tokenization | One-way or two-way tokenization can be used to mask numerical data. |

### 6.5.1.3.1 Random

Credit card number (CCN) masking is not complex. A random 11-digit number replaces the original set of digits between the 5th and 15th digit, both included. A random value ensures sufficient privacy as nobody can trace it back to the original. The first four digits along with the last one keep the utility unharmed (Table 6.6).

Now, if the CCN is the primary key of the table, then the masked value must also be propagated to the child tables where CCN is a foreign key. Such features are available in many tools. For example, some tools have a function that makes the masked value flow to dependent columns of child tables. These tools capture the interdependencies in the data, which, in case of packaged applications, it does using templates.

### 6.5.1.3.2 Scrambling

Social security number (SSN) is a 9-digit number. When these digits are scrambled, the same digits are used with positions changed to come up with a new series of digits forming a new number. There can be checks to ensure that 0 does not appear in the first position. Most tools offer a

**TABLE 6.6**

Effects of EI Masking on Testing

| Field | Original | Technique | Masked |
|---|---|---|---|
| (a) Random | | | |
|    Credit card | 4417 2303 0093 2938 | Random | 4417 3489 9823 9838 |
| (b) Scrambling | | | |
|    SSN | 348-40-9482 | Scrambling | 824-38-0984 |
| (c) Substitution | | | |
|    First name | John | Substitution | EDGAR |
| (d) Tokenization | | | |
|    Last name | Bond | Tokenization | ERQG |
| (e) Selective replace | | | |
|    Phone number | 937-239-0932 | Selective Replace | 937-874-9384 |
| (f) Flat value | | | |
|    E-mail address | Alex.smith@abc.com | Flat value | someone@example.com |

special algorithm exclusively for SSN, which may use scrambling as the underlying algorithm.

Scrambling an $n$ digit number can be done in $(n - 1)!$ ways assuming that the same digit is not selected for replacement. If there are 9 unique digits in an SSN, it can therefore be scrambled in 8! ways. This makes scrambling a good technique to mask test data. From a utility perspective, SSN has three parts [13]:

1. The first three digits are the area number
2. The next two digits are the group number
3. The final four digits are the serial number

However, unless used by government agencies for investigations, the SSN data are never analyzed in most software applications and are most commonly used as an identifying field. Thus, scrambling or even randomizing them causes no loss of utility.

### 6.5.1.3.3 Substitution

Name fields are best substituted as the replacement is done randomly. Privacy protection is good when random substitution is applied as there is no relation between the original and the replaced data.

But, as discussed earlier, if there are other dependent fields that have to be consistent with the parent, then a map needs to be maintained between the original and the masked data. This becomes a two-way tokenization, where now the token vault needs additional security measures.

*6.5.1.3.4  Tokenization*

A good alternative to substitution is one-way tokenization. One-way tokenization implements a hashing technique like SHA-256, which will replace each character in the name with another derived one. One-way tokenization is therefore deterministic. A given input value will always result in the same output, no matter where it appears.

Although one-way tokenization solves the consistency problem, one needs to ensure that the tokenization algorithm is sufficiently strong.

*6.5.1.3.5  Selective Replace*

As shown in Chapter 4, identity attacks like linkage attacks and inference attacks are possible if the adversary has sufficient background knowledge of the record owner. Thus, leaving the area code or the entire phone number as is can invite identity attacks. Here, selective replacement is useful. In case a call routing module is being tested, the area code consisting of the first three digits of the phone number is sufficient to validate the module's functioning. Thus, the last seven digits can be suitably randomized to ensure privacy.

Of course, the boundary between preserving privacy and utility is based on the application context and can be determined based on the test cases at hand.

*6.5.1.3.6  Flat Value*

A flat value for e-mail addresses is acceptable in most testing scenarios. Even if an e-mail functionality is expected as part of the workflow, a valid e-mail ID will ensure that the test predicate is adequately tested.

A flat value masks the identity of the record owner, thus giving complete privacy.

## 6.5.2  Protecting Quasi-Identifiers

While protecting EI is absolutely essential, the importance of safeguarding QI cannot be overlooked. As mentioned in Chapter 4, most threat models focus on using QI as a handle along with other supplementary information like background knowledge or external data sources. In test data, QI play a vital role in business logic, driving the transactional data. A good example is demographics of individuals, where locations contribute to establishing parameters that either allow or disallow grant of loans.

### 6.5.2.1  Essentials of Protecting QI

While protecting QI is critical, it is also important to preserve the utility of the test data. Test data utility lies in the spread of values in the QI and their respective SD columns. In Chapter 2, we stated that the analytic utility and correlation of QI with SD attributes are two important aspects considered while anonymizing QI. The case of test data QI, however, is a little more nuanced.

In test data QI, each data value is unique and offers a different flow that the program could take in its execution. Consider Figure 6.6.

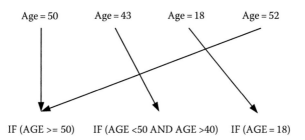

**FIGURE 6.6**
Impact of anonymizing QI.

If AGE or DATE of BIRTH is a field being used to determine what the premium is going to be for an individual, then the statements shown in Figure 6.11 are part of the code generally. These statements handle multiple conditions that combine age with other general health-related conditions to calculate the applicable premium. A slight change in AGE while anonymizing can throw the calculation out of gear. For example, some commercial tools offer a blurring method to offset the original value of an attribute within a specified range. By giving a small enough blur, the first two IF conditions may still be satisfied. But the third IF condition will never be visited by the program as the original value is what the program was looking for. In fact, if there were a condition like IF (AGE > 18 AND AGE < 21), the original value might satisfy this condition. Another possibility: consider the statement IF (AGE < 18). It could be that after blurring, a data point with value of AGE as 17 might get a blurred value of 18, thus satisfying the wrong condition.

Such interchanges of execution paths may seem trivial as we are looking at just one attribute. However, with tens of QI present in test data, such deviations can completely change the normal course of program execution and omit certain important flows that need thorough testing. This scenario is depicted in Figure 6.7.

From this discussion, it follows that perturbative techniques are not suitable for anonymizing test data QI. Moreover, individual values have high significance when it comes to anonymizing QI in test data as opposed to other areas like privacy preserving data mining, where the distribution as a whole is important and not its constituent data points.

### 6.5.2.2 Tool Offerings to Anonymize QI

The classification of data into EI, QI, and SD is missing in most tools. Consequently, the features available to anonymize QI too are either not suitable or do not maintain utility. Hence, the techniques offered by these tools overlap with those discussed in Section 6.5.1 on protecting EI. Table 6.7 lists and describes other techniques that are useful for protecting QI.

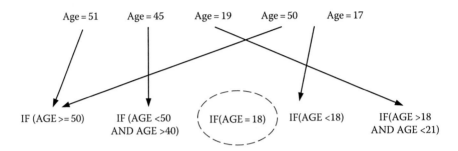

**FIGURE 6.7**
Anonymizing QI—changes in program flow.

**TABLE 6.7**

QI Anonymization Techniques

| Technique | Brief Explanation |
|---|---|
| Blurring | Fields like date are blurred. Offset values within an interval replace the original value. Test coverage is affected when code is looking for exact intervals or values. If offsets move the data from one interval to another, then test coverage changes. |
| Suppression | Data are annulled or replaced with "XXX." The obvious result is that the test coverage is severely depleted. |
| Randomization | A random value is generated to replace the original value. Based on the data format and range of original data, a number is randomly picked. |
| Generalization | The QI values are generalized to give a broader view rather than a specific view. For example, age 33 is replaced with a range 30–40 provided the data source accepts this value. |
| Group anonymization | There are techniques that work on a group of QI and not individually. This preserves relationships that exist among them and also preserves privacy effectively. |

### 6.5.2.3 How Does QI Anonymization Affect Test Coverage?

The techniques that we have discussed for the anonymization of QI in Chapter 2 and also in the previous section emphasize the importance of QI in utility. Testing relies on QI too much to compromise its value using naïve techniques of masking. Masking techniques like scrambling, substitution, flat value assignation, and so on perturb the QI to a very large extent. Table 6.12 shows the impact of blurring. Imagine the derogatory effect of using a flat value or scrambling here. The test coverage could drop by almost 50%. Yet, such are the methods often used by organizations to anonymize QI because the tools that offer them do not provide any guidance pertaining to their usage.

It is important to note that although the analytical utility of data is important while anonymizing data, in case of PPTDM, the individual values of QI hold more relevance than their overall distribution.

In Table 6.8, a piece of code looking for zip code 45435 will get invoked only with this value. Also, in case of PPTDM, the number of occurrences of 45435 is not as important as its occurrence. If this value is generalized to 45400, then we have a problem.

High dimensionality is also a major issue in anonymizing relational data [13,14]. A personal loan application contains a high percentage of QI fields that play a crucial role in the decision of approval or rejection of the loan. Let us examine a few statements that might appear in the code of a system processing a loan application. With each technique in Table 6.6, we will look at the impact on test coverage of a code snippet shown in Figure 6.8.

### 6.5.2.3.1 Blurring

Assuming that AGE is a derived attribute from date of birth and that DATE OF BIRTH is used in many other places, a possible technique to anonymize this QI would be blurring. Now, as blurring moves the original DATE OF BIRTH on either side of the original value, C1 will be satisfied for applicants

**TABLE 6.8**

Importance of Individual Values over Distribution

| Gender | City | Zip |
|---|---|---|
| M | Dayton | 45435 |
| F | Jersey City | 07302 |
| F | Owings Mills | 21117 |

```
If (AGE >60)                                          (C1)
        Deny the loan
If (EMPLOYED = FALSE)                                 (C2)
        Deny the loan
If (CREDIT SCORE >500) {                              (C3)
        If (ZIP in (a specified set))                 (C4)
                An additional set of conditions apply
        If (INCOME >=10* Annual Income)               (C5)
                A set of validations
        ...
        ...
}
If (CREDIT SCORE < 500)                               (C6)
        A different loop starts
```

**FIGURE 6.8**
Test code snippet.

whose original age was below 60. The opposite may happen too: some people with ages above 60 may still be eligible for the loan.

Although such cases may eventually even out, the fact still remains that the nuances present in the application of a 59-year-old were important for testing, which are now lost to anonymization.

### 6.5.2.3.2 Suppression

A suppressed value satisfies no conditions in the code. Therefore, any condition referring to the suppressed attribute will fail. For example, if the EMPLOYMENT STATUS of the applicant is suppressed, C2 will never be checked. Suppression, however, is used for QI that are not too important and often in conjunction with k-anonymization.

### 6.5.2.3.3 Randomization

A random or pseudorandom value when generated for a column of data will generate values with a Gaussian distribution. This value does not have the contours expected from the original attribute data. For example, a DATE OF BIRTH field with the original value of year as 1952 could get 2001 as the resultant value. This can definitely disrupt the way an application for loan gets processed.

Another flavor of randomization is additive random noise. Here, a finite noise is added to the original value to offset it. For example, if the DATE OF BIRTH is April 1, 1957, an offset of 45 days could make it either May 15, 1957, or February 14, 1957, based on whether the noise is appended or deducted.

In either case, when testing a functionality like C1 in Figure 6.11, randomizing QI data alters the program behavior. Altering these data will result in new flows or errant flows as opposed to those witnessed with original data.

### 6.5.2.3.4 Generalization

Chapter 2 shows us two ways to generalize: domain generalization and value generalization. Both these techniques lead to values that are different from those considered valid in the original data. Such an approach is not helpful in test data. Software systems, when processing data, look for specific data. For example, EDUCATION might be looking for one of 4 values as shown in Figure 6.9.

Consider the example in Figure 6.9, where the four original values of education are replaced with POST GRADUATION, GRADUATION, HIGH SCHOOL, and DOCTORATE, respectively. When the UI code processes this and passes it to the back end, a code table is referred to where the values are replaced with a unique code, possibly signifying education level. If we generalize the specific degrees to these education level synonyms, then the code will not process these inputs. Alternatively, if we create a domain generalization hierarchy, where a value like ANY_DEGREE replaces the array of values, again we lose test coverage as the code is not looking for this value at all.

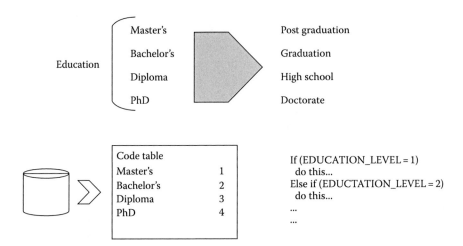

**FIGURE 6.9**
Generalization and test coverage.

### 6.5.2.3.5 Group Anonymization

In this book, k-anonymization is the only group anonymization technique we discuss that is applicable to QI. Making a set of k rows of QI indistinguishable from each other has its problems. As k-anonymization is used in conjunction with suppression, some test coverage is lost there. Besides, a high value of k means that many rows of important diverse data are being made homogeneous. This affects test coverage adversely. Conversely, a smaller value of k is not effective in protecting privacy. In Chapter 2, k was stated to be a function of various parameters in Equation 2.1

$$k = f (P_R, U_R, C_R, G_L, C) \qquad (2.1)$$

In case of PPTDM, $U_R$ is equivalent to test coverage $T_C$.

$$\text{Test coverage } T_C = f (T_P) \qquad (6.5)$$

where $T_P$ are test predicates that are defined by $T_{CS}$, the test cases. Each test case can be translated into LOC.

Thus, the choice of k needs to be determined with enough relevance given to test coverage.

Challenges in using k-anonymization have been already discussed in Chapter 2. For PPTDM, an important problem with implementing k-anonymization decides the value of k when testing with huge data sets. Another issue is that the implementation of the algorithm takes a lot of computation time.

### 6.5.3 Protecting Sensitive Data (SD)

Test data consist of reference, master, and transactional data. Almost all of SD fields are found in transactional data. Trade processing systems, loan applications, online retail websites, and so on rely on their systems to process transactions correctly. Thus, most testing of business applications is centered on transaction processing. This, brings us to the importance of SD. SD are the most important part of test data. Their elements define and reflect the current state of the system. Therefore, in the pretext of protecting privacy, it is incorrect to alter the SD, especially in the case of test data.

Outliers are often found in transactions. These could be in the form of high trade amounts, huge number of items as part of a transaction, or any other exorbitance. Outliers are interesting from a testing perspective. They give the program a chance to execute a flow far less visited than the rest. Privacy protection is also sensitive to outliers. A high trade amount with a generalized value of a geographical location can reveal that the trade has been made on behalf of the local millionaire.

With the intention of balancing privacy and utility, we use the principle of randomization (12), which adds noise to the data while maintaining the overall statistical validity of the SD. An example of this is explained in Chapter 2.

## 6.6 Quality of Test Data

Our discussion in this chapter has been on maintaining the balance between privacy and utility. After discussing the protection of privacy of the three classes of private data, we come to defining the quality of test data. What are the qualities of good test data? Can they be quantified? How can we maximize data quality? These are some questions that we try to answer in this section.

There are four fundamental considerations that define the suitability and efficacy of test data:

1. Lines of coverage
2. Query ability
3. Time for testing
4. Defect detection

In a previous work [15], two quality dimensions have been discussed as proximity to reality and degree of coverage. We agree that degree of coverage is an important measure of quality and we discuss it next. However, the proximity to reality is more of a prerequisite for having relevant test data than a measure.

### 6.6.1 Lines of Code Covered

Code coverage is a suitability measure. As was explained in Section 6.4, in PPTDM, LOC covered by test data is a definitive measure of the quality of data. In the context of PPTDM, data quality is not an absolute metric, but one relative to the test cases, as explained in Equation 6.6.

Let us consider the example of the test case "Modify Employee Record" given in Table 6.9.

Considering the test case outlined in the table, it can be assumed that each Transaction Name is serviced by a web page. Now, each web page will have a set of code at the UI level and at the processing layer, which could be a service. Functions or methods within the service process the task outlined in the test case. We will assume that each of the five steps has 50 LOC, which process this functionality.

Now let us look at the data required for this code to run on (Table 6.10).

**TABLE 6.9**

Modify Employee Record Test Case

| Step No. | Step Description | Expected Result | Other Results | Transaction Name |
|---|---|---|---|---|
| 1 | User logs into HR module | Successful login | Login error—invalid username/password | User_login |
| 2 | Enters employee record list | Display list of employees | Data security error due to insufficient privileges— stays on the same page | Employee_list |
| 3 | User selects employee record | Employee detail page is loaded | Insufficient privileges dialog box—stays on the same page | Employee_detail |
| 4 | Modify employee record | Page gets loaded with editable fields | Insufficient privileges dialog—stays on "Employee_detail" page | Modify_ employee |
| 5 | Save changes made to employee record | Page reloads with changes saved to "Employee _ detail" | Invalid values entered to fields—returns to "Modify_employee" page. | Modify_success |

**TABLE 6.10**

Tables and Columns Pertaining to Test Case

| Step No. | Table(s) | Column(s) |
|---|---|---|
| 1 | USER_TABLE | USERNAME, PASSWORD, ENTITLEMENTS |
| 2 | EMPLOYEE | NAME, EMP_BAND, etc. |
| 3, 4, 5 | EMP_DETAIL | FNAME, LNAME, SALARY FIELDS, EMPLOYMENT FIELDS, etc. |

Our test case example works only on reference data. Hence, you will only find EI and QI in these data. As the table suggests, for the code to pass this test case, three tables are required with the relevant columns carrying some valid information. Ideally, production data will have this information, and hence, the code coverage will be 250 lines. While producing the test data, it is to be ensured that all the three tables have the same kind of data available. This can be achieved by following the anonymization design principles given in Appendix A. A range of masking techniques can be used to protect the EI in these tables, while a combination of generalization and suppression can prevent linkage attacks on QI. In essence, a good anonymization design will ensure that the LOC covered are at least 250. We say at least 250 because the production data will cover only the expected results in Table 6.7. While testing, other results may need to be verified too. This means that data needed to invoke exception flows are required to be injected into the test data set. If this is achieved, more than 250 LOC can be covered, making it a highly suitable data set for testing.

In Equation 6.4, we showed how test coverage is used to calculate utility, where LOC was used as a calculated number. LOC coverage ($L_{CC}$) is therefore an absolute test data quality metric that compares the LOC covered by original data ($L_O$) to that covered by test data ($L_T$).

$$L_{CC} = 1 - \left[ \frac{L_O - L_T}{L_O} \right] \tag{6.6}$$

In the same section, we also pointed out to a situation in Equation 6.5. However, as discussed here, we know that there can be some data that when injected can enhance the value of $L_T$.

### 6.6.2 Query Ability

"Pull up all medical records, along with attendant details, that have been updated in the past six weeks and contain at least one update in patient condition from serious to critical"—This could be a filtering query fired by a head matron at the casualty ward in a hospital. When such a system is being designed, all kinds of possible filtering will be allowed to help medical practitioners get relevant data on the performance of their medicines on patients and the patients' respective responses.

Testing such an application requires precision, requiring test cases to be written to uncover all kinds of possible querying on the data. Such complex querying is also commonly used in online shopping websites, where a rich catalog of products is available arranged in various hierarchies of classification. The test cases would require data that have a wide breadth of possibilities and depth to service mass data queries, thus making the constitution of such a test data set very subjective to the software system.

Anonymization will alter a lot of QI data, making some of them indistinguishable to each other if k-anonymization is used. This means that some queries may yield a slightly different result than what the original data would have. Nevertheless, that is the price paid to preserve privacy.

Returning to the data quality discussion, query ability is a suitability measure just like lines of code coverage. Therefore, we measure query ability of test data in conjunction with that offered by the original data. This time, Equation 6.4 changes to the following form:

$Q_O \rightarrow$ Number of queries that can be run on original data
$Q_T \rightarrow$ Number of queries that can be run on test data
$Q_A \rightarrow$ Query ability of the test data

$$Q_A = 1 - \left[ \frac{Q_O - Q_T}{Q_O} \right] \tag{6.7}$$

Preparing test data to cater to all kinds of queries is a complex task. Above all, this problem is one of sampling, which is called subset creation in a test data context. Querying a particular data set from multiple perspectives is a problem often encountered in PPDM and PPTDM. As the number of queries one is looking to fire is limited and known, unlike LOC coverage, $Q_A$ will not exceed 1.

### 6.6.3 Time for Testing

Cost of quality is the cost of not executing any of the testing activities right the first time, that is, incorrect execution of a test case resulting in rework to re-execute the same test case. Incorrect execution of a test case can be due to lack of the correct test data. Until now, we have discussed two data quality measures that can be classified as suitability measures. Suitability measures act as a guideline to answering the question "What should go into the test data set?" In this section, we look at ancillary feature of test data to impact the test efficacy.

We define "time for testing" as the total time required by testers to uncover the target number of defects from a data set. Rather than dwell on testing best practices, we highlight the importance of provisioning suitable test data to abolish the curse of defect leakages and repeated test cycles.

### 6.6.3.1 Test Completion Criteria

When is testing considered complete? The chapter on higher-order testing in Myers [1] presents a good discussion on how to establish criteria for the end of testing, finally settling down to establishing a target number of defects. When defect detection slows down, it is attributed either to inadequate test cases or lack of errors to detect [1]. However, the possibility of inadequate data to uncover a defect for an excellent test case is not discussed.

### 6.6.3.2 Time Factor

While having a target number of defects to be uncovered is a good approach, the duration required to uncover them is important too. Consider the example shown in Figure 6.10.

A team takes 8 weeks to discover 323 defects at the rates shown in Figure 6.10. The curve seen here is quite normal. Assuming that all parameters of testing, for example, resources employed, their collective and individual efficiencies, test case design and test planning, etc., are kept constant, a differentiator is the test data.

$D_T \rightarrow$ Time or duration for testing
$T \rightarrow$ Testing parameters
$Q_{TD} \rightarrow$ Quality of test data

$$D_T = f\,(T, Q_{TD}) \tag{6.8}$$

If T has been optimized and is constant, then the quality of test data can bring down the time for testing. Imagine uncovering the same 323 defects in Figure 6.10 in 4 weeks. As testers need not run each test script manually, finding more defects in less time does not have any impact on the work load on each tester.

But how do we improve test data quality? Most test data challenges relate to the need for privacy. Bad data protection designs yield inferior data quality, which derails test efficacy. Good anonymization design can rescue the data from such perils by following the principles discussed in Appendix A. The result will be a reduced $D_T$ that has a ripple effect across fixing of defects, subsequent phases of testing, and eventual release to production. In effect, a good anonymization design preserves good quality of test data and speeds up time to market for any given software system.

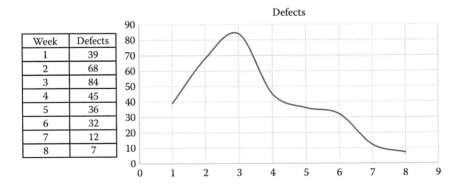

| Week | Defects |
|------|---------|
| 1 | 39 |
| 2 | 68 |
| 3 | 84 |
| 4 | 45 |
| 5 | 36 |
| 6 | 32 |
| 7 | 12 |
| 8 | 7 |

**FIGURE 6.10**
Defects over time.

### 6.6.4 Defect Detection

Another way to assess test completion is the number of defects detected over a fixed period of time. The test completion criterion criticized in Myers [1] is where a scheduled time for testing is decided after which the phases are considered ended. Though ridiculous sounding, it is used widely in the industry. During project planning, estimation models size the software application and devote a time period for testing based on prior experience in similar executions. For software vendors, it is not uncommon to feel the pressure to carry out thorough testing in a time-boxed setting. Test data quality is never more important than when defect detection rates are required to be high throughout the time window allotted to testing.

$$D_D \, \alpha \, Q_{TD} \qquad (6.9)$$

Satisfying multicondition coverage and boundary-value impact analyses help detect erroneous behavior in alternate flows of the software system. Therefore, the defect detection rate is proportional to the quality of test data.

## 6.7 Anonymization Design for PPTDM

Test data design was briefly discussed in Section 6.3. Although that discussion covered the essential ingredients for test data, one of them being the use of original data, privacy regulations impose restrictions on what can be borrowed from original data and what cannot. Therefore, most inadequacies encountered in test data are because no thought is given to fill the holes that privacy protection leaves in the test data. Inadequacies affect all the measures of test data quality discussed in the previous section. A good anonymization design takes into account privacy restrictions and utility needs to produce high-quality test data.

While the principles in Appendix A give guidelines to effective anonymization design, for PPTDM, one needs to pay special attention to the following contributing factors.

For PPTDM, the options available for anonymization are shown in Tables 6.11 and 6.12.

EI can be masked using a multitude of techniques that are available today. Consistency is needed in financial applications to maintain synchronized account numbers or loan numbers. One-way tokenization is well suited to this requirement. Similar nuances in each domain drive the decision to pick an appropriate masking algorithm that sufficiently anonymizes the EI data.

**TABLE 6.11**

Contributors to Anonymization Design of Test Data

| SNO | Contributing Factor | Explanation |
|-----|---------------------|-------------|
| 1 | Domain and classification | The same attribute may have quite different meanings when domain changes. For example, a CREDIT CARD field in an online retail website's database will be a transactional field classified as SD. However, the credit card issuing company would have the same classified as EI. If an attribute $A$ can be categorized in $n$ ways and that each of these can be then anonymized using $m$ algorithms, then the anonymized data $A'$ can be obtained in $m*n$ ways. |
| 2 | Adversary profile and location | As discussed in Table 4.3, the location and profile of adversaries are important considerations while anonymizing test data. |
| 3 | Data relationships | In PPTDM, testing may involve many applications sharing data. Relationships within and across data sources demand that the anonymization is robust and consistent. |

**TABLE 6.12**

Anonymization of Test Data

| Explicit Identifiers (EI) | Quasi-Identifiers (QI) | Sensitive Data (SD) |
|---------------------------|------------------------|---------------------|
| Substitution | Generalization | Additive random noise |
| Tokenization (One-way) | Shuffling | $l$-Diversity |
| Tokenization (Two-way) | k-Anonymization | t-Closeness |
| National identifier generator | Randomization | Outlier handling |
| Credit card generator | Blurring | |
| Mobile number | Data ranging | |
| E-mail address generator | Suppression | |
| Scrambling | | |
| Suppression | | |
| Flat value | | |

QI are important for test data utility and hence need to be anonymized using a technique such as k-anonymization, which is nonperturbative. With a minimal loss in utility and statistical properties, k-anonymization is well suited for creating test data. Complications do exist with its implementation for large data sets, but k-anonymization is by far the best suited for test data.

For SD, t-closeness is a good measure to use in the context of PPTDM. As discussed in Chapter 2, a good domain generalization hierarchy, along with a suitable value of t, will ensure that the balance between privacy and utility is maintained.

## 6.8 Insufficiencies of Anonymized Test Data

Anonymization of test data is a good approach to remain compliant with privacy regulation. However, certain circumstances do exist where anonymization is evidenced to be inadequate. In this section, we will discuss five such situations.

### 6.8.1 Negative Testing

Figure 6.11 presents a picture outlining what data are required for each phase of testing. System testing requires data satisfying both positive and negative input data to test the expected and alternate results, respectively. Original data, after anonymization, present us with just the "happy conditions" (Figure 6.11).

Alternate flows require wrong inputs, exception producing data, outliers, boundary values, and other forms of invalid attribute values. Due to the absence of such attributes, alternate flows of code do not get tested with anonymized test data.

### 6.8.2 Sensitive Domains

Complex medical records and national security documents are examples of highly sensitive domains where anonymized data will not be sufficient to advocate data sharing. Such domains are highly confidential and rely on data security mechanisms rather than anonymization to protect their data. Access privileges combined with roles govern access to this information.

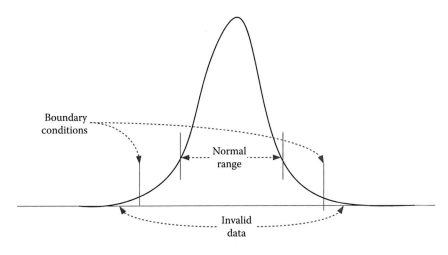

**FIGURE 6.11**
Data range.

### 6.8.3 Nonfunctional Testing

Nonfunctional requirements (NFRs) require the software system to be tested or benchmarked for performance parameters, such as response times or throughput rates on certain workload and configuration conditions. In order to create this workload, production data (transactional data) may need to be scaled manifolds. In other NFRs, security requirements need to uncover failure conditions in access rights and roles. The availability of the activity log or the lack of it affects security testing. Reliability testing of systems using mean time between failures (MTBF) or recovery testing using mean time to recovery (MTTR) require data that are not found in production systems. Thus, most nonfunctional testing phases cannot rely on anonymized test data for their data provisioning.

### 6.8.4 Regression Testing

Figure 6.1 shows the bathtub curve. The random failure phase in this curve is when the software system undergoes regression testing. These tests are conducted to test minor functional changes made to the software system periodically. During regression testing, multiple data refresh need to be done. As anonymization depends on production data, this process can turn out to be slow and also involve permissions for access to production data.

### 6.8.5 Trust Deficit

Some organizations choose not to share data via anonymization. They prefer to have data generated ground-up rather than share their original data for purposes like testing.

Each of the five situations discussed in this section can be resolved using data manufacturing or synthetic data generation (SDG). Synthetic data can aid testing of many use cases due to the absence of its relationship with original data. We discuss SDG in detail in Chapter 7 with respect to PPTDM and other areas of privacy preservation.

## 6.9 Summary

Privacy preserving test data manufacturing is a subject relevant to the way business is conducted today. We discussed how global business share their data across geographies for testing purposes and are compelled to anonymize data for this cause. But anonymized data also pose questions on utility, which, in testing terms, are measured using test coverage. Test coverage is a definitive unit to measure the efficacy of testing and, therefore, test data too are bound by it.

EI in test data are to be masked. Masking is acceptable due to two facts: first, they are rarely part of the business logic being tested and, second, perturbation of EI does not affect test coverage in any way. QI are very useful for testing and need to be handled carefully. Nonperturbative techniques are useful to preserve individual data points important for program behavior than overall preservation of the distribution. Methods pertaining to generalization need to be used judiciously so that test coverage is unaltered. Sensitive data contain the truth in the data that reflect the current state of the software system. Changes to SD should be kept to a minimum and should take effect only in cases where the field values are outliers or reveal identities by themselves.

Quality of test data is measured using considerations of suitability and efficacy. LOC coverage and the querying ability of test data are direct measures of anonymized test data that when compared with original data give conclusive evidence of test data quality. Time for testing is the amount of time required to discover a predefined number of defects. Defect detection tracking is the number of defects uncovered in a time-boxed testing exercise. Each of these measures affects testing in a significant way.

With all considerations, the anonymization of original data to produce test data still does not independently resolve regulatory or utility issues. A degree of dependence exists on externally manufactured data or synthetic data. These data possess the unique quality of being independent of the original data and thus allay fears of re-identification and privacy attacks.

# References

1. G.J. Myers, *The Art of Software Testing*, 3rd edition, October 2011, Wiley Publications.
2. Information Commissioner Office, Mission and vision as published at https://ico.org.uk/about-the-ico/our-information/mission-and-vision/ as update on July 18, 2015. Accessed April 19, 2016.
3. K. Taneja, M. Grechanik, R. Ghani, and T. Xie, Testing software in age of data privacy—A balancing act, in *ESEC/FSE'11*, Szeged, Hungary, September 5–9, 2011.
4. C.C. Aggarwal and P.S. Yu, A condensation approach to privacy preserving data mining, in *Proceedings of EDBT*, Heraklion, Crete, Greece, 2004, pp. 183–199.
5. K. Chen and L. Liu, Privacy preserving data classification with rotation perturbation, in *Proceedings of the International Conference on Data Mining*, New Orleans, LA, 2005, pp. 589–592.
6. R. Agrawal and R. Srikant, Privacy-preserving data mining, in *Proceedings of SIGMOD*, Dallas, TX, 2000, pp. 439–450.
7. J. Metsa, M. Katara, and T. Mikkonen, Testing non-functional requirements with aspects: An Industrial Case Study, in *Proceedings of QSIC*, Portland, OR, 2007.
8. A. Budi, D. Lo, L. Jiang, and L. Lucia, kb-anonymity: A model for anonymized behavior-preserving test and debugging data, in *PLDI*, San Jose, CA, 2011.

9. L. Lucia, D. Lo, L. Jiang and A. Budi, kbe-Anonymity: Test data anonymization for evolving programs, in *ASE'12*, Essen, Germany, September 3–7, 2012.
10. G.-A. Klutke, P.C. Kiessler, and M.A. Wortman, A critical look at the bathtub curve, *IEEE Transactions on Reliability*, 52(1), March 2003.
11. J. Feiman and B. Lowans, Magic quadrant for data masking technology, December 22, 2015, available at https://www.informatica.com/in/magic-quad-rant-data-masking.html. Accessed April 19, 2016.
12. M. Kessis, Y. Ledru, and G. Vandome, Experiences in coverage testing of a Java middleware, in *Proceedings SEM 2005*, ACM, Lisbon, Portugal, 2005, pp. 39–45.
13. C.C. Aggarwal, Privacy and the dimensionality curse, Springer, 2008, pp. 433–460.
14. C.C. Aggarwal and P.S. Yu (ed.), *Privacy Preserving Data Mining: Models and Algorithms*, Springer, New York, 2008.
15. J. Held, Towards measuring test data quality, in *Proceedings of the 2012 EDBT/ICDT Workshops*, Berlin, Germany, March 26–30, 2012.

# 7

## Synthetic Data Generation

### 7.1 Introduction

To this point, we have discussed masking and anonymization as the answer to privacy preservation in data mining and test data management, which were covered in Chapters 5 and 6, respectively. However, there are areas where anonymization is considered not sufficient enough to protect sensitive data (SD) and prevent threats. This is especially true in sensitive domains such as healthcare, banking, and hedge funds. The alternative we discuss in this chapter is synthetic data generation.

Scientific researchers in fields such as physics and chemistry have used artificial data to supplement the unavailability of experimental data. It is observed that although easy to create, artificial data can lead to results that are either significantly different or opposite in certain cases. Why does this happen? Why do artificially-created data not sit well with experiments? Maybe, the term *artificial* has something to do with it.

In this chapter, we will discuss the uses of synthetic data. Then, we will go into the various approaches available for explicit identifiers (EIs), quasi-identifiers (QIs), and sensitive data (SD). We will also discuss how safe it is to use synthetic data instead of anonymized data for analysis.

### 7.2 Related Work

Authenticity and natural bias are characteristics of data that there can be no substitute for. Today, researchers also focus on this aspect in a big way. Statistical disclosure control (SDC) is one such area. In [1], a great deal of emphasis is given on the use of synthetic data sets for SDC. Dreschler [1] shows that although there is an infusion of synthetic data, it is essential to maintain the statistical relevance of data while performing SDC on survey data.

Another important aspect discussed in literature is the importance of missing data. Multiple imputations [2] were introduced and later elaborated [3,4] by Rubin to show SDC's effectiveness in substituting missing data.

Even company information is sensitive in nature for data custodians when they share it with researchers. In [6], the authors discuss synthetic data methods for business data, which are often developed to facilitate the analysis, at the microeconomic level, of a range of policy issues based around business growth and performance. Anonymization of trajectories is explored in Nergiz et al. [7], where the authors use k-anonymization to demonstrate a generalized solution. They, then use randomization-based reconstruction to release a comparable trajectory to the original. This randomly generated trajectory is an example of synthetic data generated as anonymized ones may still have privacy leaks. Information discovery and analysis systems (IDAS) process large amounts of data into meaningful information. One particular research designed and developed a tool called IDAS data and scenario generator (IDSG) to facilitate the creation, testing, and training of IDAS [8].

The necessity of synthetic data arises due to high volume, high sensitivity of data, no historical data availability, and bridging incomplete data. There are tools [5] used today to generate synthetic data. They use data profiling techniques to identify what data are relevant to each test case. Some are also known to give a visual representation of the current data state and expected data for testing.

However, synthetic data generation is not limited to just relational data. There are other forms of data such as graph data, time series data, spatial-temporal data, and longitudinal data, which may require synthetic data for reconstruction, data bridging, or testing.

This chapter gives a brief overview of synthetic data generation as a good alternative to anonymization. The following section presents a definition and some uses of synthetic data. The discussion then moves on to synthetic data generation best practices with respect to EI, QI, and SD. Finally, we dwell on the question, "How safe is it to use synthetic data?" We limit our discussion to relational data sources in this chapter, but similar techniques exist to handle time series, graph, and other forms of data.

## 7.3  Synthetic Data and Their Use

Any data that are generated ground-up qualify as synthetic data. Such data are not a result of any function F that is used to transform a data set D. On the other hand, it does not mean that synthetic data do not have any relation to original data. At best, synthetic data can be based on the meta-data and general characteristics of original data. Information pertaining to row-wise individual column values is not available. In [10], data generation using deterministic rules, nondeterministic rule sets, and statistics is discussed. When these rules are well documented and the statistics of data are recorded, the synthetic data generated are of good quality and useful for their intended purpose.

Today, synthetic data are used in a wide range of applications. The foremost reason for using it is privacy preservation. SDC is an area where for privacy as well as utility reasons synthetic data are used. While [1] discusses the use of synthetic data sets for SDC, the focus is on generating missing data or replacements for units in the population that are not selected in the sample. Multiple imputations are used in such cases. Our focus here is on data that are prepared independent of the original data, albeit their characteristics are used as inputs.

The threat stream generator (TSG) project [11] claims its ability to create realistic test data sets that can be used by advanced commercial tool developers. Online retailers rely heavily on data that help them build recommender engines. Such systems require huge training data that strengthen certain patterns in order to churn out recommendations. Synthetic data are used to test such recommender engines. A good use case in testing web-based systems is discussed in [9]. Session-based systems require a series of inputs to see through a use case. Automated testing requires every piece of such a sequence, which when captured as dependencies can be used as an input to generate a synthetic workload.

In Chapter 5, we discussed anonymization techniques used for privacy preserving data mining. Although the SD in these techniques are not transformed, preserving the utility of QIs while anonymizing them is challenging. There is also a lot of legislation and scrutiny involved in protecting against linkage attacks. This makes anonymization time-consuming and expensive. Meanwhile, for a researcher or an analyst, it is the overall profile of a record owner that is used for deductions or inferences. Therefore, it is ideal if such data can be synthetically produced rather than going through the meticulous process of anonymization.

Chapter 6 discusses the shortcomings of anonymization in test data. Negative testing is an area that synthetic data can assist with. Referring to Figure 6.11, invalid data need to be generated synthetically as they do not exist in the original data. In this case, the reference is a normal range of data and boundary conditions. Anything outside of this can be generated to satisfy error and exception flows. Performance tests require higher workload compared to production data, which requires scaling of data. But such data are useful and reflect original system behavior only if workload is representative of the original data set. The representation of a synthetic workload is significantly influenced by the attributes in the workload model and the characterizations used for them [12].

Training data can also be generated using synthetic data generation. A data set used by a model for learning is called training data or training set.

After the model is built by running the learning algorithm, it is evaluated using a test set for unseen data. Thus, the difference between training data and test data is error scenarios. Synthetic data are useful for generating both training data and test data for model verification.

If an organization is skeptical about anonymization, synthetic data are very useful as it assures both the organization and its customers of good data protection.

## 7.4  Privacy and Utility in Synthetic Data

The first step in creation of synthetic data is to clearly classify the metadata. The principle of classification (1) is applicable in data.

After classification, there are a few steps that need to be followed to build a model for synthetic data generation. The model consists of rules that are created using

- Metadata information
- Referential integrity constraints
- Dependent and independent variables
- Correlated fields data
- Domain context
- Application scenarios

Synthetic data are generated according to rules. The model represents the application context in the form of instructions that help to produce useful data.

### 7.4.1  Explicit Identifiers

Creating EIs is the least complicated as very little is analyzed or tested using them. However, this does not reduce the importance of their privacy preservation.

#### 7.4.1.1  Privacy

EIs contain fields such as NAME, which are very sensitive. Substitution is one of the best techniques to replace original names with dummy ones. These data could be made relevant to a certain extent by indicating geographical or demographic characteristics to it. In the case of ID fields, privacy is rarely an issue. An ID is almost meaningless when all the surrounding data have been anonymized. Hence, a number like 12345, which is John's ID, in Table 7.1 does not have any meaning outside this table. Nevertheless, companies using only synthetic data need to give some consideration to the syntax and semantics of ID fields. Needless to say, the propagation of synthetic IDs to their respective child tables is also essential.

### 7.4.1.2 Utility

EIs are relatively unimportant, regardless of the purpose data are used for. In data mining, specific names, social security numbers (SSNs), and phone numbers are not important. It is the collective profile of record owners that are important, which cannot be obtained from EIs.

Therefore, privacy is more important to preserve in the case of EIs than utility.

### 7.4.1.3 Generation Algorithms

Synthetic data generation techniques are very specific to the field type and format. EIs could be free text fields such as names or specifically formatted ones such as SSNs. Techniques that are applicable are shown in Table 7.2.

## 7.4.2 Quasi-Identifiers

While generating EIs requires only conforming to the syntax of the field, QIs require semantics to be preserved as well. Unlike anonymization, there are no original data to work with. Hence, it is important to collect metadata to understand the syntax and statistical distribution of the original data, that is, boundary values, mean, and variances of each numerical attribute. Categorical attributes require a higher level of analysis, as their meaning or spread of values may be important.

**TABLE 7.1**

A Sample Salary Data Table

| EI | | QI | | | | SD | | | |
|---|---|---|---|---|---|---|---|---|---|
| ID | Name | Gender | Age | Address | ZIP | Basic | HRA | Med | All |
| 12345 | John | M | 25 | 1, 4th St. | 560001 | 10,000 | 5,000 | 1,000 | 6,000 |
| 56789 | Harry | M | 36 | 358, A dr. | 560068 | 20,000 | 10,000 | 1,000 | 12,000 |
| 52131 | Hari | M | 21 | 3, Stone Ct | 560055 | 12,000 | 6,000 | 1,000 | 7,200 |
| 85438 | Mary | F | 28 | 51, Elm st. | 560003 | 16,000 | 8,000 | 1,000 | 9,600 |
| 91281 | Srini | M | 40 | 9, Ode Rd | 560001 | 14,000 | 7,000 | 1,000 | 8,400 |
| 11253 | Chan | M | 35 | 3, 9th Ave | 560051 | 8,000 | 4,000 | 1,000 | 4,800 |

**TABLE 7.2**

SDG Algorithms

| SDG Technique | Brief Explanation |
|---|---|
| Substitution | Prepopulated sets of data are created. For example, first name, last name, and middle name that are directly substituted for original data. Substitution is difficult to implement when consistency is a requirement due to the randomness involved in picking the replacement. |
| Credit card, social security number, aadhar number | Format is preserved while replacing original digits and characters with randomly generated ones. The randomness needs to be carefully introduced wherever the meaning of data is not impacted. A PAN number in India has meaning for some characters in it. For example, the fourth character "P" in AAZPE3479P means the PAN belongs to an individual, whereas a 'C' in the same place means it belongs to a company. |
| E-mail address | Based on standards being followed, either an e-mail address is generated for entire record set uniquely or a common e-mail address is assigned to each row. |
| Mobile phone numbers | Most often, mobile numbers are 10-digit numbers that can be generated using a random number generator. |
| Flat value | A single value is assigned to all rows within a set. |

### 7.4.2.1 Privacy

QIs are data that help identify a record owner when combined with background knowledge or external data sources. While generating synthetic data, an important aspect is to maintain some distance between original data and synthetic data. In [13], the SDDL or the synthetic data description language is used to specify min/max constraints, distribution constraints, and iterations. For QIs to be highly private, all values need to be distorted to a certain extent that they do not compromise any individual identities as a result of external linkage. The extent of distortion can be measured using appropriate distance functions.

### 7.4.2.2 Utility

Most insurance applications have many QI fields that are processed. When these applications are tested, it is important to have a correct set of data for criteria assessment while granting loans. Synthetic data for testing need to capture all scenarios required to invoke various program flows. Similarly for data mining, analysis and the relationship between QIs and SD are important to create good data. The utility of QIs is linked to the preservation of the correlation with SD fields.

In Table 7.3, GENDER is a field that is correlated with NAME. Thus, when the substituted NAME is that of a male, the GENDER needs to correspond to it. Maintaining correlation is very important for the utility of QIs, which is done through a set of rules. For example, the rule in this table is that NAME

**TABLE 7.3**

QI Fields

| Gender | Age | Address | ZIP |
|--------|-----|---------|------|
| M | 25 | 1, 4th St. | 560001 |
| M | 36 | 358, A dr. | 560068 |
| M | 21 | 3, Stone Ct | 560055 |
| F | 28 | 51, Elm st. | 560003 |
| M | 40 | 9, Ode Rd | 560001 |
| M | 35 | 3, 9th Ave | 560051 |

is an independent variable, and GENDER is a dependent variable. These assignations need not be absolute, as the identification of dependent and independent variables is based on system behavior. The dependency determines the order of execution for a synthetic data generator.

Correlation may also exist between groups, as in a set of independent variables and a set of dependent variables. As the number of these variables increases, so does the complexity of generating synthetic data. Correlations among QI and SD fields are the most common. For example, the AGE of an individual may have a relation to the salary. SALARY could be either directly or inversely proportional to AGE. Similar examples can be found in insurance where AGE and premium are very closely related.

There are other factors that are important for utility such as statistical validity, format preservation, query ability, and test coverage (in the case of test data).

### 7.4.2.3 Generation Algorithms

Unlike anonymization, there is little to go by when it comes to synthetic data. Original data are out of bounds. All that is permitted is the metadata and a distribution-based view of the original data. Table 7.4 lists the algorithms that can be used to generate QIs.

**TABLE 7.4**

SDG Techniques for QI

| SDG Technique | Brief Explanation |
|---------------|-------------------|
| Randomization | A random value is generated to replace the original value. Based on the data format and range of original data, a number is randomly picked. This technique is applicable to date fields specifically. |
| Geographical area | Addresses and zip codes can be generated to be valid zip codes, or if the data are too clustered (like the voters list of a particular city), geographical area can be substituted against a zip code. Of course, the prerequisite is that altering the format of data is permissible. |
| Generalization | Generalizing a set of nominal categorical data values like making master's degree or PhD into postgraduate. |

### 7.4.3 Sensitive Data

SD form the most important ingredient of a data set. In data mining, facts are always attributed to SD while profiling is attributed to QIs. Numerical SD are easier to generate, as opposed to categorical ones which require additional rules to be developed.

#### 7.4.3.1 Privacy

Synthetically generated SD are similar to that discussed in QIs. Distribution of univariate and multivariate data is a good guideline to synthetically create data. Although single column data can be easily created, preserving their association with correlated data is important. The proximity of synthetic SD to its original counterpart is a debatable topic. As SD is the truth in the data, it is always desirable to have synthetic data created as close to original values as possible. However, from a privacy preservation perspective, the closer the SD to original values, the greater the privacy concerns are.

#### 7.4.3.2 Utility

Utility of synthetic data is measured in terms of its distance or departure from original values. We discuss two measures that can be used for this purpose.

##### 7.4.3.2.1 Distance-Based Record Linkage

Intuitively, distance measurement can be best explained using numerical data distributions. Consider Figure 7.1 to be the distribution of a numerical attribute to the original set being A and the synthetic data set being B.

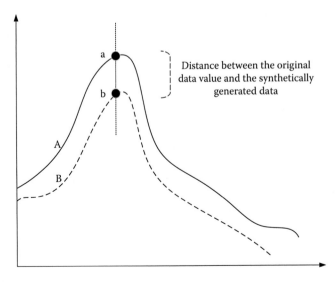

**FIGURE 7.1**
Distance measure.

The distance between the two points shown in Figure 7.1 is the difference in value for the same data point in the original and synthetic data. This record level distance d(a,b) [14] between points a and b of the distributions A and B, respectively, is shown as follows:

$$d(a,b) = \sum_{i=1}^{n} d_{Vi}\left(V_i^A(a), V_i^B(b)\right) \tag{7.1}$$

where $d_{Vi}$ is a distance assumed in each attribute $V_i$.

Based on whether the data are numerical or categorical in nature, a suitable distance measure like A threshold for this distance can assure the data generation team or the tool of sufficient privacy and controlled linkage risks.

### 7.4.3.2.2 *Probabilistic Record Linkage*

Probabilistic record linkage is discussed in Blakely and Salmond [15] in detail. The difference between distance-based record linkage and probabilistic record linkage does not differ for numerical and categorical data and requires no standardization. Weights are computed for a possible match versus a nonmatch, and using these weights, the probability is calculated that two given records refer to the same entity.

In order for the synthetic data to preserve privacy, the probabilities calculated earlier need to be kept below a threshold.

The drawback of this approach to keeping a check on privacy is that it comes with a huge computational burden.

In Figure 7.2, attributes A and B are original data, which seem to have a relationship best described as follows:

$$A \alpha 1/B \tag{7.2}$$

Knowing the range, mean, and variance of A and B, we can derive A′ and B′, respectively. Assuming that A and B are AGE and PREMIUM in an insurance setting, there would be a model that defines their relationship. Now with A′ and B′, the insurance application will expect that the relationship between A′ and B′ is the same as A and B. Unless this rule is complied with, synthetic data A′ and B′ will not be useful.

Outliers are part of SD and are interesting. These data cannot be directly acquired while creating synthetic data using the characteristics captured from the original data. The requirement for an outlier to be present is to be specified explicitly by data requesters. Similarly, boundary conditions can also be introduced to invoke a respective code while testing.

In data clustering, outliers gain prominence as they may form either sparse clusters or solitary values. This presents researchers with a unique

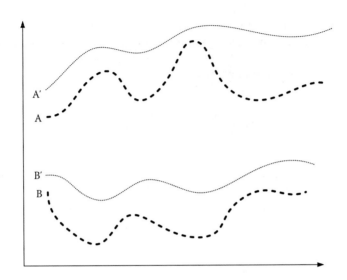

**FIGURE 7.2**
Data relationships.

perspective and an opportunity to theorize on their presence. Going back to Figure 7.2 for the attributes A and B, while generally the inverse proportionality of the two variables holds true (as assumed), at exceptionally high values of A, there might be a steep climb in the value of B, too. This would be an interesting finding for the analyst.

For categorical data, it is a bit more complicated. Consider Table 7.5.

Using the original data in this table, we find that there are five diseases totally. For the sake of demonstration, let us assume that there are 100 records having one of the five diseases shown. This metadata information about the original data is enough to generate synthetic data.

Now, we apply a good domain classification hierarchy, which generalizes that these data can be used to generate synthetic data. Again, the association of this generated SD with the respective rows is also a challenging aspect of the process, which is achieved using rules that data owners or business

**TABLE 7.5**

Patient Disease Data

| EI | | QI | | Disease (SD) |
|----|----|----|----|----|
| 23443 | ........ | 45 | ........ | Arthritis |
| 23423 | ........ | 64 | ........ | Bronchitis |
| 45662 | ........ | 32 | ........ | Lung infection |
| 75634 | ........ | 55 | ........ | Osteogenesis |
| 68643 | ........ | 86 | ........ | Asthma |

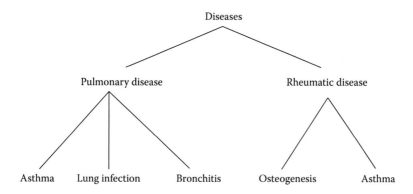

**FIGURE 7.3**
Disease classification.

**TABLE 7.6**

Synthetic Data for Disease Mirroring

| EI | | QI | | Disease (SD) |
|---|---|---|---|---|
| 83476 | ........ | 43 | ........ | Rheumatic disease |
| 93435 | ........ | 60 | ........ | Pulmonary disease |
| 45739 | ........ | 27 | ........ | Pulmonary disease |
| 12638 | ........ | 61 | ........ | Rheumatic disease |
| 34095 | ........ | 76 | ........ | Pulmonary disease |

analysts can provide. A sample domain classification hierarchy is shown in
Figure 7.3, and the resulting synthetic data are shown in Table 7.6. The speci-
ficity of the disease has been reduced to improve privacy while still providing a peripheral view of the ailment.

## 7.5  How Safe Are Synthetic Data?

In this section, we list areas where synthetic data can be used and also assess
how safe it is to do so.

### 7.5.1  Testing

Synthetic data are useful for testing in many settings. As discussed in the
last section of Chapter 6, there are a few shortcomings of anonymized data,
which can be overcome using synthetic data. Let us understand and evaluate
privacy preservation offered by synthetic data in each of these shortcomings.

### 7.5.1.1 Error and Exception Data

Invalid data produced for failure testing are done to enhance test coverage and have no repercussions pertaining to privacy. Moreover, these data are part of SD that are usually left untouched even while anonymizing the other data.

### 7.5.1.2 Scaling

The characteristics of original SD are used to scale data for performance testing. SD contain numerical and categorical data that describe the current state of the system and rarely describe the record owner. Nevertheless, a large number of SD collectively do have a chance of revealing clues about a collection of individuals or entities, but not specific ones.

### 7.5.1.3 Regression Testing

This type of testing requires multiple data refreshes as new functionality needs testing to ensure that other modules are not affected. Here, synthetic data are useful because data provisioning is much faster in the case of generation than masking and anonymization. While there are no problems with generating non-SD, EIs, QIs, and SD need to be generated carefully—especially QIs and SD, which closely mirror the characteristics of original data. This is where distance-based record linkage and probabilistic record linkage thresholds come into play.

## 7.5.2 Data Mining

In data mining, EIs are never used to derive any inference. QIs are used to profile a group of individuals or entities while SD are the data that are mined.

When synthetic data are created for EIs, they are not used for knowledge discovery and are hence safe. QI data are created using rules derived from metadata and characteristics of original data. Assuming that QIs are similar to original data, external linkage is possible with other QIs whose EIs are also available. This poses a risk of re-identification from synthetic data. Adequate distance needs to be maintained from original data while generating QIs to avoid re-identification.

SD utility takes precedence over privacy. When classifiers or clustering algorithms are applied on SD, the focus is to get results that would have been obtained, had original data been used instead.

## 7.5.3 Public Data

The disclosure risk of fully synthetic data sets is very low [1] but not zero. With public data, an intruder may perceive from synthetic data that he has identified an individual, which he does not know is made up.

Respondents to surveys usually feel that their privacy could be at risk as a result of the sharing of personal data. But as imputation models are not perfect and adversaries do not know how close synthetic data are to the original, it becomes very difficult for adversaries to make a concerted effort to re-identify the respondent.

It is important to note that partially synthetic data sets cannot offer a high-level of protection since some true values remain in the data, which makes evaluating the disclosure risk essential.

## 7.6 Summary

Synthetic data are produced using a model that is representative of a set of rules defined using program behavior. They are often used as an alternative to anonymized data due to privacy concerns. Inadequacies of original data also encourage synthetic data generation, which can fill gaps in survey data that may exist due to nonresponse. Fully and partially synthetic data sets are very useful for survey data sets. While fully synthetic data sets offer very high privacy, partially synthetic data sets refer to original data and hence require closer privacy assessment. Fully synthetic data sets are also useful when a software system is developed and tested for the first time.

EIs do not pose a big challenge while producing synthetic data as their role in program functionality or knowledge discovery is extremely limited. QIs and SD can be synthetically generated using statistical echoing of characteristics like distribution. QI data need to preserve privacy while providing utility, thereby requiring a clear demarcation of the boundary defining a balance between privacy and utility. A boundary is the amount of deviation ideal to maintain utility while preserving privacy. SD are critical for utility and mandates that the synthetic data mirror original data closely.

Synthetic data are very safe when used within set boundaries. While non-SD may be very well created, for other categories such as EIs, QIs, and SD, privacy comes at the cost of utility.

## References

1. J. Dreschler, Synthetic datasets for statistical disclosure control—Theory and implementation, Lecture notes in Statistics 201, pp. 7–10, 13–20, 41–42, 56, 2011.
2. D.B. Rubin, Multiple imputations in sample surveys, in *Proceedings of the Section on Survey Research Methods of the American Statistical Association 20–34*, American Statistical Association, Alexandria, VA, 1978.

3. D.B. Rubin, *Multiple Imputation for Non-Response in Surveys*, John Wiley & Sons, New York, 1987.
4. D.B. Rubin, The design of a general and flexible system for handling nonresponse in sample surveys, *The American Statistician*, 58, 298–302, 2004.
5. Grid Tools Datamaker, https://www.grid-tools.com/datamaker/.
6. J.H. Lee, Y. Kim, and M. O'Keefe, On regression-tree-based synthetic data methods for business data, *Journal of Privacy and Confidentiality*, 5(1), 107–135, 2013.
7. M.E. Nergiz, M. Atzori, Y. Saygin, and B. Guc, Towards trajectory anonymization: A generalization-based approach, *Transactions on Data Privacy*, 2, 47–75, 2009.
8. P.J. Lin et al., Development of a synthetic data set generator for building and testing information discovery systems in *Proceedings of the Third International Conference on Information Technology: New Generations (ITNG'06)*, Las Vegas, NV, 2006.
9. M. Shams, D. Krishnamurthy, and B. Far, A model-based approach for testing the performance of web applications, in *Proceedings of the Third International Workshop on Software Quality Assurance (SOQUA'06)*, Portland, OR, 2006.
10. X. Wu, Y. Wang, and Y. Zheng, Privacy preserving database application testing, in *Proceedings of the 2003 ACM Workshop on Privacy in the Electronic Society (WPES'03)*, Washington, DC, October 30, 2003.
11. M. Whiting, J. Haack, and C. Varley, Creating realistic, scenario-based synthetic data for test and evaluation of information analytics software, in *Proceedings of the Beyond Time and Errors: Novel Evaluation Methods for Information Visualization (BELIV'08)*, ACM, Florence, Italy, April 5, 2008.
12. D. Ferrari, On the foundation of artificial workload design, in *Proceedings of ACM SIGMETRICS*, 1984, New York, NY, pp. 8–14.
13. J.E. Hoag and C.W. Thompson, A parallel general-purpose synthetic data generator, *SIGMOD Record*, 36(1), 19–24, March 2007.
14. J. Domingo-Ferrer, V. Torra, J.M. Mateo-Sanz, and F. Sebe, Re-identification and synthetic data generators: A case study, in *Fourth Joint UNECE/EUROSTAT Work Session on Statistical Data Confidentiality*, Geneva, Switzerland, November 9–11, 2005.
15. T. Blakely and C. Salmond, Probabilistic record linkage and a method to calculate the positive predictive value, *International Journal of Epidemiology*, 31, 1246–1252, 2002.

# 8

## Dynamic Data Protection: Tokenization

### 8.1 Introduction

In the previous chapters, we discussed static data anonymization, where anonymization techniques are applied on static data or data at rest and a subset of production data is extracted and used for analysis after anonymizing it. There is another use case for data privacy—data protection methods applied during the run-time of the application—application of data protection dynamically. A number of data protection techniques can be used to protect data at run-time. One such method is tokenization. Stated simply, tokenization is a technique where sensitive data are replaced with a token having the same format as the sensitive data. A token can be generated independent of the sensitive data; tokenization is considered to provide a very high level of protection or privacy. Its main advantage is that the token is completely useless outside the context of the application. So, tokenization is ideal to protect sensitive identification information such as credit card numbers, social security numbers, and other personally identifiable information. Tokenization is used extensively in the payment card industry (PCI) and has now also been adopted across other industry verticals. In PCI, it is used to protect credit card numbers that are numerical data types. It is also possible to generate tokens for other data types. The tokens preserve the formats of sensitive data, and it will look just like the original data. So, can tokenized data be used in place of original data? Well, it depends on the application—some applications will require original data to process a transaction, and some may work with tokenized data.

This chapter covers the use cases for dynamic data protection and tokenization implementation.

### 8.2 Revisiting the Definitions of Anonymization and Privacy

In Chapter 1, we defined anonymization and privacy and showed that there is very little difference between them and they are flip sides of the same coin. A customer's record in a database can be classified into three disjoint sets of data—explicit identifiers (EIs), quasi-identifiers (QIs), and sensitive data (SD).

Static data anonymization focuses on protecting the identity of a customer and thus anonymizes or protects EIs and QIs and leaves SD in their original form so that they can be used for analytics. Conversely, privacy protects a customer's SD and leaves the identification data in their original form. Anonymity should not be confused with privacy. Anonymity does not mean privacy. For example, an adversary may not have the exact salary detail of an individual, but the knowledge that the individual is in high-income group is itself a loss of privacy for the individual. But the word "privacy" is used very loosely in the literature. There are use cases that require customers' SD or customers' privacy to be protected.

In Figure 8.1, we see that based on the role of the accessing person, the anonymization design changes. Let us look at the three user roles:

1. *Business Process Outsourcing (BPO) Employee*: A BPO employee is a support engineer who helps customers with queries about application functionality or transactional issues. The BPO employee needs to know the customers in order to service their queries or issues.

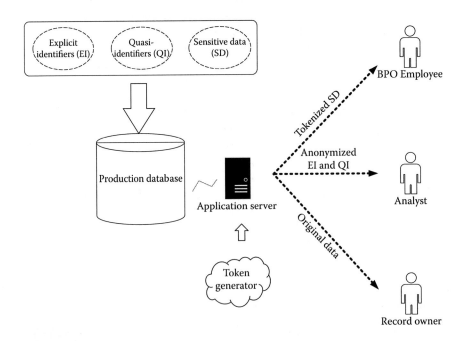

**FIGURE 8.1**
The big picture.

Thus, identity protection is not required. However, transaction details such as the credit card number used for a transaction need not be revealed. A similar example is that a hospital clerk need not know what a patient is being treated for when her job is to direct visitors to patients' ward.

2. *Analyst*: An analyst's role has been discussed at length in Privacy Preserving Data Mining (PPDM). Her needs are limited to SD, which form a large part of the analysis. QI requirements can also be generalized so that an overall profile of an individual is acquired.

3. *Record Owner*: A record owner is someone who logs in to view their own data. After proper authentication, original data can be displayed.

## 8.3 Understanding Tokenization

There are many methods that can be used to protect data: data masking, encryption, and tokenization. Masking and encryption have been used for a long time, and tokenization is relatively new. Tokenization has many benefits over other techniques. The following example illustrates this difference. Take a credit card number of a customer. In static data masking, the credit card number is masked. Masking is an irreversible process. The original data cannot be recovered from the masked value. However, tokenization is a two-way process in which the original data can be recovered. The masking of credit card numbers is shown in Figure 8.2. It is important to note that this field is classified as SD here.

Masking completely destroys the utility of a masked value, whereas tokenized data can be used in a transaction after swapping the original data with a token, or they can be used as they are if the application supports. Figure 8.3 illustrates how tokenization is implemented.

There are two types of tokenization:

1. Dependent tokenization
2. Independent tokenization

This classification is based on how a token is generated and its relationship with the original data.

### 8.3.1 Dependent Tokenization

Figure 8.2 illustrates a credit card number and a corresponding token for the 11 digits of the card number. So far, there has been no mention whether

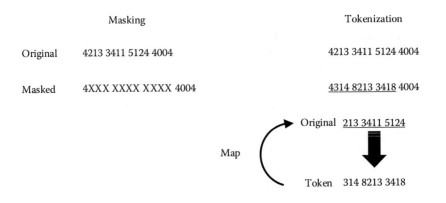

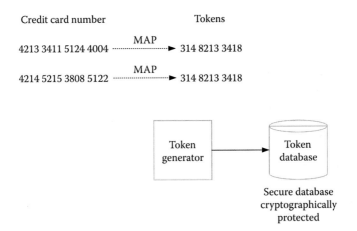

**FIGURE 8.2**
Difference between data masking and tokenization.

**FIGURE 8.3**
Implementing tokenization.

these 11 digits are dependent on the credit card number or not. In dependent tokenization, a token is generated based on original data. The token can be a random number, a hash, or an encrypted value. A dependent token is not very strong as there is a relationship between the token and the original data.

So, is an additive random noise the same as a dependent token? An additive random noise is based on the original data and has similar statistical

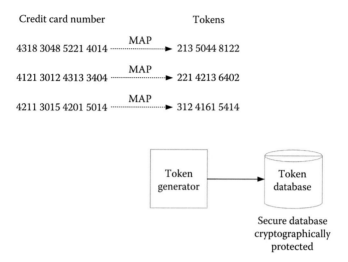

**FIGURE 8.4**
Generation of independent tokens.

properties as the original data, whereas a token does not have similar statistical properties as the original data. Therefore, a well-designed token is stronger than a random noise.

### 8.3.2 Independent Tokenization

In independent tokenization, tokens are generated independent of the original data. The tokens have absolutely no relationship to the original data. In this case, a unique token is generated for every data element in the sensitive data set. The token is then mapped to the data element. Figure 8.4 illustrates this process.

In the process, the token generator generates tokens—in the case of credit card numbers; the tokens could come from a random number generator. It is to be ensured that tokens are not duplicated. The token database contains mapping between the sensitive data and its token.

## 8.4 Use Cases for Dynamic Data Protection

Some very relevant use cases are as follows:

a. Business operations—Privacy preserving business operations
b. Ad hoc reports for regulatory compliance

### 8.4.1 Business Operations

Many large industries such as banks, insurance, financial services, and manufacturing outsource their business operations to BPO organizations located either in their own countries or in countries such as China, Brazil, and India. Customers of these companies contact these BPOs for assistance (Figure 8.5).

Business applications and customers are in the same country, and business operations are in a different country. Data protection acts such as European Union (EU) Data Protection Act and Swiss Data Protection Act (FADP) enforce that customer-sensitive data should not cross the geographical boundaries of the country. In such case, how can business operations access customer data and assist their customers? This is where tokenization can help. When applied during run-time, customer-sensitive data such as credit card numbers and account numbers can be replaced with tokenized numbers. Based on the application, a tokenized number can be used in a transaction or the token is replaced by the original data before the transaction. An associate in business operations will not be able to differentiate between the original sensitive data and the tokenized version. This helps in preserving the privacy of the customer and also complies with the regulation. By outsourcing business operations to low-cost countries and using tokenization, companies make huge savings.

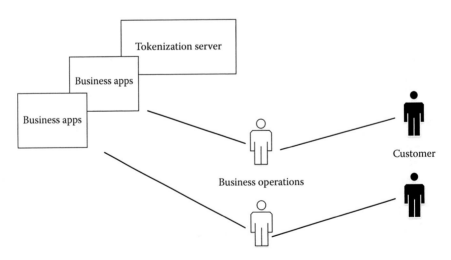

**FIGURE 8.5**
Use case—Outsourcing business operations.

### 8.4.2 Ad Hoc Reports for Regulatory Compliance

Companies in the United States should comply with the Sarbanes–Oxley Act. External auditors who audit companies generate ad hoc reports to check for compliance. The reports contain customer-sensitive data that should be protected. Data protection should be applied at run-time or dynamically. The use of tokenization ensures that customer-sensitive data are replaced with tokens, and there is no disclosure.

## 8.5 Benefits of Tokenization Compared to Other Methods

The paper by Stapleton and Poore [1] compares various methods of data protection with respect to credit card numbers (primary account number [PAN]). The focus of this paper is on the strength of the various methods in protecting PAN. But there are more benefits of tokenization than just its strength.

Some of the benefits of tokenization are as follows:

1. *Consistency*: In a networked set of applications, a data element appearing in multiple applications is transformed consistently.

2. *Format preserving*: Tokens have the same format as the sensitive data, which means applications need not be modified to handle tokens.

3. *Supporting different data types*: Tokens were initially used in credit card number protection, which is numerical, but as tokenization is now adopted across industry verticals, it supports different data types.

4. *Strength*: Conceptually, tokenization should provide high levels of security compared with other methods as tokens are generated independent of sensitive data. Just as encryption is dependent on the safety of keys, tokenization's strength depends on the security of the token database. If the token database is hacked, then tokenization is broken.

5. *Tokenization is reversible*: It is possible to get back the original sensitive data from the tokenized data.

6. *Cost*: Static data anonymization is very difficult to implement as there is a detailed process to be followed, but tokenization is much simpler. The overall cost for tokenization is relatively less.

## 8.6 Components for Tokenization

Tokenization has emerged as a popular mechanism to protect data in the retail, healthcare, and financial world today. A reason for its popularity is the flexibility in its implementation. As we explore the tools providing tokenization, we will understand its advantages as well as some minutiae regarding its implementation in an enterprise setting. While understanding the components involved in implementing tokenization, we will simultaneously discuss tools on tokenization as well as pros and cons of tokenization itself.

Figure 8.6 depicts the components that are part of an independent tokenization implementation. We discuss only the relevant components here.

### 8.6.1 Data Store

A data store is a collection of tokens available for replacement. For each request from an application, a token is picked from the data store based on a predetermined logic (e.g., random selection). Then the data store maintains this association between the original data and the token. The token, which replaces the original data, acts as an alias and is used within the application until the need for the original data arises again, at which point again the data store is referred to.

As this data store maintains the association of original data and tokens, it needs to be secure. The data store stores the data in an encrypted format and the keys used for this encryption are managed within the enterprise key management environment. Some important challenges in maintaining the data store are security of the data store, high volumes of data, tokens of different sizes, performance, scalability, and so on.

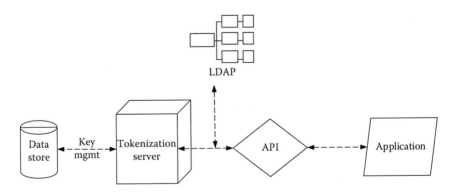

**FIGURE 8.6**
Components of tokenization.

### 8.6.2 Tokenization Server

The tokenization server receives requests from the application. The request is always accompanied by a parameter. In case of persistence, an original data value is passed to the tokenization server, which in turn returns a token after storing the token-value pair in its data store. In the other case, where an application needs to back the original value, the token is passed to the tokenization server to retrieve the original value, which is then possibly used to process a transaction.

## 8.7 Summary

This chapter provides a very brief overview of tokenization and how it can be used for dynamic data protection. Tokenization is an evolving technique and is slowly being adopted across industry verticals. It will have a lot of tractions in emerging areas such as Internet of Things (IoT).

## Reference

1. J. Stapleton and R.S. Poore, Tokenization and other methods of Security for card holder data, *Information Security Journal: A Global Perspective*, 20(2), 91–99, 2011.

# 9

## Privacy Regulations

Privacy preservation is discussed in this book for one important reason: Regulations. We turn our attention now to compliance regulations that govern the use of personal data. Most privacy preservation endeavors are aimed at complying with regulations at a country, region, or global level. Organizations also have their own privacy policies. In this chapter, we understand some of the most important privacy laws that businesses encounter while working with their data.

## 9.1 Introduction

Data collected from a large population give the collecting agency great insights into the demographics, behavior, preferences, and other characteristics of the population. The insightful nature of these data also makes it a lucrative source of gaining intelligence for external enterprises. In the past, agencies shared these data with external private partners, with the permission of the participants, in the form of fine print clauses. Today, this practice has come under a lot of scrutiny due to the kind of analysis done by private players to enhance business intelligence and create targeted marketing campaigns. Survey data are a highly sought-after data source. Now, many countries have an ethical code that governs the production of official statistics. The International Statistical Institute (ISI) has a declaration on professional ethics [2], which states in its ethical principle #12 that the interests of subjects need to be protected by having appropriate measures to prevent data being released in a form that allows a subject's or respondent's identity to be disclosed or inferred.

Mining of retail, financial, and healthcare data is commonplace today. While inferences made from such data are highly useful in our daily lives, it is equally important that the identity of the participants in these data is protected. Global agencies are also engaged in such analysis, thus bringing privacy preservation to the fore. Chapter 5 discussed the challenges of protecting personal data while mining.

Test data manufacturing is another area where companies struggle to protect privacy. As testing is outsourced to partner companies often located in different geographical regions, the capability of creating data that are good for testing and devoid of personal identification information is in high demand today. Needless to say, test data are scrutinized by not just parent companies but also by countries, which have privacy laws regarding the use of data within and outside their boundaries. The European Union has been active in defining rules for protecting personal data [3] and is refining the Data Protection Directive of 1995. The regulation (EC) No. 45/2001 of the European Parliament and the Council of December 18, 2000 [4] mentions in Article 9 the adequacy of protections that need to be in place in third countries. In the Swiss Federal Act on Data Protection (FADP) [5], Article 12 of Section 3 states in paragraph 2c that disclosure of sensitive data or personal files to a third party cannot be done without prior justification. With regard to transborder data flow, Article 6 prohibits data sharing with a country that has privacy laws that are not equivalent of the Swiss laws.

Additional specialized laws prohibit certain fields of data such as payment card numbers. Online businesses today rely heavily on instant transactions carried out using payment gateways, which are a secure medium for obtaining authorization from banks to complete a transaction. In this process, the card information is shared across multiple parties, making the cardholder's information vulnerable to attack. The Payment Card Industry Data Security Standard (PCI DSS) [6] is a comprehensive data security standard used to govern properly the way in which card data are handled in the payment card industry. PCI DSS requirement #3 protects stored cardholder data. The logging of transactions at the merchant's end does include all payment card details. Apart from this, consumers are prompted to allow or disallow storing card details for future transactions by the merchant. The PCI DSS aims at securing these data.

With regard to handling consumer data in a highly interconnected world, many regulations have been proposed, one of which is the Federal Trade Commission's report on Protecting Consumer Privacy in an Era of Rapid Change [7]. After a preliminary report published in December 2010, the final report was released in March 2012. As part of its final privacy framework and implementation recommendations, the report states in principle B of its privacy by design category that comprehensive data management procedures need to be maintained by companies throughout the life cycle of their products and services. Consequently, all activities performed with data at development, testing, production, and analysis stages are supposed to have privacy factored during the design stage rather than have it embedded later as an afterthought. In the same report, there is also mention of the lack of consistency in privacy standards that arise out of data being shared across borders. If there are a set of basic privacy principles that apply globally, the discord between regional privacy regulations can be managed. The report also puts forth nine privacy principles: the 2004 Asia-Pacific Economic Cooperation ("APEC") Privacy Framework [8].

The Organization for Economic Cooperation and Development (OECD) states in its basic principle #17 that transborder flows of personal data are not restricted if (a) the other country substantially observes these guidelines or (b) sufficient safeguards exist, including effective enforcement mechanisms and appropriate measures put in place by the data controller to ensure a continuing level of protection consistent with their guidelines [9].

Domains also command their own rules of data privacy. Therefore, there are often multiple privacy regulations that function in conjunction with each other. There are also laws such as the Health Insurance Portability and Accountability Act (HIPAA) [1] that have an absolute say in how healthcare data are used and shared in the U.S.

In this chapter, we will discuss various privacy regulations and their intricacies in data protection. We deal with each law from three perspectives: data sharing, data protection guidelines, and anonymization standards. We will also present our views of the recommended privacy design for compliance.

## 9.2 UK Data Protection Act 1998

The Data Protection Act 1998 (DPA) is an act of parliament of the United Kingdom. Although not introduced as a privacy law, the DPA lays down guidelines on how personal data are to be processed. In [17], a total of eight principles on how data are processed are listed, which address various aspects including how data need to be protected when transferred to a country or a territory outside the European economic zone. Compliance with the DPA is regulated and enforced by an independent authority, the Information Commissioner's Office, which maintains guidance relating to the act.

### 9.2.1 Definitions

The DPA has defined various entities in the data protection exercise [18]:

1. *Data Controller*: a person who (either alone or in collaboration with others) determines the purposes for which and the manner in which any personal data are, or are to be, processed

2. *Data Processor*: a person (external to the data controller) who processes the data on behalf of the data controller.

3. *Data Subject*: an individual who is the subject of personal data.

Personal data are defined in the DPA as data relating to a living individual who can be identified

a. From those data

b. From those data and other information that is in the possession of, or is likely to come into the possession of the data controller and includes any expression of opinion about the individual and any indication of the intentions of the data controller or any other person in respect to the individual. Some attributes explicitly mentioned in the DPA are shown in Table 9.1.

If NAME, ADDRESS, and other explicit identifier (EI) fields are not mentioned explicitly, one can assume that they are naturally part of "personal data." Schedules 3 and 4 state that processing of personal data "is carried out with appropriate safeguards for the rights and freedom of data subjects." Appropriate safeguards point to privacy preserving mechanisms such as anonymization, encryption, or synthetic data generation.

The eight fields shown in Table 9.1 have not been discussed earlier in this book. So, let us see what techniques can be applied to them and how the resultant data would look (Table 9.2).

A number of schedules available in the DPA define various sections of the law pertaining to the data protection commissioner, appeal proceedings, inspections, public records, educational records, and so on. However, the primary goal is to ensure that the rights of the data subject are protected and that he/she is in control of what part of his/her data are shared, in what format, and for what purpose.

## 9.2.2 Problems in DPA

The DPA was enacted in 1998, at a time when data were shared by survey agencies, healthcare agencies, etc., with governmental or nongovernmental

**TABLE 9.1**

Sensitive Attributes as per DPA

| S. NO | Attribute | Classification |
|---|---|---|
| 1 | Ethnicity | QI |
| 2 | Political opinions | QI |
| 3 | Religious beliefs | QI |
| 4 | Affiliations to trade unions | SD |
| 5 | Health condition (physical and mental) | SD |
| 6 | Sex life | QI |
| 7 | Crime background | SD |
| 8 | Legal background | SD |

**TABLE 9.2**

Anonymization Options for Sensitive Personal Data

| Attribute | Assumption/ Notes | Technique | Result |
|---|---|---|---|
| Ethnicity | A finite set of values | Shuffling | Shuffling often fails, as Asian and African names are very suggestive of ethnicity. Though it does not reveal the identity, it lets the intruder know that data have been anonymized. |
| | | Generalization | Generalization tends to make some rows indistinguishable. If k-anonymization is used, along with suppressed rows, some data might get the same value for ethnicity. This has an impact on utility. |
| | | Suppression | Utility is adversely affected. |
| Political opinions | A limited set of values such as liberal and conservative | Shuffling | Correlated data may exist. For example, political party as a field may be part of SD. The political opinion need to match with the political party. Thus, utility is affected. |
| | | Generalization and suppression | Same case as ethnicity. |
| Religious beliefs | A finite set of values | Shuffling | The religion "Hindu" cannot have a religious belief as "Atheist." Correlated data need a careful privacy design. Utility is impacted. |
| | | Generalization and suppression | Same case as ethnicity. |
| Affiliations to trade unions | A list of values— could be a large field with many names | Outliers only | Bordering QIs and SD, but as affiliations change or add up over time, we classify it as SD. Being SD, it is important for the task being performed (testing, mining, etc.). Domain generalization hierarchy could be used to generalize very revealing affiliations. In most cases, data should be kept as is. |
| Health condition (physical and mental) | Highly sensitive | None | Health condition is SD and important for the assessment or analysis. Hence, no anonymization should be applied except for outlier handling. |

*(Continued)*

**TABLE 9.2** (*Continued*)

Anonymization Options for Sensitive Personal Data

| Attribute | Assumption/ Notes | Technique | Result |
|---|---|---|---|
| Sex life | Could be elaborate in health data or just activity levels in other domains | Shuffling, generalization, or suppression | Correlation restrictions apply here too, which make shuffling preserve privacy but give up utility. Generalization is preferred when used in conjunction with suppression for other fields. Suppressing this field will result in loss of utility. |
| Crime background | Highly sensitive and descriptive in nature | Outlier handling | A field could contain a list of case numbers, which is maintained elsewhere, or have the description of each crime instance there itself. In either case, being SD, the record should not be anonymized. Specific case numbers within the field could be suppressed, though. High-profile case descriptions should be handled as outliers. |
| Legal background | Highly sensitive and descriptive in nature | Outlier handling | Same as crime background. |

organizations for the purpose of analysis or publication of reports. Today, companies share their data with their partners for convenience, monetary or procedural benefits, and so on. Outsourcing as a business model was not widespread at the time this law was enacted. Hence, most references to data sharing do not directly refer to this model. Even in the amendments made as part of the Coroners and Justice Act 2009 [19], #174 do not explicitly mention outsourcing as one of the data sharing models that the commissioner should assess and monitor regularly.

Personal data, as defined by the DPA, do not include specific guidelines for attributes such as name, address, and identifiers such as national insurance number and postal codes. This loose definition of personal data limits the capacity of organizations in formulating policies for the protection of the attributes mentioned earlier. In the new world of a global marketplace, data are the biggest asset. Companies buy data from agencies to get into the psyche of consumers, placing them into buckets, classifying their behaviors, and building profiles based on their transactions.

Sensitive personal data shared across countries such as India, China, or Russia find many service partners who play the role of data processors. This poses a serious security as well as privacy threat to the data subject and needs to be addressed in future amendments of the UK Data Protection Act.

## 9.3 Federal Act of Data Protection of Switzerland 1992

The FADP, first enacted in 1992, aims to protect the privacy and fundamental rights of people when their data are processed. Applicable to individuals and federal bodies, the act defines personal data as all information relating to an identified or identifiable person. Like the UK DPA, sensitive personal information is again defined in a similar fashion protecting personal details with regard to ethnicity, beliefs, health, and legal standing.

The Swiss FADP is particularly careful in articulating cross-border disclosure guidelines in Article 6. Item a. of Article 6 explicitly states that personal data may be disclosed abroad only if sufficient safeguards, in particular contractual clauses, ensure an adequate level of protection. These safeguards must be informed to the federal data protection and information commissioner. Proper authorization to data and detailed provisions on minimum standards of data security can be found in Article 7. Guidelines for third-party processing of data are laid down in Article 10a, which designates the instructing party as the responsible entity for ensuring compliance and security.

Although not updated, the FADP produces annual reports with details on new technology advances and the posture adopted. We discuss only the relevant findings of the latest report [21].

### 9.3.1 Storing Patients' Records in the Cloud

Many doctors have their patients' medical data hosted on a cloud. FADP recommends that cloud service and its providers be located in Switzerland, and they must be able to provide the doctors with a contractual guarantee that no patient records will be transferred outside the country. If the doctors want to share these data for statistical purposes, they can do so only after the data have been made "totally anonymous."

The interpretation of "totally anonymous" is that all EIs and quasi-identifiers (QIs) should conceal the patient's identity. Anonymization principles (2,13) help achieve masking of EIs and anonymization of QIs. Only outlier records need to be protected. For example, a patient with an extremely rare disease could be identified by a neighbor who works in the company analyzing this patient's data.

Such rare data can be generalized. Ebola in Figure 9.1 could be replaced with a value such as "Infectious Viral Disease." Of course, as a result, analysts may lose the perspective of the gravity of the disease, which is a utility issue.

### 9.3.2 Health Questionnaires for Job Applicants

Health questionnaires should be specific to job positions, and responses should be assessed by a medical practitioner and not the employer. At the end

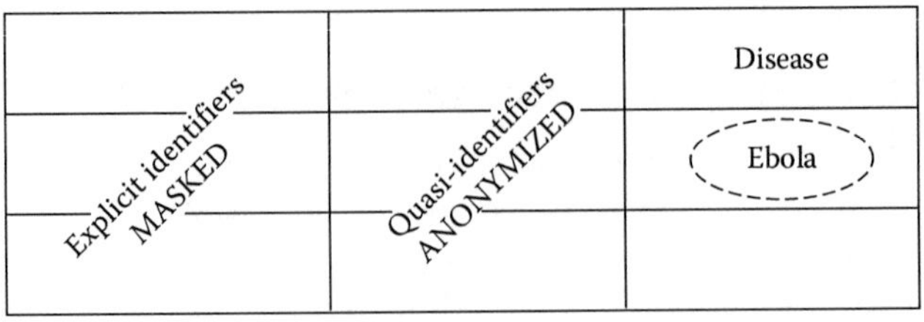

**FIGURE 9.1**
Rare disease.

of the evaluation, only the doctor is entitled to say whether an applicant is suitable for the position, for example, if the illness would directly impair the applicant's working capacity or prevent him from carrying out his duties.

### 9.3.3 Transferring Pseudonymized Bank Customer Data Outside Switzerland

The FADP states that pseudonymization is a special process whereby all the elements that allow the data subject to be identified are replaced by a neutral identifier or pseudonym. The pseudonym is stored in a separate correspondence table together with identification elements so that the authorized user is able to correlate the data with the data subject who is therefore identifiable within the meaning of the DPA. This can be thought of as a two-way tokenization mechanism. However, it is also true that a person with access to the correspondence table (or the vault maintaining the tokens) is able to identify the subject.

The law has been designed to enforce transparency when a data subject's data are outsourced to a different country for processing, which ensures that consent is taken and not assumed.

## 9.4 Payment Card Industry Data Security Standard (PCI DSS)

The Payment Card Industry Data Security Standard (PCI DSS) was developed to enhance cardholders' data security and facilitate the adoption of consistent data security measures globally [6]. As is evident, the standard is focused on the business process that handles payment cards and ensures the security of this information throughout the payment life cycle. With high focus on network and system security, access control, and vulnerability management guidelines, the PCI DSS is a security standard rather than a privacy standard. Nevertheless, the protection of cardholders' information is critical part of the overall data protection exercise. In our discussion of PCI

DSS, we keep our focus only on the privacy aspect of cardholder data, which is addressed in specific requirements of the standard.

PCI DSS applies to two kinds of data:

1. Cardholder data
2. Sensitive authentication data

Table 9.3 shows a nonexhaustive list of attributes that fall into these categories.

Requirement 3 of PCI DSS is specific to the protection of cardholder data. As guidance to compliance with requirement 3.1, the only cardholder data that may be stored after the authorization of a transaction are the primary account number (PAN) (rendered unreadable), expiration date, cardholder name, and service code. Authentication data such as pins and full track data are prohibited to be stored at any level after the execution of a transaction. Requirement 3.3 mandates that PAN be masked when displayed. Table 9.4 shows what is permissible as per PCI DSS and what is not.

These guidelines are combined with access privileges, which also ensure data security. Only authorized personnel have access to original complete PAN. It is important to note that requirement 3.3 is only applicable to the visual access of the payment card data. For data that are stored in a data source, requirement 3.4 states that PAN is to be made unreadable when it is stored in a physical data source. Now, the approach recommended by PCI DSS is one-way hashing using an industry-tested and accepted algorithm. However, this guideline makes card data unreadable and hence not capable of being queried. Such an implementation prevents applications from having visual control enabled by access privileges, somewhat defeating the very purpose.

**TABLE 9.3**

PCI DSS Applicability

| Cardholder Data | Sensitive Authentication Data |
| --- | --- |
| Primary account number (PAN) | Full track data (magnetic stripe data or equivalent on a chip) |
| Cardholder name | |
| Expiration date | CAV2/CVC2/CVV2/CID |
| Service code | PINs/PIN blocks |

**TABLE 9.4**

Payment Card Data

| Original | Masked | Evaluation |
| --- | --- | --- |
| 4628 8344 5902 0094 | **4628 8309 8347 0094** | **Permitted** |
| 3876 9344 9110 0211 | *3876 9344 8942 0211* | *Violation* |
| 6289 0332 5832 9428 | *6289 0332 0038 9428* | *Violation* |

**TABLE 9.5**

Anonymization Scenarios of Card Data

| S. No. | Solution | Scenario |
|--------|----------|----------|
| 1 | Random number generation or flat value | When there is no processing expected on these data other than just record keeping, then random number generation with format preservation can be employed. A flat value is the cheapest solution in case no processing is expected. |
| 2 | Card-type preserving data generation | ISO/IEC 7812-1:2012 specifies a numbering system for the identification of card issuers, the format of the issuer identification number (IIN), and the primary account number [20]. The generator could keep the card mathematically valid and conform to the Luhn algorithm. |
| 3 | Suppression or removal | For scenario 1, another option is to suppress the field's value, which makes the utility of the field 0, but as there is no functionality around it, the test coverage is largely unaffected. If the field is not used by any line of code, the field could be removed altogether. |

Requirements 6.4.1–6.4.4 address the intimate relationship between production and test environments, which is also an important concept in this book. Card information such as PAN should never be allowed to get into test data sources as is. Most often, test data are created by borrowing some portion of production data. PCI DSS dictates that all PAN data should never be transferred to test beds. This standard stops short of advising what could be a good way to have these data created in test environments. In Table 9.5, we summarize a few scenarios.

## 9.5 The Health Insurance Portability and Accountability Act of 1996 (HIPAA)

The Health Insurance Portability and Accountability Act of 1996 (HIPAA) privacy rule was issued to ensure that individuals' health information is properly protected while allowing the flow of the information to provide and promote high-quality healthcare and to protect the public's health and well-being [1]. According to the rule, "protected health information" (PHI) consists of the following categories of data:

- Health condition of patients, physical or mental from the past, present, or the future
- The healthcare that is provisioned
- Payment information for the healthcare provisioned to the patient

There is also a provision on de-identified health information and its definition. De-identified data, as per HIPAA privacy rule, are that which cannot by itself be attributed to an individual. These data can be obtained by either statistically determining that there are no possible ways to use these de-identified data to positively point to an individual or by suppressing a field or a set of fields that point to characteristics that could lead to the identification of the individual.

As per the HIPAA privacy rule, de-identification of PHI is to be achieved using one of the following two ways:

1. Covered entity removes all direct identifiers, reduces the dimensionality of data, and restricts the distribution of the data set itself through a data use or restricted use agreement.
2. Safe harbor method that lists direct identifiers and other identifiers who need to be removed from the data set.

HIPAA is difficult to implement as there are separate rules for privacy, security, enforcement, and others. In [10], a framework has been presented to assess the gap between healthcare systems and HIPAA regulations and policies.

Let us examine the merits of HIPAA. In the example shown in Table 9.6, we have a set of records that are part of clinical information maintained by a healthcare provider. On compliance with HIPAA, the data that will be released will look like the following.

The data produced in Table 9.7 are a result of compliance using the safe harbor method. Gender is part of demographic information that need not be de-identified. The disease is the information that is released. Zip code is de-identified using the rule that the first three digits when combined into a geographical unit should not be part of a set of predefined set given by HIPAA. Thus, rows for identifiers 103, 104, and 105 have zip codes starting with 000.

The data thus produced are now usable for research and can be shared with a third party. Now, the released fields are gender, zip code, and illness. As shown in Benitez and Malin [11], a voter list could have the same fields with

**TABLE 9.6**

Data Set of Healthcare Provider

| Identifier | Name | DOB | Gender | Zip Code | Illness |
|---|---|---|---|---|---|
| 101 | Catherine Bale | 3/12/1958 | Female | 78234 | Diabetes II |
| 102 | Sherwin Joe | 10/02/1967 | Male | 28132 | Paralysis |
| 103 | Kevin D'Mello | 03/07/1989 | Male | 99344 | Hypertension |
| 104 | Gloria Periera | 11/07/1975 | Female | 83030 | Myopia |
| 105 | Vishal Zute | 21/12/1979 | Male | 20301 | Bronchitis |
| 106 | Sean Mortimer | 04/12/1978 | Male | 20301 | Lung cancer |

**TABLE 9.7**

Published Data

| Gender | Zip Code | Illness |
|--------|----------|---------|
| Female | 78234 | Diabetes II |
| Male | 28132 | Paralysis |
| Male | 99344 | Hypertension |
| Female | 00030 | Myopia |
| Male | 00001 | Bronchitis |
| Male | 00001 | Lung cancer |

names in there and could also contain spatial data, which helps an attacker zero in on a particular record. A classic example is that of Sweeney [12] deciphering the identity of the governor of Massachusetts from health records and a voter list.

### 9.5.1 Effects of Protection

HIPAA-compliant data are difficult to re-identify, making them very private. Of course, they have their ill effects, too.

In Table 9.6, the persons identified by 105 and 106 have illnesses of bronchitis and lung cancer, respectively. Let us assume that there are 1000 records with these zip codes. Now, as these are suppressed as per HIPAA, an analysis correlating the illnesses with the geographical information can no longer be done. Furthermore, if the illnesses in this zip code are all related to breathing or the lungs in particular, then the analysis that could link the health condition with a health hazard in the area could prove to be vital. This example also represents a set of clustered data where records having similar illness characteristics are grouped only to find that the zip codes also have a similar grouping. But once the data are de-identified as per the HIPAA privacy rule, this relationship is lost. In [13], the authors point out that HIPAA's impact on medical research could jeopardize the studies of drug safety, medical device validation, and disease prediction and prevention.

Medical QIs are useful in understanding the profile of a patient. As SD provide disease-related details that are not anonymized, QIs are very important for this analysis. In our opinion, HIPAA's stringent approach to anonymizing QIs affects analyses, in that the inferences or relationships observed are weaker than what could have been done with data produced as per a research-friendly privacy policy.

### 9.5.2 Anonymization Considerations

HIPAA is designed to protect the interests of the individuals whose health records are being maintained and shared. As Figure 9.2 shows, there are various perspectives at play in this debate on privacy. Business associates are completely

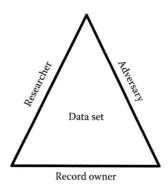

**FIGURE 9.2**
Perspectives on data set.

focused on the utility of the data, which means that they want almost all the original attributes to be shared with them in the same format. At the same time, adversaries look for the slightest possibility to put multiple data sources together and understand how individual data are represented, thus revealing identities. A good anonymization design should take care of the interests of the record owner and the researcher and ensure that the adversary is disillusioned.

### 9.5.2.1 Record Owner

Record owners have the following privacy perspective on their data:

a. HIPAA ensures that EIs such as name, social security number, and address are de-identified. Hence, QIs such as date of birth, date of admission or discharge, and zip code are the primary targets of attackers. k-Anonymity anonymizes QIs such that values are indistinguishable from at least k − 1 other records in the same data set. Risk of re-identification is present as k-anonymity is not robust enough to prevent homogeneity attacks.

b. Even though the privacy design is successful in limiting the disclosure of sensitive data, there still remains the problem that HIPAA may not have any control over an individual's data in the outside world, for example, social networks and blogs.

c. An adversary can be a neighbor or an acquaintance who can obtain background information about an individual's habits and lifestyle. A neighbor with the knowledge of your hospital visiting schedule could possibly infer your illness.

d. Geo-spatial data from cell phones combined with de-identified health records are capable of creating a complete profile of a patient, which can be exploited for marketing campaigns that target the patient's treatment needs.

### 9.5.2.2 Business Associate

A business associate has the following utility perspective on the data:

a. The utility of data is highly valuable. Especially, the illness data studied for relationships with location, ethnicity, age, and demographic information are vital for high certainty in findings.

b. The ability to query the data in the same way as original is important. During de-identification, if the data are smoothened to remove specifics, for example, if the date of birth is replaced by just the year, then queries that are run using original data are no longer effective (Table 9.8).

c. De-identification should not alter the correlation that exists within the data. Such perturbation can lead to inaccurate conclusions and interfere with research goals.

d. Zip code data suppression is highly restrictive in nature due to loss of the complete utility of geo-spatial information that may help detect or analyze causal relationships between the environment and epidemic illnesses.

### 9.5.3 Anonymization Design for HIPAA

A privacy design starts with the correct classification of attributes in a data set. In [14], the classification of a data set is given as identity attributes, sensitive attributes, and nonsensitive attributes. Notably, nonsensitive attributes consist of age, gender, race, education, occupation, height, eye color, and so on. Although the authors go on to point that the nonsensitive data are the ones that result in vulnerabilities as shown by [12], the naming of this category itself varies from our view. If they help re-identification they cannot be nonsensitive. Our classification terms this as QIs. And yes, these pose the most serious threat to personal data. Hence, our privacy design needs to take special care of QIs in anonymization.

The principles of Appendix A guide us in our quest for a good anonymization design for HIPAA. Value-based anonymization explained in principle (9) is very important due to the range of values that one may encounter in illnesses. Data on diseases such as "EBOLA" and "AIDS" are certainly bound

**TABLE 9.8**

Smoothing of Date

| ID  | Date of Birth |     | ID  | Date of Birth |
|-----|---------------|-----|-----|---------------|
| 101 | 3/12/1958     |     | 101 | 1958          |
| 102 | 10/02/1967    |     | 102 | 1967          |
| 103 | 03/07/1989    |     | 103 | 1989          |

to offer more clues about the identity of an individual than "FLU." An application of principle (8) shows that certain illnesses are gender specific and cannot be reassigned to any other row at will.

In Table 9.9, if "Victor" is assigned "uterus infection," it would make the data semantically incorrect, thus violating principle (8). One could also think of a correlation between the *illness* and *gender*, in which case principle (7) will provide an insight.

Table 9.10 shows anonymized data for the six rows of data of Table 9.9, with other attributes included. Name, SSN, and Mobile fields have been masked using substitution, format preserving randomization, and shuffling, respectively. Age, city, and zip code have undergone 3-anonymization. Illnesses have been selectively suppressed.

It is interesting to note that while masking EI is inconsequential for PPDM as well as PPTDM, the 3-anonymized QI will not be useful in PPDM. Aggregate conclusions drawn from the 3-anonymized data will be different. For PPTDM, though, these data are acceptable for testing. The only utility loss for PPTDM is the *illness* value of ID = 5.

Table 9.11 demonstrates how the *date* fields of *date of birth* and *date of admission* into a hospital are classified and anonymized. Principle (8) gives us clear guidance that although the attribute category is the same, the date of birth is

**TABLE 9.9**

Example for Principles 8 and 9

| ID | Name | Gender | Illness |
|----|------|--------|---------|
| 1 | Maria | Female | Breast cancer |
| 2 | Lincoln | Male | Fractured leg |
| 3 | Victor | Male | Prostate cancer |
| 4 | Gloria | Female | Uterus infection |
| 5 | Molly | Female | AIDS |
| 6 | Evan | Male | Flu |

**TABLE 9.10**

Example of ADP #5

| ID | Name | SSN | Mobile | Age | City | Zip Code | Illness |
|----|------|-----|--------|-----|------|----------|---------|
| 1 | Simona | 345-04-3485 | 910-387-4589 | 36 | Union City | 94587 | Breast cancer |
| 2 | John | 320-04-5126 | 408-302-9852 | 19 | Owings Mills | 21117 | Fractured leg |
| 3 | Shane | 236-06-9328 | 201-098-4897 | 19 | Owings Mills | 21117 | Prostate cancer |
| 4 | Tina | 619-08-9672 | 607-393-3879 | 36 | Union City | 94587 | Uterus infection |
| 5 | Dora | 721-39-9341 | 843-492-5790 | 19 | Owings Mills | 21117 | — |
| 6 | Luke | 901-02-8780 | 925-855-8973 | 36 | Union City | 94587 | Flu |

**TABLE 9.11**

Example for ADP #8

| Address | Date of Birth | City | Zip Code | Hospital Address | Date of Admission | Date of Discharge |
|---|---|---|---|---|---|---|
| 33 Oak St. | 01/06/1979 | Union City | 94587 | 5 Mill Ave. | 03/06/2015 | 03/06/2015 |
| 4 Canton Rd. | 12/01/1995 | Owings Mills | 21117 | 34 Presidio Parkway | 05/08/2015 | 05/08/2015 |
| 9 Hill St. | 01/06/1979 | Union City | 94587 | 55 Paseo Padre | 08/14/2015 | 08/16/2015 |
| 21 Elm St. | 12/01/1995 | Owings Mills | 21117 | 2 Stevenson Rd. | 07/30/2015 | 08/02/2015 |
| 6 Wells Ln. | 01/06/1979 | Union City | 94587 | 11 Stonemark Ct. | 12/28/2014 | 01/03/2015 |
| 7 Pier Rd. | 12/01/1995 | Owings Mills | 21117 | 33 Zink Rd. | 07/12/2015 | 07/15/2015 |

QI while dates of admission and discharge are SD. Similarly, the address of an individual is an EI, while the address of the hospital is an SD. Now, once classification is done, we can follow principles (3) and (5) to anonymize the data. In the case of PPDM, the SD address and dates would remain the same. In the case of PPTDM, the date of birth is k-anonymized.

### 9.5.4 Notes on EIs, QIs, and SD

A de-identification mechanism, as per HIPAA, is one of the ways to protect data. There are various techniques needed to achieve satisfactory standards of anonymization.

#### 9.5.4.1 Explicit Identifiers

Principle (2) clearly states that all EIs need to be masked. It is a rare phenomenon that EIs require special attention while masking, but such situations do come up. For example, there can be account numbers with characters that represent a region, customer type, or account type. In India, a PAN, which is used to track an individual's financial transactions, has a format of XXXXX0000X. The fourth character [15] represents "entity type" and can have one of 11 alphabets, each representing the status of a PAN holder. For example, "P" stands for individual.

Similarly, categorical data may also have statistical relevance. Let us look at Table 9.12. For simplicity, we present only selected fields.

The values for Last Name in each row in Table 9.12 are the same because the people mentioned in the data might be related. This is an important fact in two ways:

1. The Connors may be part of a family that suffers from an infectious disease. The data need to have this clue maintained after anonymization.

2. If the data set consists of 100 records with more than 30 records having "Connor" as the last name, it shows that a major portion of this subset of data are part of a cluster based on the ZIP code. An analysis needs to be done as to why they appear in this set and

**TABLE 9.12**

Statistical Validity in EIs

| ID | First Name | Middle Name | Last Name | Zip Code | Illness |
|----|-----------|-------------|-----------|----------|---------|
| 1 | John | Eric | Connor | 45324 | ............. |
| 2 | Sarah | Eric | Connor | 45324 | ............. |
| 3 | Eric | Emanuel | Connor | 45324 | ............. |
| 4 | Megan | Eric | Connor | 45324 | ............. |
| ............ | ............. | ............ | ............. | ............ | ............. |

how the illness or treatment is applicable to such a large number of individuals with the same last name in a particular geographical area. Is there a reason to this finding? Are the Connors living near some form of a health hazard? Or is this a genetic disorder running in the family?

### 9.5.4.2 Quasi-Identifiers

QI anonymization is the most important aspect of a privacy design, because this is the most vulnerable among the three categories of PHI. The vulnerability lies in the possibility that the external source of data will enable adversaries to correlate the data and establish the identity of individuals (Table 9.13).

As shown in principle (5), there are various factors that drive the way QIs are anonymized and that the whole process is highly contextual in nature.

### 9.5.4.3 Sensitive Data

SD are meant to be preserved in their original form when shared with business associates. However, situations do arise that require outliers in the transactional data to be handled. The result of such an intervention is two-fold. The interesting aspect of the outlier is that it alters a fact in the data if doctored. However, it also protects the record owner, whose SD are an outlier, from being identified as a result of the anomalous nature of the transaction. Let us examine some fields in SD that may require some form of intervention.

In Table 9.14, we list a few examples of how there are extraordinary circumstances where even SD fields require anonymization to be performed at an individual row level. However, there is always a trade-off that makes such selective anonymization debatable as it invariably affects utility.

## 9.6 Anonymization Design Checklist

Principle (8) states that the context drives the anonymization design. Thus, all the designs mentioned earlier at an individual field category level need to be considered in the light of the overall context of the intended use of the data, which is the guiding factor for anonymization.

Most privacy laws lay down guidelines as to what are personal data, how to secure them, and what principles are to be enforced. However, achieving compliance with them is often based on the five items listed in Table 9.15, which is a checklist for designing anonymization.

**TABLE 9.13**

Anonymization Design—Quasi-Identifiers

| Category | Attribute | Algorithm | Rationale |
|---|---|---|---|
| QI | IP address | Format-preserved value generation, flat value, controlled randomness (location descriptor maintained), suppression, and removal | An IP address identifies a machine connected to a network such as the Internet. This is a QI field that can point to an individual if supporting temporal data are available. Subnet values could be maintained with the other values anonymized to de-identify data from a record owner. |
| QI | Zip code | Geo-spatial replacement of zip code (nearby zip code assignment), contextually similar zip code replacement, shuffling, suppression, partial suppression, and removal | Considering that zip codes are clustered geographically, a random replacement from the same cluster is acceptable. If a specific characteristic is investigated, then the context can be used to group zip codes and a random replacement could be done. Shuffling preserves statistical validity from a data set perspective but loses correlations, if any. |
| QI | Vehicle identification number (VIN) | Randomization, partial randomization, suppression, partial suppression, and removal | QI and VIN identify a vehicle but do not provide ownership data independently. In cases, where type of vehicle is important for accident or ergonomic illness cases, then the type of vehicle may need to be maintained. However, these are rarely based on the VIN, and the data would generally have separate fields describing the vehicle make and models. |
| QI | License plate number | Format-preserving replacement, randomization, partial randomization, suppression, partial suppression, and removal | A license plate number is independently unable to identify individuals. Only department of motor vehicles (DMV) data can provide the link. For example, every U.S. state has a different convention for license plates. For example, in [16], Montana has its own codes, which require to be maintained while anonymizing the data. In India, each state has a two-letter code, such as "MH" which represents Maharashtra, that a typical license plate number starts with. |
| QI | Health plan beneficiary number | Format-preserving tokenization, randomization, suppression, and removal | This number is specific to the healthcare provider and government databases. While anonymizing, referential integrity is to be maintained. Otherwise, the number has no meaning when taken out of the healthcare context. |

*(Continued)*

**TABLE 9.13 (*Continued*)**

Anonymization Design—Quasi-Identifiers

| Category | Attribute | Algorithm | Rationale |
| --- | --- | --- | --- |
| QI | Device identifier and serial number | Randomization, partial randomization, suppression, partial suppression, and removal | A device identifier is meaningless outside the context of healthcare and products space. Individual privacy is not compromised until it gets correlated to another data set with treatment details. Hence, it is a QI. |
| QI | Dates related to individual profile | Blurring, randomization, and additive or multiplicative noise | Examples of dates that are linked to individual profiles are dates of birth or death. Other dates such as the date of undergoing a one-off procedure are also included. However, a chemotherapy date is more of a transactional date, since chemotherapy is performed as a course of four or six sessions. Date fields are very important for the statistical validity of anonymized data. |

**TABLE 9.14**

Anonymization Design—Sensitive Data

| Category | Attribute | Algorithm | Rationale |
| --- | --- | --- | --- |
| SD | Illness | Suppression *or* domain generalization hierarchy-based value assignation | An illness that is very rare, such as Ebola, could easily identify an individual. Such diseases are reported in the media, and even though they do not reveal the name of the individuals, all other QIs such as origin, age, and location details are generously reported. Such data can be suppressed. Alternatively, a value based on domain generalization could be assigned. |
| SD | Body part | Shuffling and substitution | Although the body part can be anonymized, this piece of information is vital to the utility of the data. Hence, most data consumers require it to be left unaltered. |
| SD | Payment information | Randomization, additive noise, and shuffling | Payment information can remain as is in most cases. However, if an illness is rare and requires high payment, any medical practitioner is capable of identifying the nature of illness. For example, if an internal ear procedure costs a patient $15,000, and the illness is anonymized while leaving the body part information as is, then an otorhinolaryngology specialist could easily identify the illness. |

**TABLE 9.15**

Steps for Anonymization Design

| S NO | Checklist Item |
|------|----------------|
| 1 | What is the intended use of a data set? |
| 2 | What is the domain, context, and application scenario? |
| 3 | Who are the users of data and what are their profiles? |
| 4 | Have adversaries, threats, and attack models been identified? |
| 5 | What are the possible correlated data sets available that can be matched with the source? |

## 9.7 Summary

Privacy regulations are the main reason anonymization is done. Each region and domain have relevant laws that restrict the use of personal data in their original form. In this chapter, we have explained some of the guidelines specified by privacy laws and also understood ways to comply with them.

## 9.8 Points to Ponder

- How does one handle payment card data in a healthcare data set?
- When are date fields part of SD?
- If a bank's data are outsourced to India from Switzerland for testing, which guideline will be in effect? The OECD or FADP?
- A clinical trial is carried out over a period of 10 years. How would you classify the data of the volunteers?

## References

1. Summary of the HIPAA privacy rule, available at http://www.hhs.gov/sites/default/files/privacysummary.pdf by US Department of Health and Human Services. Prepared by Office of Civil Rights on 05/03. Accessed April 19, 2016.
2. Declaration on Professional Ethics, adopted by ISI Council in July 2010, Reykjavik, Iceland https://www.isi-web.org/index.php/news-from-isi/296-declarationprofessionalethics-2010uk. Accessed April 19, 2016.

3. Commission proposes a comprehensive reform of the data protection rules, available at http://europa.eu/rapid/press-release_IP-12-46_en.htm?locale=en, a European Commission Press Release on 25th January 2012 at Brussels. Accessed April 19, 2016.

4. Regulation (EC) No 45/2001 of the European Parliament and of the Council of 18 December 2000. Published by the Official Journal of the European Communities on 12.1.2001. Accessed April 19, 2016.

5. Data Protection Act, Switzerland, available at https://www.admin.ch/opc/en/classified-compilation/19920153/index.html published by The Federal Council, the Portal of the Swiss Government on June 19, 1992 (Status as of January 1, 2014). Accessed April 19, 2016.

6. Payment Card Industry (PCI) Data Security Standard-Requirements and Security Assessment Procedures, v3.1 Page 5, April 2015. Published by PCI Security Standards Council, LLC 2006–2015. Accessed April 19, 2016.

7. Protecting consumer privacy in an era of rapid change: Recommendations for businesses and policymakers, Fed. Trade Comm'n, March 2012, available at https://www.ftc.gov/sites/default/files/documents/reports/federal-trade-commission-report-protecting-consumer-privacy-era-rapid-change-recommen dations/120326privacyreport.pdf.

8. APEC Privacy Framework of 2004, available at http://www.apec.org/Groups/Committee-on-Trade-and-Investment/~/media/Files/Groups/ECSG/05_ecsg_privacyframewk.ashx. Published by APEC Secretariat, Singapore in 2005. Accessed April 19, 2016.

9. OECD Guidelines governing the protection of Privacy and Transborder flows of Personal Data-11, available at http://www.oecd.org/sti/ieconomy/2013-oecd-privacy-guidelines.pdf. C(80)58/FINAL, as amended on July 11, 2013 by C(2013)79. Accessed April 19, 2016.

10. R. Wu, G.J. Ahn, and H. Hu, Towards HIPAA-compliant Healthcare Systems, in *IHI'12 Proceedings of the Second ACM SIGHIT International Health Informatic Symposium*, Miami, FL, January 28–30, 2012.

11. K. Benitez and B. Malin, Evaluating re-identification risks with respect to the HIPAA privacy rule, *Journal of American Medical Informatics Association*, 2009, p.170. Accepted December 14, 2009. Accessed April 19, 2016.

12. L. Sweeney, k-anonymity: a model for protecting privacy, *International Journal on Uncertainty, Fuzziness and Knowledge-Based Systems*, 10(5), 557–570, 2002.

13. A. Evfimievski et al., Privacy preserving mining of association rules, in *Proceedings of the Eighth ACM SIGKDD International Conference on Knowledge Discovery and Data Mining*, New York, 2002.

14. L. Motiwalla and X. Li, Value added privacy services for healthcare data, in *IEEE Sixth World Congress on Services*, Miami, FL, 2010.

15. Income Tax Department—Permanent Account Number, available at http://www.incometaxindia.gov.in/tutorials/1.permanent%20account%20number%20(pan).pdf. Published by Income Tax Department, Department of Revenue, Ministry of Finance, Government of India as amended by Finance Act, 2015. Accessed April 19, 2016.

16. License Plates—Department of Justice of Montana, available at https://dojmt.gov/driving/license-plates/. Prepared by Motor Vehicle Division, State of Montana, Department of Justice. Accessed April 19, 2016.

17. Data Protection Act 1998, Schedule 1, Part 1 Principles, available at http://www.legislation.gov.uk/ukpga/1998/29/schedule/1/part/I. Delivered by The National Archives. Accessed April 19, 2016.
18. Data Protection Act 1998, Original available at http://www.legislation.gov.uk/ukpga/1998/29/pdfs/ukpga_19980029_en.pdf. Published by TSO (The Stationary Office) printed in 1998 reprinted incorporating corrections in 2005. Accessed April 19, 2016.
19. Coroners and Justice Act 2009, available at http://www.legislation.gov.uk/ukpga/2009/25/contents. Delivered by The National Archives. Accessed April 19, 2016.
20. Standards Catalogue ISO, available at http://www.iso.org/iso/home/store/catalogue_ics/catalogue_detail_ics.htm?csnumber=66011. Published on 2015-07-01 by Registration Authority c/o RA/MA (ABA) Washington DC. Accessed April 19, 2016.
21. 22nd Annual report 2014/2015 of the Federal data Protection and Information Commissioner (FDPIC), available at http://www.edoeb.admin.ch/dokumentation/00153/01251/index.html?lang=en. Complete report available in German and Frensh at BBL, Vertrieb Publikationen, 3003 Bern Art. Nr. 410.021. Accessed April 19, 2016.

# Appendix A: Anonymization Design Principles for Multidimensional Data

## A.1 Introduction

Anonymization design is an optimization approach, and it is necessary to have some guiding principles to come up with an appropriate design. Any optimization exercise is a complex one. Anonymization as a data protection technique is relatively new and its design depends on many factors, which have been discussed in Chapter 1. In such circumstances, it is necessary to have guidelines or best practices on design to help the practitioner. We have come up with a catalogue of principles or best practices that can help in anonymization design. Each principle is structured into two parts—rationale and implications. The first part details out what that principle is and how to use it for anonymization design, and the second part tells what happens if you do not follow the principle. Each principle is explained using examples. There are many data structures that we have covered in this book—multidimensional, transaction, graph, time series, longitudinal, and spatiotemporal. In this Appendix, we discuss anonymization design principles for multidimensional data, which are the commonly used data structure.

## A.2 Anonymization Design Principles

1. Principle of classification—Classify the data set D into EI, QI, SD, and NSD with clear boundaries between them.

2. Principle of concealment—Completely mask EI.

3. Principle of specialization—Understand the application domain to decide on the anonymization design.

4. Principle of consistency—Ensure consistency in masking data across applications in a domain.

5. Principle of utilization—Understand the application scenario to decide on the anonymization design. For example, analytical utility of QI in data mining may not be required in TDM.

6. Principle of threat modeling—Identify possible threats for a given environment, setting, or data type.

7. Principle of correlation—Maintain correlation between attributes. For example, locality and zip code or DOB and age.

8. Principle of contextual anonymization—Understand the context. (From whom are you trying to protect the data? What is the environment?)

9. Principle of value-based anonymization—Understand the semantics of the data in the context of the application so as to apply the correct or appropriate anonymization technique on the data.

10. Principle of data structure complexity—Anonymization design is dependent on the data structure.

11. Principle of correlated shuffling—Maintain correlation between related attributes while shuffling data. For example, correlation between locality, city, and zip code.

12. Principle of randomization—Maintain statistical properties (like distribution) when randomly perturbing the data.

13. Principle for protection against identity disclosure—Define a privacy model to prevent identity disclosure via record linkage.

## A.2.1 Principle of Classification: Classify the Data Set D into EI, QI, SD, and NSD with Clear Boundaries between Them

### A.2.1.1 Rationale

Given a table T with data set D, the first step in anonymization design is to classify the data into EI ($EI_i$, $EI_{i+1}$,..., $EI_n$), QI ($QI_j$, $QI_{j+1}$,..., $QI_m$), SD ($SD_k$, $SD_{k+1}$,..., $SD_p$), and NSD (Table A.1).

This classification is an essential first step as it will help in determining which attributes must be masked and which attributes must be identifiable.

**TABLE A.1**

Classification of EI, QI, and SD Fields

| Explicit Identifiers | | | Quasi-Identifiers | | | Sensitive Data | | | |
|---|---|---|---|---|---|---|---|---|---|
| ID | Name | DOB | Gender | Address | Zip Code | Account Number | Account Type | Account Balance | Credit Limit |
| 1 | Ravi | 1970 | Male | Fourth Street | 66001 | 12345 | Savings | 10,000 | 20,000 |
| 2 | Hari | 1975 | Male | Queen Street | 66011 | 23456 | Checking | 5,000 | 15,000 |
| 3 | John | 1978 | Male | Penn Street | 66003 | 45678 | Savings | 15,000 | 30,000 |
| 4 | Amy | 1980 | Female | Ben Street | 66066 | 76543 | Savings | 17,000 | 25,000 |

Classification is extremely challenging when dealing with a data set of high dimensionality. For example, a personal loan application of a bank has over 200 fields; a mortgage loan application has many more fields. In such a situation, the following questions arise:

- What constitutes EI?
- What constitutes QI and SD?
- How do you determine the boundary between QI and SI?

What constitutes EI?

- All identifiers that directly identify the record owner. Examples of EI are name of the record owner, social security number, driving license number, passport number, insurance ID, and any other attribute that can directly identify the record owner. It is a relatively easy task to pick out the EI.

What constitutes QI?

- Attributes in the data set that can be traced to or linked to an external publicly available data source are termed as quasi-identifiers. They are generally composed of demographic and geographic information of the record owner. It is difficult to clearly quantify the amount of publicly available information, especially in the current era of social media.

How do you determine the boundary between QI and SD?

- It is very difficult to define a clear boundary between QI and SD. The reasons could be the dimensions of QI and also the complexity of the business domain. Let us assume that an HR personnel is the adversary, then the background knowledge of the adversary is more than what is present in the external source. It is important to understand from whom we are trying to protect the data. This helps sometimes to draw a boundary between QI and SD.
- Another example from the mortgage domain illustrates the difficulty in identifying QI and the boundary between QI and SD. Consider Table A.2. The table contains the geographical information of the record owner's current residence and that of the property he has acquired. Both these addresses are available in a public data source. According to our earlier definitions of QI, both these addresses should be included in the QI and be de-identified. By anonymizing the address of the acquired property, the analytic utility of the data set is reduced, but not doing so will lead to identity disclosure.
- So, are there any rules to be used for identifying QI?

**TABLE A.2**

Sample Mortgage Table

| ID | Name | Gender | Address | Zip Code | Address of the Property | Zip Code |
|----|------|--------|---------|----------|-------------------------|----------|
| 1 | Hari | Male | Park Street | 560033 | South Street | 560068 |
| 2 | Jane | Female | King Street | 560053 | Beach Road | 560003 |

### A.2.1.2 Implications

- Incorrect identification of EI, QI, and SD attributes could lead to privacy loss or utility loss.
- Are phone numbers and e-mail addresses EI or QI?

## A.2.2 Principle of Concealment: Completely Mask EI

### A.2.2.1 Rationale

- In a data set D, EIs are identifiers that uniquely identify a record owner. Examples of EI are names (first name, middle name, last name), social security number, driver's license number, tax ID, passport number, insurance ID, etc.
- Not masking any EI attribute could violate the record owner's privacy. That is why it is very critical to identify the boundary between EI and QI. Are telephone—landline and mobile—numbers and e-mail addresses EI or QI? A mobile number in the name of the record owner uniquely identifies the record owner and therefore must be marked as EI and masked. What about other fields like landline number (residence, office) and e-mail ID?
- Anonymization has two broad techniques to preserve privacy—masking and de-identification. Masking is a perturbative technique generally applied on EIs. De-identification uses more of nonperturbative techniques and is usually applied on QIs. De-identification techniques should preserve the analytical utility of QIs.
- As a rule, all EIs are completely masked. Masking is a technique where the data are completely perturbed. Techniques like encryption, hashing, and substitution completely perturb the data so that there is no resemblance to original data. This is what most authors recommend. We recommend a technique called one-way tokenization, which can be used to mask the attributes of all EIs while preserving their format, providing a higher level of data protection, and also delivering on referential integrity requirements.

### A.2.2.2 Implications

- Incorrect identification and masking of EI will lead to the loss of privacy of the record owner.

## A.2.3 Principle of Specialization: Get an Understanding of the Application Domain to Decide on Anonymization Design

### A.2.3.1 Rationale

- A good understanding of the domain (Business) is needed to come up with the right anonymization design. To illustrate this, consider the following example tables from two different domains (Tables A.3 and A.4).

In Table A.3, it is obvious that there is a strong correlation between geographic data and SD fields [1].

Before releasing the data, the QI fields are to be anonymized. By anonymizing QI fields, the correlation between the geographic data and the income is lost, which means the truth in the data is destroyed. If the data are separated from the business application, then the data have no context or meaning.

With reference to Table A.3, if geographic identifiers are anonymized, then it will prevent its legitimate use by analysts. An important point to note here is that an application has different characteristics; in a given context, some data sets may be more sensitive than others.

In Table A.4, there is no correlation between geographic information and the sensitive attribute "disease." Of course, there are exceptions to this

**TABLE A.3**

Sample Survey Data

| Name | DOB | Address | Zip Code | Salary |
|------|-----|---------|----------|--------|
| James | 1980 | M.G. Road | 56001 | 100,000 |
| Eric | 1985 | M.G. Road | 56001 | 120,000 |
| Hari | 1979 | Park Street | 56068 | 60,000 |
| Amy | 1977 | Park Street | 56068 | 50,000 |

**TABLE A.4**

Sample Healthcare Data

| Name | DOB | Address | Zip Code | Disease |
|------|-----|---------|----------|---------|
| James | 1980 | M.G. Road | 56001 | Hypertension |
| Eric | 1985 | M.G. Road | 56001 | Flu |
| Hari | 1979 | Park Street | 56068 | Diabetes |
| Amy | 1977 | Park Street | 56068 | Cancer |

observation when an epidemic strikes a particular region and many in that locality suffer from the same illness.

In the first data set, it is the aggregate privacy that needs to be protected, while for the second it is the individual privacy. It is worth noting here that it is not possible to have one anonymization design that would meet the requirements of both application domains.

### A.2.3.2 Implications

- Incorrect anonymization design will result in loss of information or in other words, loss of utility.

### A.2.4  Principle of Consistency: Ensure Consistency of Masked Data across Applications in a Domain

### A.2.4.1  Rationale

- Applications in a domain are never silos. They are all integrated to solve business problems. The same set of sensitive data, for example, names, identifying attributes like SSN, and passport number, are generally present in most of the applications in the business domain. All of these common data should be consistently masked; in other words, the masked value of a data element should be the same across all the applications. This is an important requirement in integration testing. All applications in the chain having the same masked values will ensure successful integration testing.

### A.2.4.2  Implications

- Not conforming to principle of consistency will result in failed integration testing.

### A.2.5  Principle of Utilization: Anonymization Design Depends on the Application Scenario

### A.2.5.1  Rationale

- As stated in Chapter 1, one of the factors that affect anonymization design is application scenario.
- Anonymized data are provisioned for various purposes like data mining and analytics, or as test data or training data. What should be the characteristics of the anonymized data for each of these purposes?
- Data mining has three major functions: classification, clustering, and association mining. Regardless of which privacy preserving method or anonymization is chosen, it should support the above three

functions without any significant deviation in the analysis results. Anonymization techniques should support query answering and classification accuracy and maintain statistical distribution, cluster quality, and association among correlated data sets. Data mining is exploratory in nature, and you really do not know what you are looking for. As you mine you uncover a lot of knowledge buried in the data. In such a case, you really do not know which data attributes require protection and which do not.

- PPDM uses the aggregate property of the data set.
- In PPTDM, test cases are provided that clearly specify what data are required for testing purposes and only those are extracted and anonymized. PPTDM relies more on data masking.

Consider an example.

- In a company, it is quite common to see employees in a particular level or band draw very similar salaries and what you notice in the table is a cluster of similar salaries. If you are provisioning this data as test data then you do not need all of the records, only a couple will do and the rest can be suppressed. Whereas, if you are mining this data, then the cluster provides useful insights into the characteristics of the system (Table A.5).

### A.2.5.2 Implications

Many common anonymization algorithms or techniques are applied across these applications. For example, shuffling can be safely used in both PPDM and PPTDM. Applying random perturbation (both additive and multiplicative) in PPDM will be fine, but one has to be careful with its application in PPTDM. Random perturbation changes the value of the data, which may become unsuitable as test data.

### A.2.5.2.1 Note

Why are we discussing two very diverse application scenarios (PPDM and PPTDM)? Throughout the book, it can be observed that there are a number of data protection technique options like perturbative, nonperturbative, and

**TABLE A.5**

Sample Salary Table

| ID | Name | Salary |
|----|-------|--------|
| 1 | John | 20,000 |
| 2 | Hari | 20,000 |
| 3 | Swamy | 20,000 |
| 4 | Lisa | 20,000 |
| 5 | Jane | 20,000 |

group anonymization methods. Our finding in the literature on anonymization was that there is detailed coverage of the functions of these algorithms but no clear-cut guidelines on where and how to use them. For example, can we use k-anonymization for test data, or how to use data shuffling? We felt that a discussion on the appropriate usage of these techniques is warranted and we have tried to cover them as much as possible in this book.

### A.2.6 Principle of Threat Modeling: Identify Possible Threats for a Given Environment, Setting, and Data Type

#### A.2.6.1 Rationale

We examine threats at the following levels:

##### A.2.6.1.1 Location and Actor (Adversary) Complexity

- Location and actor complexity includes background and external knowledge. Most of the existing work in this area is focused on external and background knowledge of external adversary. Our approach is to classify the adversaries into either internal or external to the organization. Another related aspect that needs to be considered is the location of the adversary. Adversary classification is discussed in detail under threat modeling section in Chapter 4.

- The next level of threat exists at the data structure level. The more complex the data structure is, the more vulnerable it is to threats.

Finally, anonymization algorithms should have the following properties:

- Should not be vulnerable to well-defined privacy definitions; for example, k-anonymization is vulnerable against homogeneity attacks.
- Must be robust.
- Should provide the required performance.
- Must be scalable—Should provide required performance as data size grows.
- Should provide a balance between privacy and utility.

#### A.2.6.2 Implications

There is no one anonymization design that fits all privacy and utility requirements.

- Anonymization design depends on many factors and not considering them into the design could lead to privacy loss. As an example, consider a multidimensional database provisioned for analysis to an internal employee (could be an internal adversary). It is difficult to model his background knowledge—difficult to predict how much he or she knows about the data. In such cases, it is sometimes necessary to anonymize some of the fields in the sensitive data set, for example, salary or disease, which would result in lower levels of utility.

## A.2.7 Principle of Correlation: Maintain Correlation between Related Fields during Anonymization

### A.2.7.1 Rationale

- In many cases, attributes in QI are correlated, for example, address and zip code. Similarly, there could be correlation between attributes in QI and SD. For example, in life insurance data, the age of the policy holder is related to the premium he pays. The premium is also a function of health issues and habits like smoking, drinking etc. In this case, age is a QI attribute and premium is an SD attribute. Therefore, any anonymization method should ensure that the transformed data set maintains the correlation in the original data set (Table A.6).

Use techniques like shuffling (rank order correlation) to ensure privacy and utility by preserving the relationship between data attributes (Table A.7).

In Table A.6, the premium amount is correlated with age, health issues, and smoking and drinking habits of the policy holder. This is a very strongly correlated data set wherein there is correlation between the QI and SD attributes and also within the SD attributes. So, how do you anonymize this data set

**TABLE A.6**

Original Correlated Data Set

| ID | Age | Premium |
|----|-----|---------|
| 1  | 21  | 504     |
| 2  | 23  | 345     |
| 3  | 45  | 1305    |
| 4  | 55  | 550     |
| 5  | 32  | 768     |
| 6  | 41  | 984     |
| 7  | 50  | 1450    |
| 8  | 35  | 735     |
| 9  | 40  | 920     |
| 10 | 30  | 450     |
| 11 | 25  | 600     |
| 12 | 38  | 912     |
| 13 | 48  | 1392    |
| 14 | 33  | 759     |
| 15 | 37  | 592     |

**TABLE A.7**

Shuffled Table That Maintains Correlation
among Attributes, Utility, and Privacy

| ID | Age | Premium |
|----|-----|---------|
| 1  | 55  | 1450 |
| 2  | 50  | 1392 |
| 3  | 48  | 1305 |
| 4  | 45  | 984 |
| 5  | 41  | 920 |
| 6  | 40  | 912 |
| 7  | 38  | 768 |
| 8  | 37  | 759 |
| 9  | 35  | 735 |
| 10 | 33  | 600 |
| 11 | 32  | 592 |
| 12 | 30  | 550 |
| 13 | 25  | 504 |
| 14 | 23  | 450 |
| 15 | 21  | 345 |

without losing the correlation among the attributes? This is a challenging problem; anonymization must ensure that the transformed data set should support any requirements of clustering or classification or any further analysis.

### A.2.7.2 Implications

- A naive anonymization approach, for example, a randomization method on the age attribute can completely destroy the relationship between age and premium, resulting in a data set that has very low utility.

### A.2.8 Principle of Contextual Anonymization: Understand the Semantics of the Data in the Context of the Application so as to Apply the Correct/Appropriate Anonymization Techniques on the Data

#### A.2.8.1 Rationale

- Anonymization technique should focus on the semantics of the data and not just on the syntax.
- In the principle on threat modeling, we considered the anonymization design in the context of the location, the user, and the presence of additional knowledge. Semantics of the data is another dimension that needs to be considered while anonymizing.
- For example, consider a mortgage application in a bank. A sample mortgage application data table will have the following fields (Table A.8):

**TABLE A.8**

Sample Mortgage Table

| ID | Name | Gender | Address | Zip Code | Address of the Property | Zip Code |
|----|------|--------|---------|----------|-------------------------|----------|
| 1  | Hari | Male   | Park Street | 560033 | South Street | 560068 |
| 2  | Jane | Female | King Street | 560053 | Beach Road   | 560003 |

- There are two address fields in the table. The first one is the address of the customer and the second one is the address of the property he has purchased. If you go by syntax then all address fields will be anonymized similarly. But you need to consider the semantics of the fields in the context of the mortgage application. The second address field—the address of the property—is SD, whereas the first one is a QI. In this case, both the address fields are very sensitive from the application perspective and should be protected. The address of the property should be anonymized without compromising its utility for analysis purposes. The first address field is a QI attribute and can be generalized without affecting the utility significantly.
- The first important step is to classify the attribute—the address of the property as an SD and then appropriately anonymizing it without compromising its utility. So, the big question is how to anonymize this field effectively?

### A.2.8.2 Implications

- Applying a syntax-based anonymization will lead to the loss of utility of the anonymized data set.
- Every attribute in an application has some specific meaning in the context of the application, and this meaning, or semantics, should be retained in the anonymized data set.

### A.2.9 Principle of Value-Based Anonymization: Anonymization Design Should Be Flexible to Provide Different Levels of Protection Based on the Sensitivity of Attributes in an SD Data Set

### A.2.9.1 Rationale

- Anonymization design should be flexible to provide different levels of protection for different sensitive values and not just uniform protection for all the values in the SD data set [2].
- For example, in a healthcare database, the attribute "disease" can contain diseases like AIDS, flu, diabetes, and so on. Here, AIDS is more sensitive than flu. Therefore, data protection mechanism must be stronger for AIDS than for flu.

Table A.9 lists a sample healthcare data table. In Table A.10, AIDS as a disease is more sensitive than other diseases and therefore must have stronger protection than flu, which is common.

### A.2.9.2 Implications

- Having the same level of protection for all the values tends to over-protect the sensitive data. For example, flu is a common ailment during winter and AIDS could be an outlier (only few individuals have AIDS), then the anonymization design must be flexible to suppress AIDS, which is more sensitive, and retain flu as is, to increase the utility of the released data.

## A.2.10 Principle of Data Structure Complexity: Anonymization Design Is Dependent on the Complexity of the Data Structure

### A.2.10.1 Rationale

- The most common data structure that we encounter is the relational table, also called multidimensional data. Most of the anonymization techniques developed so far focus on protecting multidimensional data. The techniques focus on preventing identity and sensitive data disclosure.

**TABLE A.9**

Sample Healthcare Table

| ID | Name | Disease |
|----|--------|----------|
| 1 | Mike | Flu |
| 2 | Jane | Diabetes |
| 3 | Mary | AIDS |
| 4 | Thomas | Flu |
| 5 | Jude | Flu |
| 6 | Kane | Flu |

**TABLE A.10**

Sample Healthcare Table with Suppressed Data

| ID | Name | Disease |
|----|--------|----------|
| 1 | Mike | Flu |
| 2 | Jane | Diabetes |
| 3 | Mary | — |
| 4 | Thomas | Flu |
| 5 | Jude | Flu |
| 6 | Kane | Flu |

- Multidimensional data structure is a simple data structure and provides a smaller "surface area" for attacks, which leads to a simpler anonymization design when compared to other complex data structures, such as graph, longitudinal, time series, spatiotemporal, and transaction. The more complex the data structure, the more avenues it offers to attacks. Table A.11 summarizes the different structures and possible avenues of disclosure [3–5].

## A.2.11 Principle of Correlated Shuffling: Maintain Correlation between Related Fields/Attributes While Shuffling Data

### A.2.11.1 Rationale

- Shuffling is a very powerful technique that can be used on all data types like categorical, numerical, and strings. Shuffling means exchanging data values among the attribute column.
- When anonymizing correlated data columns, it is important that when shuffling one of the column data all the related data are shuffled so that they remain correlated. For example, when locality, city,

**TABLE A.11**

Data Structure Complexity, Attack Type, and Protection Method

| Data Structure | Privacy Attacks | Anonymization Approach |
|---|---|---|
| Multidimensional data (relational data) | Identity disclosure<br>Attribute disclosure | Randomization<br>k-Anonymization<br>l-Diversity<br>t-Closeness |
| Transaction data | Sensitivity of the transaction<br>Attribute<br>Record linkage | Randomization<br>Band matrix method<br>Coherence<br>$k^m$-Anonymity |
| Graph data | Identity disclosure<br>Link disclosure<br>Sensitive content<br>Disclosure<br>Graph metrics | Random perturbation<br>k-Anonymization<br>Clustering |
| Longitudinal data | Identity disclosure<br>Sensitive data disclosure | k-Anonymization<br>(K-C) Privacy |
| Time series data | Identity disclosure<br>Attribute disclosure<br>Filtering<br>Regression analysis | Random noise<br>Generalization<br>k-Anonymization<br>Aggregation<br>Suppression |

and zip code are correlated, shuffling just the zip code will break its relationship with other related fields and render data of low utility.

- Rank order shuffling could be considered to ensure a good balance between privacy and utility.

### A.2.11.2 Implications

- The truth in the data set will be lost if correlation is not maintained among related fields while shuffling.

### A.2.12  Principle of Randomization: Maintain the Statistical Properties (Univariate and Multivariate) Like Distribution While Adding Noise to the Data Set

### A.2.12.1 Rationale

- Random perturbation or random noise is generally added to numerical data (continuous data) to hide the sensitiveness of the data. Consider $x_i$ as the original data and $n_i$ is the additive random noise, then the final perturbed data are

$$P_i = x_i + n_i$$

- Ensure that $n_i$ is correlated and has a mean of zero. This results in the mean and covariance of the original data set and perturbed data set being equal.
- $P_i$ is the perturbed data that have no resemblance to original data but maintains the statistical properties of $x_i$.

### A.2.12.2 Implications

- If $n_i$ is not correlated with $x_i$, then $n_i$ can be easily filtered out and $x_i$ can be identified, that is, the original data can be recovered. This means loss of privacy.

### A.2.13  Principle for Protection against Identity Disclosure: Define a Privacy Model to Prevent Identity Disclosure via Record Linkage

### A.2.13.1 Rationale

You need to consider the following aspects while anonymizing QI:

- Prevent record linkage—Ensure that the QI is not linked to any external data source and the record owner is re-identified.
- Outlier records—Ensure that outlier records in the data table are sufficiently protected and do not lead to re-identification.

- Utility of anonymized data—Ensure that the transformed data retain their analytic utility.
- Naive transformation techniques like random noise and shuffling, which are perturbative in nature, may protect QI but render them with very low utility. The truth in the data is lost with these masking techniques. Therefore, nonperturbative techniques like generalizations should be used, which transform data to semantically similar format, thus retaining the analytic utility of QI. Another issue that you need to deal with is the masking of outlier records. It is not easy to mask outlier records. Therefore, the approach to transformation is to construct groups of anonymous records that are transformed in a group-specific way [6].
- Perturbative methods of masking destroy the truth in the data set, whereas nonperturbative methods preserve the truth in the data set. Nonperturbative techniques are used to implement group-based anonymization like k-anonymity.

Consider a data table DT having QI (q1,..., qm).

- k-Anonymity is satisfied when each tuple in a table DT is indistinguishable from at least k-1 other tuples with respect to QI.

Consider the original data table DT and the k-anonymous tables given as follows:

| ID | ZIP Code | Disease |
|---|---|---|
| (a) Original table | | |
| 1 | 560001 | HIV |
| 2 | 560005 | Flu |
| 3 | 560035 | Cancer |
| 4 | 560031 | Flu |
| 5 | 560002 | Diabetes |
| 6 | 560006 | BP |
| 7 | 560034 | HIV |
| 8 | 560031 | BP |
| (b) k-Anonymous table (k = 4) | | |
| 1 | 560000 | HIV |
| 2 | 560000 | Flu |
| 3 | 560030 | Cancer |
| 4 | 560030 | Flu |
| 5 | 560000 | Diabetes |
| 6 | 560000 | BP |
| 7 | 560030 | HIV |
| 8 | 560030 | BP |

*(Continued)*

| ID | ZIP Code | Disease |
|----|----------|---------|
| (c) k-Anonymous table (k = 2) | | |
| 1 | 560000 | HIV |
| 2 | 560010 | Flu |
| 3 | 560040 | Cancer |
| 4 | 560030 | Flu |
| 5 | 560000 | Diabetes |
| 6 | 560010 | BP |
| 7 | 560040 | HIV |
| 8 | 560030 | BP |

Table (a) is the original data table and table (b) is the transformed table, which is the k-anonymous table with k = 4. Zip code, which is a QI, is anonymized by generalizing to prevent record linkage (Figure A.1).

- The quasi-identifier is generalized to semantically similar data, thus protecting against record linkage and retaining the analytical utility of the data.
- Parameter k defines the level of privacy. A higher value of k means more privacy and less utility. The probability of linking the record owner to his actual record's QI is 1/k.
- If you look at tables (b) and (c), you will see clusters of data. In table (b) you see clusters of four data points and in table (c) clusters of two data points. As the value of k goes up, the number of data points in each cluster increases. This would result in each cluster

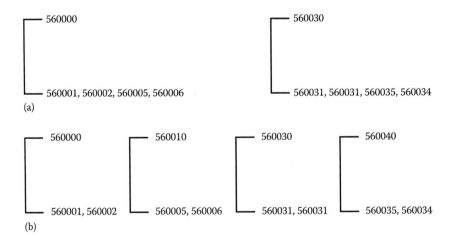

(a)

(b)

**FIGURE A.1**
Generalization of quasi-identifier (zip code). (a) Domain Generalization Hierarchy, Generalization Step size = 1,4-anonymity. (b) Domain Generalization Hierarchy, Generalization Step size = 1,2-anonymity.

containing generalized data values whose distance from the original value would be higher compared with a cluster having a lower value of k. Therefore, a lower value of k results in the higher utility of the k-anonymous data but at the cost of lower privacy. So, how is the correct value of k chosen for the given data table size?

### A.2.13.2 *Implications*

- Perturbative masking reduces the utility of the masked data.
- Nonperturbative masking like generalization preserves the utility of the data.
- Group-based anonymization, for example, k-anonymization provides protection against record linkage, outlier record protection and higher utility of transformed data.

---

# References

1. N. Shlomo, Accessing Micro data via the internet, Joint UN/ECE and Eurostat work session on statistically data confidentiality, Working paper No. 6, Luxemburg, April 7–9, 2003.
2. B.-C. Chen, K. LeFevre, and R. Ramakrishnan, Privacy skyline: Privacy with multidimensional adversial knowledge, Technical report #1596, University of Wisconsin, Madison, WI, July 2007.
3. G. Ghinita, Y. Tao, and P. Kalnis, On the anonymization of sparse high dimensional data, in *Proceedings of the 24th IEEE International Conference on Data Engineering (ICDE)*, April 2008, Cancun, Mexico, pp. 715–724.
4. Y. Xu et al., Anonymizing transaction databases for publication, in *ACM KDD'08*, August 24–27, Las Vegas, NV, 2008.
5. M. Terrontis et al., Privacy preserving anonymization of set—Valued data, *Proceedings of the VCDB Endowment*, Auckland, New Zealand, 1(1), 115–125, August 2008.
6. C.C. Aggarwal and P.S. Yu (eds.), *Privacy Preserving Data Mining: Model and Algorithms*, 2008, New York, Springer.

# Appendix B: PPTDM Manifesto

Privacy preserving test data management (PPTDM) is the process of creating high-quality data for diverse phases of testing with goals to protect data privacy, retain data utility, and maintain high test coverage.

A good PPTDM strategy enables organizations to optimize their time and effort spent on testing and improves both cost-effectiveness and time to market.

## Guiding Principles

Data privacy laws drive privacy preservation of test data

Document privacy goals

Document testing goals

Understand the domain and context of the application

Uncover the behavioral aspects of the original data and their trends

Maintain referential integrity

Maintain logical relationships within/across systems

Maintain the consistency of masked data across both upstream and downstream applications

Use test data tokenization for sensitive data

Anonymize test data based on semantics

Test data anonymization design should be independent of the underlying database technology

Create anonymization design based on location, actors, and entitlements

Analyze all threat models applicable

Mask EI, anonymize QI, and maintain SD as is

Use anonymization techniques to maintain the correlation among related attributes

# *Index*